# REFORM IN SOVIET POLITICS

Lessons of recent policies on land and water

# REFORM IN SOVIET POLITICS

Lessons of recent policies on
land and water

THANE GUSTAFSON

# CAMBRIDGE UNIVERSITY PRESS

*Cambridge*
*London   New York   New Rochelle*
*Melbourne   Sydney*

Published by the Press Syndicate of the University of Cambridge
The Pitt Building, Trumpington Street, Cambridge CB2 1RP
32 East 57th Street, New York, NY 10022, USA
296 Beaconsfield Parade, Middle Park, Melbourne 3206, Australia

First published in 1981

Printed in the United States of America
Typeset by Rainsford Type and Graphics Ltd., Ridgefield, Connecticut

*Library of Congress Cataloging in Publication Data*
Gustafson, Thane,
Reform in Soviet politics.
Includes index.
1. Russia – Politics and government – 1953 –
2. Land use – Russia – Planning. 3. Water resources
development – Russia. 4. Environmental policy – Russia.
5. Agriculture and state – Russia. I. Title.
JN6526 1981.G87   320.947   80–24286
ISBN 0 521 23377 1

*to the memory of my grandfather*
CHAPIN JONES

# CONTENTS

# PREFACE

How shall we understand the Soviet system and the ways time works on it? One of the purposes of this book is to wrestle with the question, How would we know a significant change in Soviet politics if we saw one? At a minimum, significant change means some alteration of a regime's basic stuff, whether defined as "the authoritative allocation of values" or "who gets what, when, and how." For change in Soviet politics to be significant, it must touch on the sources and instruments of the state's power and authority.

A generation ago, the synthesis achieved by Merle Fainsod in his book *How Russia Is Ruled* commanded a degree of agreement among his colleagues that no scholar is able to muster today. Western writers on Soviet politics now run the gamut from those who believe that the Soviet Union has not changed since Stalin's day to those who see evolving in Russia a measure of pluralism or at least a certain diffusion of power away from the central leadership. Each one has his own formula, aimed at capturing the essence of the system: "participatory bureaucracy," "institutional pluralism," "pluralism of elites," "directed society," "authoritarian system with a dysfunctional totalitarian residue," "welfare authoritarianism," and one could mention many more. In recent years, instead of synthesis and common ground, there is growing acrimony. What accounts for the loss of the earlier consensus?

It springs not so much from disagreement about facts – all Western Sovietologists work much the same mine and refine what they can from the same low-grade ore – but rather from different ideas about political theory, particularly about power, which unfortunately are not usually stated explicitly. That is not a criticism one can make of *How Russia Is Ruled*. Fainsod drew for his theoretical foundation on the work of C. J. Friedrich and others on totalitarianism, and his view of the Soviet state as totalitarian runs through every line. To be sure, his use of the term *totalitarian* was carefully balanced, reflecting the complex picture of Soviet society and administration that Western scholars had derived from Soviet documents captured in World War II and from countless interviews with former Soviet citizens who remained in the West after the war's end. Fainsod's Russia was totalitarian but not monolithic. "The pressure from above is ruthless and unremitting," he wrote, "and evasion from below is resourceful and not unavailing." Nevertheless, such evasion did not affect the essence of the system; it operated, Fainsod believed, entirely within the limits imposed by the ruling priorities of the party leadership.

The virtue of the totalitarian model, no doubt one of the reasons for its long appeal, is precisely that it defines a totalitarian regime by the way it forms and holds power. That is putting first things first. But to judge whether significant political change is at work, one must then ask further questions that a taxonomic model does not ask, such as the following: As the underlying society and economy of a totalitarian polity evolve, do its ultimate sources of power – the motives in people's minds (fear, faith, self-interest, and so forth) – evolve too and is the regime able to retain control of them? Do the changing society and economy produce new instruments of power and are they appropriable by anyone but the established rulers (as land grants and purchased offices proved to be in earlier ages)? What *kinds* of power are generated by a totalitarian regime at various stages of its existence, and are they equally effective at each stage in serving the leaders' goals? Questions such as these lead to specific and researchable tests. They may not reduce the disagreements among Western observers, but they may make it possible to identify more precisely what underlying conceptions of power the disagreements are really about.

One such test, the central theme of this book, is reform. Here I do not mean the self-improvement campaigns to be found in every issue of *Pravda*, but rather the purposeful attempt of a political leadership to remove a danger to itself, not by stopgap measures or repression but by developing new policies. Any leader who embarks on a new policy is well aware (we are talking about professionals of power, after all) that by altering established priorities, structures, functions, and procedures, or people, he may alter and thereby endanger the basis of his own power. Any reform amounts to a deliberate attempt to consolidate or rescue what the leaders consider essential while offering up the nonessential for sacrifice, hoping that the forces of change that they have loosed can be kept under control.

Any attempted reform is therefore a diagnostic tool for observing power at work. By observing what prompts a reform to start, we see what the political leaders regard as sufficiently threatening (and therefore basic) to warrant the effort and risk of an attempted change. By observing where reform stops (or, at least, where the leaders attempt to stop it), we see the point at which the initial motives of the leaders are balanced by their growing fear of the reform itself. By their ability to respond to threats while safeguarding their positions, to channel the course of reform without losing control of it, we gauge the sources and instruments of the leader's power and the degree to which those may be changing. Through the kinds of power the leaders attempt to deploy in each situation, and the success of each kind in furthering the reform, we gauge the aptness of the instruments available to them. And finally, if one is able to follow the debate and conflict surrounding a reform, one can gauge the strength of the various participants and determine whether they have power, or influence only.

Reform, of course, is not the only test of power relations in a political system. Moreover, focusing on reform amounts to making an implicit choice among competing definitions of power. According to some, power should be measured by the final outcomes it produces in society. Other definitions start from the view that power can be reliably traced only by watching both outcomes *and* the conflicts that produce them. If there has been no observable contest, then one cannot be sure from the outcome alone whether there has been an exercise of political power or some other cause, such as values widely shared by everyone involved or frustration of the leaders' policies by nature. This book tends to adopt the second definition as the only reliable guide to power. To judge the direction in which the Soviet political system is moving, it is not enough to observe the policies that the system is producing; one must also observe the process by which those policies are formed and implemented, and whether their final shape matches what the leaders intended at the outset. Using reform as a test of changing power relations is one way of doing that.

This book has gone through several molts. It began its earliest stage as a series of seminar papers on Soviet environmental and natural-resource politics, written under Merle Fainsod between 1970 and his death in 1972. It subsequently became a doctoral thesis comparing American and Soviet organizational responses to change in the politics of water management and large public works, based on a year of research in the Soviet Union. Five years of teaching Soviet and American politics then led to a broader concern with power and political change, an invaluable postdoctoral apprenticeship that gradually prodded the book toward its present appearance. Several return trips to the Soviet Union under the U.S.–Soviet Joint Agreements in effect during the latter half of the 1970s enabled me to conduct interviews and gather material for additional chapters. In the end, not much is left of the original Ph.D. thesis, a wry warning to graduate students.

I have incurred many debts along the way, and it is a great pleasure to have the opportunity to express publicly my appreciation to those who have advised, encouraged, and criticized this project at its various stages. I wish to thank first of all Arthur Maass of the Department of Government at Harvard University, under whose painstaking care and kind encouragement this book evolved, and whose line-by-line criticism of successive and innumerable drafts was the best part of my graduate and postdoctoral education. Special thanks are also due to Jerry Hough, who was my first teacher of Soviet politics while I was a member of his first class, the autumn that Khrushchev fell. Over the years since, he has provided many valuable suggestions and important observations for this book, but more important, he has been the most stimulating influence in the field and a constant source of new thoughts for everyone in it.

Not the least satisfying part of writing this book has been to discover the true meaning and value of the invisible college of scholars. I have benefited from the advice, help, and cheerfully donated labor of a large and talented group, including particularly David Albright, Arthur Alexander, Abram

Bergson, Seweryn Bialer, Paul Cocks, Loren Graham, Anatolii Gokhshtein, Gregory Grossman, Werner Hahn, Roy Laird, Gail Lapidus, Robert Legvold, Stephen Marglin, Pat Micklin, Nancy Nimitz, David Powell, Harry Rigby, Theodore Shabad, and Judith Shklar.

I have profited also from the help of many a fellow student and friend, whose work I follow with pleasure and respect, hoping only that in the last few years I have grown as much as they. Particular thanks go to George Breslauer, Valerie Bunce, Timothy Colton, Michael Mandelbaum, Bruce Parrott, Christophe Riboud, William DeSmedt, Peter Solomon, Susan Solomon, and Enders Wimbush. I am also indebted to my former graduate students, who are already promising colleagues: Mary Ruth Coleman, Patrick Flaherty, Peter Hauslohner (honoris causa), Geoffrey Levitt, Gregory Miller, and Bruce Porter. Two particularly able friends made valuable comments on later drafts, and I am especially grateful to them for inspiration: Steve Lemsen and Mark Beissinger.

The research and writing for this book could not have taken place without the help of many institutions and their members. From beginning to end I have enjoyed the steady and generous support of my former teachers and colleagues in the Government Department of Harvard University, where I spent ten rewarding years. The Russian Research Center, the Center for Science and International Affairs of the Kennedy School of Government, the Environmental Systems Program, the Seminar on Science and Public Policy, all of Harvard University, were happy and productive places to work. I am grateful to their staffs and members, and to the hospitality of their directors, Adam Ulam, Abram Bergson, Paul Doty, Graham Allison, Grant Schaumburg, Robert Dorfman, Harvey Brooks, I. Bernard Cohen, and Don K. Price. For the opportunity to travel and study in the Soviet Union at various times from 1972 to 1979, I am indebted to the International Research and Exchanges Board, the National Academy of Sciences, the Environmental Protection Agency, the National Science Foundation, Metasystems, Inc., the Rand Corporation, the USSR Ministry of Higher Education, the USSR Academy of Sciences, the USSR Ministry of Reclamation and Water Management, and the USSR Ministry of Power and Electrification, as well as the USSR State Committee on Science and Technology. Particularly helpful and hospitable were the officials and scholars of the Institute of Water Problems and the Institute of Geography of the USSR Academy of Sciences, the Ukrainian Academy of Sciences, and the State Universities of Moscow and Kiev. Finally, I am deeply grateful for the support of the Gildersleeve Wood Foundation and its capable director, C. Silver.

*Charlottesville, Virginia*                                                                      T.G.
*15 January 1981*

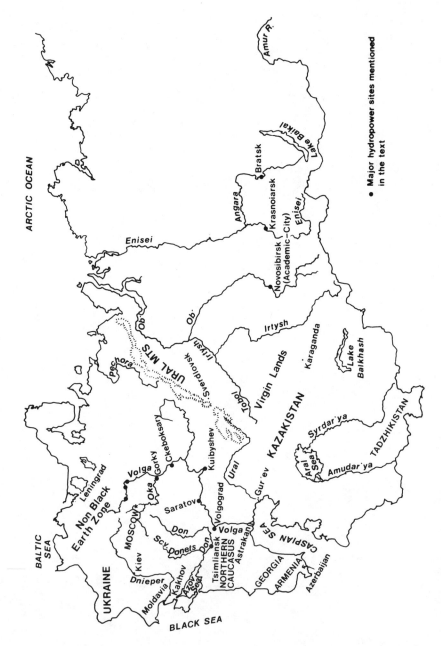

Map of Soviet Russia showing major hydropower sites.

# 1
# CHALLENGE OF THE
# THIRD GENERATION OF
# SOVIET POWER

This is a book about reform in Soviet politics and government. The reader may well ask, "What reform?" After fifteen years of a conservative, indeed virtually immobile regime under Brezhnev, what reforms can one talk about, other than those that shriveled in the bud or may await Brezhnev's departure to blossom? Yet the Brezhnev leadership committed a substantial share of its attention and energy to making one major change: It was the first Soviet government to address decisively, through a massive program of investment, the perennial blight of the Soviet economy, the problem of agriculture. The countryside consistently commanded the top civilian priority of the Brezhnev period, as the regime launched and sustained year after year a broad program of basic reconstruction and modernization. Here, then, is an exception to the overall immobility of the rest of the domestic scene. Its intrinsic importance aside, what does it tell us about the Soviet political system itself and about its capacity for reform? As Brezhnev's agricultural policy was apparently so different from that of his predecessors, does it reflect in any sense a deeper evolution? Does it contain any evidence of an underlying change in the relationship of knowledge to power in Soviet politics or in the instruments by which new policies are implemented? In short, if the Brezhnev agricultural policy is a reform, what does it imply for our understanding of the Soviet political system as a whole?

That is the subject of this book. The reader will not find here a systematic survey of agricultural policy but a set of connected case studies, through which we seek to understand basic political questions: How did the Soviet leaders come to admit that their traditional approach to agriculture had failed? How was a political coalition gradually formed behind a new one? Why did it then evolve the way it did, finally coming to include a broad range of associated policies for conservation, land and water use, and many more? How were the new policies carried out and with what effects? Through the answers to these questions we may begin to gauge the blend of reforming energy and conservative inertia with which the Soviet elite approaches its third generation of power.[1]

That third generation will face very different problems from the first two, and the Brezhnev experience in agriculture gives a foretaste of how difficult they will be. For fifty years the Soviet Union has built industrial and military might through a unique command system. Whether because of this system or in spite of it, the Soviet Union has become the world's second industrial, and perhaps first military, power. But now the last two decades of the twentieth century bring problems that threaten to slow or even halt the country's growth, calling into question the command system's most basic features. For fifty years economic growth was fed primarily by migration from the countryside and the mobilization of new raw materials. Whatever it may have wasted along the way, the command system gathered these resources quickly and put them where the leaders wanted them. But the new materials available today are both poorer in quality and located far from population centers, and manpower too is growing short. Soviet leaders could once squeeze consumption decade after decade, relentlessly building up capital stock. But now that strategy too is beginning to weaken, for consumers are also workers, and their frustrated expectations show up in poor labor discipline and stagnating labor productivity. The traditional system of planning and incentives rewarded quantity of output above all. Now the country finds that, because of its long neglect of quality standards and innovation, too much of what it produces is shoddy and backward, is unable to satisfy its own citizens, to compete in world markets, or perhaps even to provide the broad technological base required for the broad range of tomorrow's weapons systems. Each year brings new warnings: declining rates of economic growth, diminishing gains in factor productivity, a lengthening technological lag in many critical sectors, rising consumer resistance, and a thriving black market. After two generations of virtually single-minded heavy industrialization, the Soviet elite must confront the evidence: The next generation in the Kremlin must deal decisively and differently with the requirements of a developed industrial economy.[2]

But is the Soviet political system, now one of the world's longest established and most conservative, capable of making such basic changes? The political system grew up with the command economy and ever since the 1920s each has been shaped by the other, to such a point that both the political system and much of its power derive from its job of overseeing the command economy. They form virtually a single whole, whose strong points lie in its ability to produce a concentration of effort rather than a balance, quantity more than quality, uniform solutions over custom-tailored ones, enthusiasm and storming rather than measure and moderation, and vertical integration instead of horizontal. The levers of this system are primarily political rather than economic: Administrative allocation replaces the market; targets and directives replace price signals; and the movement of physical goods, channeled by supply orders, counts more than the movement of money. But political levers, as a recent work puts it, "have strong thumbs and weak fingers."[3] Much of the work of the political system traditionally consists of daily intervention to offset the thumb's defects. The result is a unique Soviet formula of dual government by party and state, which, though it arose initially through improvisation, has not changed much in fifty years. Half of it, the system of ministries and state committees, operates and coordinates the command system. The other half, the party apparatus, paralleling the first from top to bottom, counteracts the worst of its side effects and keeps it on course. This system has ensured for two generations the concentration of effort that the leaders required, and by comparison with all but a handful of countries, it has been successful and remarkably stable.[4]

Through this system the Soviet political elite have risen and succeeded, and they know no other. In the absence of an acute crisis, can they be expected to countenance any reform that would change their familiar world and the basis of their power? They would be unusual people indeed if they did not find merit in the functions that put them where they are, and this will be just as true of tomorrow's leaders as it is of today's. Can such an elite really address the social and economic problems now gathering before them?

That depends on what is required of them. What exactly makes this third-generation Soviet economy different from that of the first two? First, the period of revolutionary mobilization is long over. The state watches in resigned frustration as an increasingly affluent and independent-minded population migrates, consumes, works, and multiplies to suit itself. Of course the Kremlin could use force, and if hard-pressed enough it may yet do so. But that would cost the leaders dearly in terms of values they manifestly share with the rest of the population. One has only to look at how much the Brezhnev regime has invested in housing, livestock, automobiles and large appliances, imported consumer goods and food subsidies to see that today's leadership increasingly bases its sense of its own legitimacy on its ability to increase the public welfare. Can one seriously imagine such a conservative and materialistic leadership thrusting its conservative and materialistic population back into the terror and turmoil of the 1930s? However much the Kremlin may rail against the irrationality of its citizens' behavior, it has apparently resigned itself to coping as well as it can through incentives and exhortation, which means, in practice, that it is constrained from using its awesome powers of coercion.[5]

Second, the resources needed for further economic growth are growing scarcer – both conventional resources like land, labor, and minerals, and more subtle quantities like the stock of foreign technology that is easily assimilable or the waste-diluting capacity of seas and river basins. There are no uncommitted and easily accessible reserves on which to draw. So resources must be used more efficiently. In political terms, this means tailoring policies to local conditions and short-term changes in weather, supplies, world markets, and so on; limiting waste; accepting dependence on international trading partners so as to exploit the country's comparative advantages; and developing ways to shift resources rapidly among competing uses. The implication, once again, is that in their choices of policies and instruments the leaders are constrained.

Third, the entire Soviet economy now operates at a much higher technological level than it did a generation ago, and the tasks it performs are more demanding. Therefore the leadership increasingly requires high-quality work from a large fraction of the population. A better-educated and better-informed labor force must be stimulated, not coerced, and this too constrains the choice of the political instruments that can be used.

Another way of describing the constraints on the leaders in their use of the traditional instruments of a command economy is that the uneven, unbalanced development those instruments tend to produce is less and less tolerable, not least to the leaders themselves. What is the good of a modern computer network, for example, if the country's telephone system is too unreliable to be used for data transmission?[6] Of what value is the world's most advanced welding technology if half the supporting operations are still performed by hand?[7] The Soviet Union today is an industrial giant whose tractors, airplanes, and computers stand idle in large numbers for lack of spare parts and skilled technicians; whose population still spends a portion of each day standing in line for food or consumer goods; whose increasingly mechanized agriculture still lacks rural roads and processing plants. In these paradoxes we see the gathering consequences of an unbalance deliberately maintained for two generations.

In sum, the challenge of the Soviet economy in its third generation is this: An increasingly affluent and independent-minded population, scarce and remote resources, and ever more advanced and demanding technologies require new policies and mechanisms to promote greater balance, quality, attention to detail, fast and flexible response, efficient use of resources, and innovativeness. Without them, the Soviet economy cannot continue to grow.

If the beginning of reform is to recognize that a problem exists, then the Kremlin under Brezhnev has made more progress than one might think. Brezhnev himself, especially since 1968, has hammered away at the vital importance of technological innovation, productivity, and higher standards of quality.[8] His words at the Twenty-fifth Party Congress could be found in nearly all of his speeches of the last ten years:

> Comrades, in order to carry out successfully the diverse economic and social tasks facing the country, there is no other way than that of promoting the rapid growth of labor productivity and achieving a steep rise of efficiency in all areas of social production. Emphasis on efficiency – and this must be repeated again and again – is the key component of our entire economic strategy.
>
> We shall have to rely not on enlisting additional labor power but solely on increasing labor productivity.
>
> In the past we simply could not give due attention to infrastructure, in particular, to the construction of roads and storage facilities. We shall now have to engage in this work and do it seriously.
>
> The revolution in science and technology requires radical changes in the style and methods of economic work, a determined struggle against sluggishness and red tape.[9]

As the 1970s give way to the 1980s, the same sentiments echo throughout the country, in the press and in the speeches of other Soviet officials. Managers and specialists debate the pros and cons of various incentives, economic levers, indicators and prices.[10] Western management techniques, theories of organizational development, and computerized data-processing systems have become the fashion[11] The Soviet literature on the reasons for lag in technological innovation is abundant and frank.[12] The newspapers and journals are full of items about reducing the waste of metal, recycling process wastes, saving energy, uncovering caches of unused supplies and equipment, and finishing uncompleted projects. Perhaps the most popular word of the Brezhnev period is *kompleksno*, which translates (depending on the context) as multiple purpose, integrated, balanced, comprehensive, or ecologically sound. If talk necessarily led to action, the Soviet Union might be on the verge of the millennium.

Some of the talk has indeed led to action. The price system has been revised several times, with considerable overall improvement,[13] and there is constant tinkering with new target indexes and incentive systems.[14] Interesting experiments are under way in the management of technological innovation.[15] Economic planning has become more realistic and professional, and the targets of five-year plans under Brezhnev have been geared more closely to what the country can realistically attain. The leadership has deliberately slowed the rate of increase of capital accumulation, which by the 1960s had reached one-third of the national product, and it is promoting a more egalitarian welfare system and distribution of incomes.[16] Housing has expanded greatly; and the spread between the highest and lowest incomes has been reduced,[17] at least in comparison to the highly inegalitarian bias developed under Stalin. The principle of comparative advantage in international trade is increasingly accepted officially, and its corollary, economic interdependence, is making its way through the elite,[18] sometimes with surprising results. For example, for such a strategic material as aluminum, the Soviet Union has allowed itself to be dependent to a remarkable degree on foreign sources of bauxite, a development that would have been unthinkable in Stalin's time.[19] The economic and legal aspects of industrial production get more attention than they once did; contracts in particular are experiencing a revival as an instrument for regulating the relations between enterprises.[20] Two of the fastest-growing professions in the country are economics and law.[21] Despite the Brezhnev regime's conservative and stodgy image, it has encouraged a great deal of what one might call establishment soul-searching.

This is all abundant evidence that at least part of the ruling elite has convinced itself of the need for important changes. But for all the discussion and experimentation there has been very little actual reform. Most novelties, bravely launched in a fanfare of official publicity, have been easily derailed, co-opted, contained, or outlasted by the established ministries and state committees, and the leaders have not made any great effort (as far as outsiders can judge) to save them. The economic reform of the mid-1960s lost much of its force after 1968, and though it is still part of the official program, it is in effect a dead letter.[22] Reorganization of industrial production into corporationlike "associations" (*ob"edineniia*), that is, replacing the traditional vertically integrated directorates (*glavki*) with more horizontally integrated and profit-oriented units, has been deformed by ministerial resistance to the point where in most instances the associations either resemble the *glavki* in all but name, or have failed to develop beyond the stage of paper reform.[23] Computerized management and planning, after a decade of enthusiasm, have led to little so far except expensive experiments and considerable disillusionment.[24] Ministry research institutes, placed on a cost-accounting basis in the last ten years to make them more responsive to the needs of industrial producers, have often simply turned into job shops.[25] The overall supervision performed by the State Committee on Science and Technology is criticized as ineffectual.[26] Enterprise managers at the local level and the *glavki* above them remain as resistant to innovation as before,[27] and the diffusion of new products and processes continues to be slow.[28] Lastly, the basic system of targets, indicators, incentives, and prices, though much criticized, has not changed much either. Planning, though more modest and realistic, remains the same incremental, bargained affair it has traditionally been, despite the advent of computers;[29] and techniques like input-output analysis, though much heralded at first, have made only modest headway.[30] New performance indicators, such as profit or volume of production actually sold, turn out to have side effects of their own, as awkward (and sometimes the same) as the indexes they replaced. The word of the day may be *kompleksnost'* but the word that still describes reality is *vedomstvennost'*, the narrow departmentalism of the specialized bureaucracies. There has been no lack of starts, yet it is remarkable how few of them have been pursued. Reforms are never officially buried, but the life goes out of them. Important issues remain suspended for years. Reform is everywhere and yet nowhere. The political leaders may fume in the pages of the press, but they are apparently unable to overcome, or even to make much effort to overcome, the inertia and conservatism of the traditional institutions.

Why have the Soviet leaders failed to persist in the reforms they seem to perceive as so necessary? Faced with such a question, one instinctively reaches for the broad answers: The answer, some may say, lies in Brezhnev's personality, or the character of the dominant coalition in the Kremlin, or some peculiarity of the distribution of power within the current elite. Others may feel that the political system itself is somehow petrified, unable to respond to its problems with effective reforms. Both of these explanations arise out of a common view of Soviet development: that while the Soviet economy and society are evolving, the political system and the political elite are not, and that unless the latter can make basic changes, dire things will happen.[31]

There is nothing wrong with such explanations; they may even be correct. But they require a long jump, to say the least, between fragmentary evidence and sweeping conclusions, and, unfortunately, we Western observers of Soviet affairs all too often find that jump irresistible. We are too quick to infer vast political consequences from economic and social causes without being particularly precise about what connects one to the other. We have not done enough thinking about what kinds of political changes, short of sweeping systemic reform, might be enough to enable the political system and its elite to maintain themselves. Between sweeping reform or reaction, on the one hand, and petrification and collapse, on the other, we leave little middle ground; and we make little allowance for the unspectacular process of trial and error by which most established political systems somehow manage to cope with their crises and blunder on. Can one avoid these pitfalls? Probably not altogether, but one can at least ask oneself the following three test questions: First, what established political system ever addresses all of its problems simultaneously? If we wish to judge accurately the precise mixture of reforming vigor and hardening of the arteries in the Soviet political system under Brezhnev, we must look where the regime has chosen to devote most of its attention and resources. Second, what established political system launches reforms when its problems are still on the horizon? The last fifteen years have been a comparatively benign period in Soviet economic life, and most of the problems of the third-generation Soviet economy are only beginning to be felt. Many members of the elite, seeing the country quiet at home and powerful abroad, may understandably feel no particular urgency about reforms nor agree on the sources of the country's problems. Third, what established political system embarks on major systemic changes before exhausting the milder or safer alternatives? In sum, to gain a realistic idea of the capacity of the Soviet political system to solve new problems, we must look first of all for sectors of policy that meet the following three criteria: They must be sectors in which the political leadership perceives a clear and present threat, in which earlier policies have manifestly failed and to which the leaders give sustained attention and high priority.

We have not far to look, for there have been only two fields of policy under Brezhnev that meet these criteria: military technology and agriculture.[32] It is the former, of course, that has drawn the world's attention. The most spectacular and ominous achievement for which the Brezhnev regime will be remembered is the modernization and expansion of the Soviet armed forces. But the more significant and difficult policy, as a test of the adaptiveness and reforming energy of the Kremlin, is agriculture.

Agriculture meets all three test questions raised above. First, the Brezhnev agricultural policy was prompted by the clearest threats. Although crop failures and even famine are nothing new in Russian experience, such occurrences in the 1960s were especially bad. Extremes of weather, aggravated by neglect and bad management, caused major losses in 1963, 1965, and 1969. More to the point, the rising standards of the Soviet population turned these periodic failures into a distinct political danger. Food riots broke out in several places, mainly over shortages of meat. The need to turn to foreign markets for grain became a regular humiliation and a drain of foreign currency. In the eyes of the leaders of the mid-1960s, agricultural problems endangered at once domestic stability, national security, and economic growth.

Second, the traditional approach had manifestly failed. It was based on the assumption that a modern agricultural sector could be created with a minimum of investment, if only one could find the right combination of organization and incentives. When that failed, agricultural policy degenerated into political pressure and a vain search for shortcuts, which worsened an already serious misallocation of scarce agricultural resources.

Third, agriculture has undoubtedly received the leaders' sustained attention and priority, for over the past fifteen years, agriculture, conservation, and related programs have been the fastest-growing sectors of the Soviet economy – faster growing, in fact, than the military. Their share of the country's capital investment budget now stands at 27 percent, twice what it was in the early 1950s.[33] This would be a remarkable shift of resources for any major industrial power, but it is especially so for a country that until recently gave agriculture the lowest priority and whose leaders built their careers almost entirely around industry.[34] In the scale and scope of the effort, in the number of people and regions affected, the only precedent that stands comparison with it is the beginning of the heavy industrialization of the 1930s.

Even more remarkable, however, are the changes that have taken place in the style and the design of agricultural policy. Largely gone are the gimmickry and quackery, the administrative tinkering and political pressure, the erratic funding of Soviet agricultural policy in earlier years. After ten years of debate, development, and expansion, virtually all aspects of agricultural investment are getting top-priority support. The Soviet leadership has launched and maintained for more than a decade a major program of reclamation and conservation, modernization of animal husbandry, sharply increased investment in the underlying structure required for modern agriculture, and improvement of rural living standards. For the first time, it has begun a real environmental program to protect scarce land and water. Not only have the leaders' investment priorities changed but seemingly also some of their most deeply ingrained habits and attitudes toward agriculture and natural resources.

Consider now what it has meant in political terms to attempt to undo forty years of neglect. Agriculture was the orphan of the Stalin period. The resources, the expertise, and the political power that in a country like the United States went into modern agriculture flowed instead in the Soviet Union toward other sectors. Cropland was flooded for hydropower, taken over by cities and industry, and allowed to erode and deteriorate. Soviet chemists made explosives, not fertilizers. Electricity went to the cities, not the countryside (only now is the Soviet Union conducting a program of rural electrification analogous to that of the United States in the 1930s).[35] Water resources were developed for power, transportation, and industrial production, instead of irrigation. The generations of talented rural graduates who might have become agronomists, plant breeders, or soil scientists went to the cities instead and became engineers. In short, forty years of neglect of agriculture became part of the very structure of society, of the appearance of the land, and of the shape of the political system. To redirect priorities back toward agriculture has inevitably been slow, difficult, and attended by constant conflict.

Therefore, if we wish to test the political vigor and reforming ability of the political system under Brezhnev, there is no better place to begin than

with agriculture. To initiate, design, and implement the new policy required first of all the forging of a strong pro-agricultural coalition in the
Politburo and the government elite, that is, among a group of men not much
accustomed to taking agriculture as seriously as industry. Second, it required giving some respect and recognition to the advice of specialists
whose disciplines only a few years before had been lightly regarded and
developing, as a result, new attitudes toward land, water, and other natural
resources. Finally, by far the biggest requirement was to move power, skills,
and resources from industry to agriculture. This has meant disrupting
established lines of status, priority, and habit at all levels throughout the
country, from Gosplan (the State Planning Committee) at the top to local
irrigation districts at the bottom. This has been no mere redirection of
policy but a massive transfer of political clout, positions, and prerogatives.
Just to carry out that much has been a major challenge.

But is this a "third-generation" reform? Earlier we summed up the requirements for managing the increasingly sophisticated, but constrained,
Soviet economy under the words *balance, quality, long horizons,* and *efficiency.* Is there any sign in the initiation, design, and implementation of the
Brezhnev agricultural policy that the political leadership really recognizes
these requirements and is able to adapt to them? The difficulty of this
question is that the job of rescuing and reconstructing Soviet agriculture
calls for a mixture of both the heroic *grands moyens* of Stalinist industrialization and the carefully measured and tailored approach of modern industrial management. On the one hand, given the abysmal condition of Soviet
agriculture in the 1950s, the degraded state of the soil, the primitive rural
infrastructure, the low status of agricultural sciences and professions, and
the scarcity of skilled labor, the core of the new program has necessarily
consisted of a vast effort of capital investment and training, precisely the
classic task that every Soviet leader and official has grown up on. In this
respect the Brezhnev agricultural policy is the last of the great Soviet
industrializing campaigns, and presumably the natural tendency of everyone concerned is to carry it out in the familiar way.

But modern agriculture is also a quintessentially third-generation undertaking in all three of the senses described earlier. The growing tendency of
Soviet people to move, work, and reproduce to suit themselves puts even
more pressure on the farm than on the city. If rural living conditions and
incomes remain substandard, young and skilled farmers simply leave.
Water and good land are in short supply. And the country's rising requirements for high-quality performance are as great in agriculture as they are in
sophisticated high-technology industries. New grain varieties, for example,
must get exactly the right combination of sun, moisture, and fertilizer to
produce high yields and good nutritional quality. Improper irrigation and
drainage will poison a field with salt in a few years. New machinery must be
serviced; new seed varieties must be tested; the modern "agroindustrial
complex" (to use the Soviet term) requires reliable supplies, good access,
power, and communications. In sum, modern agriculture is demanding in
the same ways that modern industry is, but it is also more delicate. Unless

the Brezhnev agricultural policy manages to incorporate major elements of a third-generation approach, it will not succeed beyond a very modest, but very expensive, level.

Any one of the major components of the Brezhnev program could be used to illustrate the combination of second- and third-generation reforms contained in it, but none engages so many of these requirements simultaneously, none illustrates better the ambition and scope of the new policies than the effort to free Soviet agriculture from drought. That struggle will be the focal point of many of the conflicts and debates described in this book. Uncertain rainfall is the greatest single hindrance to Russian agriculture. Sixty percent of the Soviet grain-growing area suffers some loss from inadequate moisture, on the average, in three or four years out of ten.[36] This makes Soviet agriculture highly unpredictable, a nightmare for those who manage it and for those who depend on it. In the late 1960s and early 1970s, for example, procurement sales of grain to the state were only half as large in the worst years as in the best ones. The central aim of the Brezhnev policy has been not only to increase overall yields but also to stabilize them. Hence, an extraordinary emphasis on irrigation.

Foremost on the list of crops to stabilize is grain. This has meant bringing irrigation to the European part of the USSR, where it had been little used before. The traditional focus of Soviet irrigation had been on Central Asian cotton; it has now shifted decisively to the production of grain in the Ukraine and the southern regions of Russia.[37] By the mid-1980s, such newly irrigated areas could produce a dependable addition to Soviet grain output of up to 30 million tons a year, compared with only 4 million tons from irrigated lands in 1965.[38] The irrigation program stands as the centerpiece of what might be called the "southern strategy" in the Brezhnev policy (in contrast to a "northern" strategy of drainage, liming, as so on, in areas like the non-black-earth zone [*nechernozem'e*], north and west of Moscow). The southern strategy has to recommend it longer growing seasons, more sunlight, richer soils, and relatively more plentiful manpower. But its one great drawback is a lack of water.

As a result, the southern strategy is technically and politically tricky. Building thousands of miles of irrigation canals and developing the capacity to use them require nothing less than a new industrial base, specialized in the production of concrete forms, earth-moving equipment, plastic sheeting, sprinklers, pumps, and so on. Construction teams must be assembled, housed, and fed. Farmers must learn irrigated agriculture, particularly how to avoid poisoning the land with excess moisture and salt. Competing water users like hydropower and industry must be cut back to liberate water and pollution must be controlled, for soon the presently available sources of water will be developed and committed. New seed varieties are needed; and the proper combinations of fertilizer and water must be determined for each variety and location. All of these policies must operate smoothly and in the proper sequence for the southern strategy to succeed.

The reader will have noted in this list a mix of both traditional and third-generation tasks. Building the irrigation system is difficult enough.

But liberating water for it while maintaining a balance with the needs of other important users, getting farmers to irrigate correctly, obtaining higher yields without losing nutritional content, preventing heavy metals and chemicals from reaching the fields – these are precisely the third-generation challenges we have been talking about, and they will determine the success or failure of the program.

If the political system fails in them, then there remain two alternatives: to curtail the southern strategy or to bring down additional water from the north. Neither alternative is particularly palatable, the first because the southern strategy is essential for a stable buffer of grain, upon which Soviet animal husbandry is exceptionally dependent (other types of fodder are still relatively undeveloped);[39] the second because diverting northern rivers would involve some of the most expensive and ambitious engineering ever undertaken by man.[40] As a result, the southern strategy is a high-stakes wager on the ability of the political system to implement an efficient and balanced program, the very essence of a third-generation challenge.

The crucially scarce resource whose allocation and efficient use will spell the success or failure of the southern strategy is not money, but water. The Soviet Union can be thought of as a single plateau with a low divide in the middle, separating the country into a north and south face. One of nature's injustices to the Soviet Union is that more than 88 percent of the country's freshwater is located in the north and east, whereas the south and west get only 12 percent.[41] According to one Soviet authority, by the year 2000 the water needed for irrigation in the southern half of the European USSR, together with the amounts necessary to maintain the levels and ecological conditions of the Caspian and Azov seas, will exceed what the area's rivers supply in an average year.[42] In Central Asia, irrigation already takes 75 percent of all the water consumed in the Aral Sea basin, and experts warn that if more water is not available by the 1990s, further development will cease.[43]

But for the observer of Soviet politics, the scarcity of water proves to be a bonanza, for it forces into a single political arena a crowd of powerful and thirsty actors. In the southern half of the USSR, hydropower, industry, waterways, transportation, and agriculture all depend heavily on water. (See map p. xiv.) The disagreements among these groups are loud and often bitter; but most important of all, they are public. Soviet sources that are silent on traditional subjects of power politics (like money) become positively garrulous on the subject of water. The politics of water give a more vivid and detailed insight into the operations of the Soviet political system than any other single scarce resource. This most crucial issue of the Brezhnev agricultural reform, upon which hinges the fate of the southern strategy, provides much of the illustrative material for the themes of this book. Our fundamental subject is not water or agriculture as such; rather, it is the capacity of the Soviet political system to initiate and carry out reform. The central issue is whether its leaders can meet the challenges of economic modernity as we have just described them.

What are the political implications of that challenge? Under Soviet conditions, the demands of a third-generation economy lead to a political dilemma.

On the one hand, to deal with them adequately, the leadership must elicit from people at all levels of Soviet society the kinds of behavior that will produce "quality and efficiency" (as the current Soviet formula goes) in a third-generation economy: to accept risks (those of promoting innovation, for example); to take broader account of the costs and consequences of their actions (such as those of not meeting contracts for intermediate goods); to adapt to complex, shifting, or uncertain conditions; and to take greater responsibility for the quality of their performance – in short, the political system must elicit not simple obedience but high-quality and intelligent participation, not just in a few high priority sectors but throughout the economy.

Yet the special dilemma of reform in Soviet politics is that the inducements that might elicit such participation must operate in a political system based largely and essentially on negative powers, that is, powers that aim to contain and control people's behavior and make it predictable. Negative power, as I am using the term here, means not so much police power (although police power is a part of it) as it does a deeply rooted network of centralized signals, incentives, and commands that inhibits people at all but the very top levels of society from perceiving accurately the true costs of alternative actions, from taking risks or responding energetically to uncertainty, from taking the broad or long view, or from responding to problems and opportunities by adjusting rapidly their plans, their instruments, or their location; and most of all, from taking initiative. The system encourages instead caution and passivity or at best a kind of virtuosity in extracting the maximum safe advantage for the individual or his immediate circle from the incentives and signals presented to them. It is not for nothing that the literary hero closest to Soviet hearts is Ostap Bender, the agile con artist of *The Twelve Chairs* and *The Golden Calf*.[44] The existing network of prices, procedures, and incentives gives most people little to lose from the inefficient operation of the system and little to gain in exchange for the risk and work that would be required to do things differently. Negative controls create a safe, if inefficient, world that is by now deeply rooted in people's habits and attitudes and that competes directly with more positive instruments.

In the last ten or twenty years, to be sure, Soviet leaders have not made full use of the negative powers available to them (at least as far as the bulk of the population is concerned). It is at least plausible to suppose that this reflects a tacit acknowledgment on their part that it is impossible to deal with the demands of modern economy by the coercive methods that even under Stalin did not work particularly well. But can they develop different ones? The political system may be so fundamentally based on the resources and instruments of negative control that the positive instruments required to deal with the problems of a modern economy cannot be developed without threatening the source of position and privilege in Soviet society, not only at the top but at every level.

Before concluding that reform is impossible, we should remember that any state system is based on some combination of positive and negative powers, and that to some degree the two are always antagonistic and must somehow be accommodated to one another. In this sense the problem of reform in Soviet politics is only a particularly acute form of the problem that must be solved by any ongoing political system. One must not assume in advance, therefore, that the Soviet political system is inherently unable to turn the universal trick, at any rate to the extent necessary to develop the half measures and second bests with which political systems manage to cope with their problems.

But there is coping and coping. How can we tell the difference between mere short-term temporizing and effective long-term responses to the challenges of a modern economy? Any Soviet leadership, whether that of Brezhnev or his successors, as it goes about developing a new policy, must address certain generic problems:

1. How to bring new ideas (and useful criticism of old ones) into legitimate currency within the Soviet elite

2. How to translate new ideas into programs that can be added to the political agenda

3. How to form a new elite consensus and/or a commanding political coalition around new ideas

4. How to implement new ideas

5. How to gain accurate and useful information about problems arising along the way

By examining, in specific cases, the way these five tasks are carried out, one can begin to judge how deep a new policy goes and what its deeper political consequences may be, that is, whether it involves some change in the relationship of knowledge and power in the political system and some evolution in the resources and instruments of power upon which the leadership can draw. Given the requirements of a third-generation economy, these political challenges of reform will be the same for any future Soviet leaders, regardless of whether the leadership happens to be broadly reform-minded or inclines, on the contrary, to shrink from reform in all but one or two areas (as the Brezhnev leadership did). That is why the study of even limited reform in an otherwise conservative regime yields insights that are broadly applicable to the whole political system, regardless of who succeeds Brezhnev to the Kremlin in the 1980s.

These questions dictate the plan of this book. It is divided into two parts. The first chapter discusses the origins of the Brezhnev program in the Politburo: How persuasion, key alliances, and crisis combined by the end of the 1960s to form a strong – perhaps even too strong – pro-agricultural coalition. The next four chapters deal with the roles and uses of experts in the initiation and evolution of the Brezhnev program and question the significance of their influence on the leaders' thinking. Chapter 2 examines the ways in which authority was established around the new program. Chapter 3 describes the rise of an environmental protest movement and the part that movement played in making environmental issues a legitimate part of the official agenda and an important component of the southern strategy. Chapter 4 shows the part that the revival of economics, and especially the rehabilitation of an interest rate on capital, played in inhibiting the political clout of hydropower, agriculture's chief competitor for scarce water and land; and questions the significance of economic analysis in planning capital investment in the new agricultural policy. Chapter 5 recounts the twenty-year debate over proposals to divert northern waters to the south and explains why such proposals may now be on the verge of official adoption, to save the southern strategy. Finally, Chapter 6 discusses how the position of specialists, advisers, and establishment protesters has evolved under Brezhnev, the scope and limits of their influence, their role in bringing new ideas to the state agenda, and the fate of their advice once new policies have been adopted.

Part II deals with implementation. Chapter 7 shows why agriculture's competitors have been able to obstruct and delay the transfer of water and priority over water use to irrigation. Chapter 8 describes the difficulties of enforcing a waste-treatment program, the resistance of industry, and its consequences for the southern strategy. Chapter 9 analyzes why the reclamation program itself has strayed off course, producing skyrocketing costs but little progress in improving or stabilizing yields. Together these three chapters show why the leaders' efforts to promote smooth reallocation and the efficient use of water for the southern strategy have lagged, driving Moscow closer to the classic second-generation solution of bringing more water to the south through massive engineering. Chapter 10 generalizes about the leaders' problems with implementation, arguing that their efforts to correct them through traditional instruments of power have not enabled them to get their way at the price and pace they need.

Though much of this book deals with public debate and conflict among specialists and conflict among state agencies, it is not a book about interest groups or a defense of the view that the Soviet political system is evolving toward pluralism. Instead, the key question here is whether the Soviet political system, born and formed as it was during the first two generations of the Soviet period, can develop resources and instruments of power appropriate to the third, and what will happen to its policies if it cannot.

# 2
# BUILDING AUTHORITY AROUND A NEW AGRICULTURAL POLICY

Nowhere is there a greater contrast between the first two Soviet generations and the third than in agriculture and the programs that support it. In effect, Stalin's priorities have been reversed. Agriculture no longer subsidizes industrial growth; instead, it is now industry that subsidizes agricultural reconstruction and modernization.[1] At the beginning of the 1960s, nothing would have seemed less likely than such a drastic turnabout. The Soviet regime's bias against agriculture appeared built into the very structure of planning and administration. How then was the Soviet leadership able to change direction so dramatically?

The argument of this chapter is that the change took fifteen years of painful trial and error, a long learning period in which several things evolved together: the elite's attitudes toward agriculture, but also, at a deeper level, their views on natural resources, large undertakings, and on the complex demands of policy making in a mature industrial system. The gradual evolution of new policies suggests that another kind of learning was also taking place: how to build authority and agreement in a political system no longer inspired by fervor or (at least in everyday establishment politics) ruled by fear.

Officially, the new program dates from the March 1965 plenum of the party Central Committee, convened some five months after the fall of Nikita Khrushchev.[2] At that session, one bitter speech after another repudiated Khrushchev's agricultural policies. His last desperate reforms, particularly one that divided the party apparatus into separate agricultural and industrial wings, were annulled.[3] Within a year, agricultural reconstruction and reclamation began expanding phenomenally.

Yet the fact is that most of the post-1965 programs actually began under Khrushchev, and their underlying strategy can be traced back to 1962 or even1958.[4] The authors of the new policy in 1965 were not new either. By and large, they were Khrushchev's Politburo without Khrushchev.[5] During 1958–64, several of them had been noticeably cool to the idea of allocating more money to agriculture.[6] In fact, Brezhnev had to labor for five more years after 1965 before there jelled a stable coalition in favor of higher agricultural investment.

What, then, brought forth the new coalition and the underlying change in the thinking of the Soviet leadership? To answer this question, we must look back to well before the plenum of March 1965; in particular, we must look at Krushchev himself.

## Khrushchev

Krushchev's role in agricultural policy was disastrous and yet indispensable. By repeated and resounding failure, he discredited the worst of the Stalinist approach to agriculture, clearing the way for something new. To appreciate how important this is, we must look back to the 1950s. Traditional Soviet agricultural policy, as inherited from Stalin, was a blend of pressure and impatience, of stubborn optimism, and of willful ignorance. Whatever their differences in detail, Soviet leaders had shared the belief that agriculture could be set in the right direction without a major restructuring or a permanent increase in agriculture's share of the investment budget. This opened the way to gimmickry. Soviet leaders were easily won over by quacks like Lysenko who promised miracles for nothing, whether by exploiting new lands, the latest crop or cropping system, reorganization, or change of personnel. Loud promises got more support than sound agronomy.

In these views and ways, Khrushchev belonged to his generation. Over the years, there was little in the traditional arsenal that he did not try, and many of the traits for which we remember him best come from his endless schemes for the countryside: his colorful harangues and pungent scoldings, his love of the spectacular gamble, his tub-thumping campaigns and whirl-wind inspection tours, his endless and frantic reorganizations, his weakness for miracle crops and agronomic nostrums, and especially his fatal habit of taking every good turn in the weather as a vindication of his policies.[7] Khrushchev may have carried this style to its extreme, but it was not different in kind from what the entire Politburo had grown up on.

Yet Khrushchev also differed from his rivals of the 1950s in one important respect – his passionate interest in agriculture. Because agriculture was his constant preoccupation, he kept the local party apparatus busy on agricultural problems and favored the careers of apparatchiki with agricultural, rather than industrial, experience. In this way, he contributed to the subsequent post-1965 majority for agriculture, for when his successors ended his bifurcation of the apparatus into separate industrial and agricultural branches, the men appointed first secretaries of the *oblast'* party committees (as well as afforded membership in the CPSU Central Committee) turned out to be largely the pre-bifurcation incumbents of those posts, men with experience in agriculture.[8] By forcing his colleagues and the entire party apparatus to focus their attention on agriculture, and by keeping them so focused for a decade, Khrushchev drove the entire Soviet leadership through a collective education.

Nothing captures this painful and protracted learning process better than the Virgin Lands program launched in 1954, Khrushchev's most famous agricultural gamble. He justified this bold move to open up tens of millions of acres of prairie land in Kazakhstan as an emergency maneuver, a temporary expedient to hold the line while mechanized, intensive agriculture devel-

oped in European Russia. This was Khrushchev at his daring and imaginative best. But in its military cast, its ambition and haste, its appeal to
patriotism and youthful energy, it was a classic Stalinist venture, vulnerable to the classic Stalinist excesses. Like many another temporary measure, the Virgin Lands program soon became permanent, displacing what it
had been intended to buy time for. As it expanded, it starved the rest of
Soviet agriculture, especially in the non-black-earth zone in the northern
half of the European USSR. What had been a good gamble until 1958
mushroomed into a very bad one by 1963. This was Khrushchev at his
worst.

We have a remarkably frank front line assessment of these events in the
autobiography of Fedor Morgun, now first secretary of the CPSU's Poltava
obkom and a member of the CPSU Central Committee.[9] From chairman of
a state farm cut out of uninhabited prairie in 1954, Morgun rose by the
mid-1960s to become head of agriculture for the entire Tselinnyy Kray in
the Virgin Lands. Although he never mentions Khrushchev's name, Morgun
shows in devastating detail how the late leader's policies drove soil fertility
steadily downward, leading eventually to the disastrous crop failure of
1963. Constant pressure from above to increase the area under the plow led
to a steady and ultimately fatal reduction in fallow. Soon the fields were
infested with weeds. Attempts to deal with them by plowing them under
only made matters worse. The steady, dry winds of Kazakhstan whipped up
the soil into dust storms that reached as far as European Russia. Farm labor,
discouraged by declining yields, migrated back to Europe. New arrivals,
attracted at great expense, brought with them the agricultural habits of the
Ukraine and Belorussia, ill-suited to the dry, fragile soils of the Virgin
Lands. What kept the fateful cycle going, Morgun stresses again and again,
was short-sightedness, agronomic stupidity, and willful disregard of facts –
all a result primarily of relentless political pressure from Moscow.

Leonid Brezhnev, as first secretary of the party organization in Kazakhstan,
was in charge of the Virgin Lands program in its first two years. In his official
autobiography, he takes pains to show that his own approach was very
different from Khrushchev's.[10] Brezhnev writes that he and his Kazakh
colleagues listened carefully to scientists. They responded to local conditions, heeded the advice of soil scientists in laying out the state farms, and
planned for the future from the start. As early as 1955, Brezhnev was
following the advice of the advocates of late sowing and ample fallow.[11]
But what went wrong? "There is a more terrible enemy of the land than the
plow and weeds," Brezhnev writes: "It's the practice of imposing on it every
conceivable kind of 'recommendation' from above."[12] Surprisingly, he
mentions Khrushchev by name, but surprisingly, too, he treats the late
party leader rather gently, even though portraying him as impulsive and
impatient.[13] Bearing in mind that we are dealing here with a highly official
biography, we need not take at face value Brezhnev's description of his own
role – he was above all supremely lucky to get out of Kazakhstan when he
did – but the account is valuable for stressing the ways in which the
Brezhnev policy claims to be different from Khrushchev's.

Was the great gamble worth it? Morgun believes it succeeded, and so does Brezhnev. For a total investment of 21.1 billion rubles in Kazakh agriculture from 1954 to 1977, Brezhnev observes, the Soviet Union got more than 250 million tons of grain, and the Virgin Lands are now an established going concern. But were significant alternatives forgone as a result? Martin McCauley, in his work, *Khrushchev and the Development of Soviet Agriculture*, examines carefully all the possible alternatives and comes to the striking conclusion that there really were none. None, that is, that the leaders of the 1950s were prepared to pursue seriously.

Technically, the main alternative open after Stalin's death was to concentrate on raising yields in the European USSR – the strategy the Soviets call intensification. G. M. Malenkov, Khrushchev's principal rival in 1953–5, favored this approach, yet there is no evidence that he or anyone else in the Soviet leadership during that period was willing to devote the time and resources to make it work.[14] Khrushchev in his memoirs claims that he too favored intensification but that the country lacked the necessary supporting industrial base (for the manufacture of machinery, fertilizer, etc.) and skilled manpower. Meanwhile, a great crisis loomed, and something had to be done quickly.[15] Given those assumptions, the Virgin Lands scheme was tempting indeed.

Nevertheless, there was a great deal of opposition to it in 1953–5, and Brezhnev describes the issues in some detail. Some objected that the Virgin Lands program would make the country even more a hostage to bad weather than it already was; others felt that scarce manpower and equipment should not be drawn away from the European USSR, where they were already in short supply. "Here and there in the villages of Smolensk province," grumbled old Marshal Voroshilov, "people are still pulling the plows themselves." But Voroshilov soon came around, Brezhnev writes, once he saw the results. "What a good thing [it is] we came here!" Voroshilov later exclaimed on a visit to Kazakhstan; "You should draw a yellow cross on those machines, the color of that wheat!"[16] What Brezhnev discreetly passes over is that the grumbling over the Virgin Lands continued throughout the party and government long after the venture was launched. Morgun mentions the sarcastic comments he heard on visits to party functions in Moscow,[17] and McCauley discusses a debate after 1964 over whether to scrap the whole program.[18] But Brezhnev refers only to steady support from the CPSU Central Committee and the Politburo.[19]

For all their muttering against the Virgin Lands project, what were the opponents proposing instead? Intensification without major investment amounted to going nowhere, an empty formula. Khrushchev at least had a plan to meet a clear crisis. He caught the imagination and promised quick, tangible results. But both he and his opponents appear to have agreed on one thing: There was no question of making quantum increases in agricultural investment. We can see that much from the sums of money involved then and since: The Virgin Lands project ended up costing 21 billion rubles in twenty-five years, but the intensification strategy pursued since 1965 will cost fifty times that over a similar period. This enormous difference shows how much has changed in the leaders' attitudes since the mid-1950s: The Soviet leadership of the 1970s was willing to spend hundreds of billions and wait decades (though their successors in the 1980s may be less so); Khrushchev, his rivals, and his colleagues of the 1950s were not, and there was no serious disagreement among them on that point.

Some Western specialists will disagree. Sidney Ploss and Carl Linden, writing soon after Khrushchev's fall, saw Khrushchev as a consistent supporter of increased agricultural investment throughout his rule.[20] What prevented him from succeeding was the opposition of military and heavy-industrial interests. In this interpretation, two events were crucial. The first was the near-coup of 1957, in which Khrushchev found himself outvoted in the Politburo and saved himself only by hastily summoning an emergency meeting of the Central Committee, which ousted the would-be ousters. According to Ploss, Khrushchev's narrow escape forced him to sacrifice his ambitious plans for agriculture in exchange for support from the military and the party apparatus against his enemies in the Politburo.[21] The other key point was in 1961-2, when Khrushchev redoubled his agitation for more agricultural spending and supposedly failed, once again because he was opposed by the advocates of continued heavy spending for the military and heavy industry.

This interpretation, if correct, would have two important implications. First, that during the entire decade of Khrushchev's rule, the attitudes of the top elite toward agriculture did not evolve and that most of them remained consistently opposed to increased investment in agriculture. If this is true, then it is difficult to understand how both Khrushchev and Brezhnev managed to gain additional resources for agriculture in the 1960s (as we shall see they did), when Khrushchev was already weak and (after 1964) Brezhnev was not yet strong. The second implication is that power politics overshadowed concern for sound policy in the Kremlin, and the issue boiled down to a simple matter of Khrushchev versus the steel-eaters, in which Khrushchev was repeatedly forced to soft-pedal his views on policy to save his political position. When he failed to do so, this view implies, he so offended established conservative interests that their anger contributed substantially to his fall.

It now appears that this interpretation is mistaken. The pattern of funding for agriculture in those years, and particularly the share of agriculture in the total investment budget, tells another story: Agricultural investment (as a percentage of total investment) declined during Khrushchev's strongest years and rose again as he weakened in the 1960s – hardly the pattern one would expect if Khrushchev was the lone defender of agricultural investment throughout his rule.

George Breslauer's careful analysis of Khrushchev's speeches points to a more likely explanation: Until 1960, he was convinced that the solution to the country's agricultural problems lay not in more investment but, rather, in better organization and mobilization of the farmers. And when agricultural investment plunged, from 1956 to 1960, to levels not seen since the late 1940s (perhaps as low as 12 percent of the total investment budget),[22] there is no evidence that Khrushchev opposed the decline. Far from being the embattled advocate of greater agricultural investment in the late 1950s, Khrushchev stood firm *against* pressure for greater investment coming from what he termed the "agricultural organs," who had "worked out fairly extensive proposals for the development of all branches of agriculture in the Soviet Union." Khrushchev added, "We rejected these proposals."[23] Such language suggests that Khrushchev himself led the way in cutting agricultural investment after 1955. It also suggests that a part of the Soviet elite had already begun the slow change in their agricultural views that culminated in a new consensus in the 1960s.

There are problems as well with the view that Khrushchev, agriculture's friend, was trying to cut back the military. It is now clear in retrospect that the late 1950s were a major turning point in Soviet military policy, the beginning of the vast program of expansion and modernization that has created the mighty military machine we see before us now. No government whose top leader was locked in perpetual conflict with the military could have achieved such a systematic and thorough restructuring. We know, from other Western sources on the subject, that Khrushchev was often at odds with the traditional land forces and tried to reduce their power.[24] But for the military as a whole, Khrushchev presided over a major increase in investment. Given his views on agriculture during the 1950s, there was no conflict or inconsistency between his aims for the one and his aims for the other.

But by the end of the decade Khrushchev was gradually moving toward very different opinions. From 1960 on, he came around to the view that only massive investment in infrastructure would solve the agricultural problem. In a note to the Presidium in October 1960, Khrushchev wrote, "obviously we did not act completely correctly when we began to cut capital investments" – which is as close as any politician can afford to come, while still in office, to admitting a mistake.[25] At the January 1961 plenum of the Central Committee, Khrushchev went on to urge, "now our country has such powerful industry and such powerful defense that it can allot more funds for developing agriculture."[26] And at the same plenum, he began criticizing those who have "now developed an appetite for giving the country as much metal as possible."[27]

The interpretations of Khrushchev referred to earlier see such statements as the opening shots of a head-on confrontation between Khrushchev and the military-industrial complex, a confrontation that Khrushchev lost. His subsequent reorganizations and maneuvers, in this view, were largely a reaction to that loss, a desperate second-best effort to wring miracles from the countryside without additional resources. But the figures on investment, once again, tell a different story. The fact is that agriculture's share of overall investment increased substantially from 1961 through 1964, recovering to nearly the record level of 1955. In other words, once Khrushchev and his allies had decided that additional agricultural investment was essential, they got it. In view of Khrushchev's weakening political position at the time, that must mean that agriculture did *not* face uncompromising opposition from the bulk of the top elite. And if Khrushchev still appeared

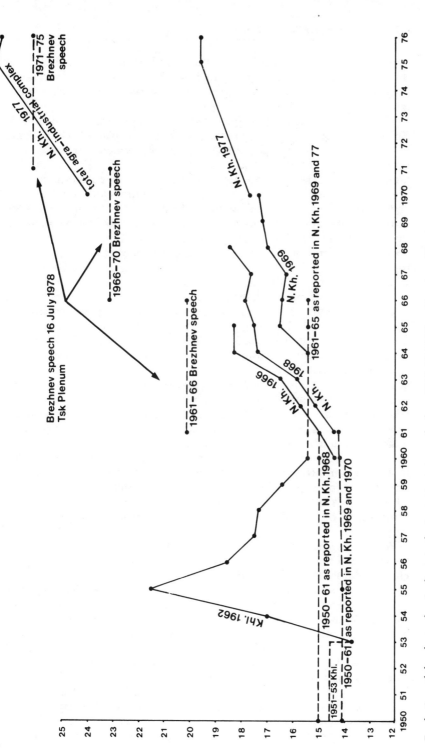

Evolution of the share of agriculture in the Soviet investment budget, 1950–75. N.Kh. – Narodnoe Khoziastvo.

ambivalent about increasing agricultural investment, alternately leading the movement and following behind, it was because he himself was under pressure from a pro-agricultural lobby that was trying to get him to move faster still.

The essence of the difference between these two ways of looking at Khrushchev stands out clearly in the way each one explains his behavior at the Central Committee plenum of March 1962, which both see as very important but for different reasons. For Ploss and Hahn, the March 1962 plenum was a serious defeat for Khrushchev. He came into the plenum breathing fire, determined to pry loose more resources for agriculture, but departed without much to show for it. Tatu's interpretation is much the same, except that in addition he blames Khrushchev's poor preparation and improvisation.[28] For Breslauer, on the other hand, Khrushchev was under pressure from pro-agriculture forces, who, encouraged by signs of support from the leader, deluged him with claims for more agricultural investment, which he then had to hold off.

The second interpretation seems more plausible on three counts: First, it is consistent with the fact that a major increase in planned agricultural investment actually did take place from 1961 to 1964. Second, the Breslauer interpretation paints Khrushchev himself in the most likely colors – ambivalent and contradictory. Third, it does not require the strained assumption that an agricultural lobby simply appeared from nowhere in 1965 but suggests instead that it had been building gradually for several years.

But if Khrushchev had come around by 1964 to two of the most important features of what we now call the Brezhnev program, and if there was growing pro-agricultural sentiment in the elite, why was he unable to build a durable coalition around it himself, one that might have kept him in power?

A revealing symptom of Khrushchev's problem is that while he was able to win big commitments for agricultural investment in the official plans, he was unable to make them stick in the course of implementation. Part of Khrushchev's difficulty was the enormous difference between the resources promised by the Kremlin for agriculture and those that actually found their way into the field.[29]

What was the obstacle? According to Khrushchev, it was primarily Gosplan and the executives of heavy industry who were frustrating him.[30] He complained long and loud about "men in steel blinders," who cry "Steel! Steel!" and "whose hands tremble at the thought" of reallocating large sums from industry to agricultural chemistry.[31] Now, to be sure, such surreptitious reprogramming is a chronic problem in Soviet agricultural policy. Much of the off-farm production for agriculture is performed by ministries whose main tasks lie in heavy industry and defense. Under the pressure of taut plans, they are tempted to cover their main targets by reprogramming resources away from agriculture, and Gosplan, which is organized internally by major branches of industry, shares their bias. Brezhnev complained about this as often as Khrushchev did and in much the same language. But the revealing difference is that Brezhnev was more successful, especially after 1970, in doing something about it. This suggests that the ultimate source of

Khrushchev's problems was not Gosplan alone but rather the signals coming to Gosplan from Khrushchev's colleagues in the Council of Ministers and the party leadership, as well as the failure of the local party apparatus, increasingly alienated from Khrushchev after 1962, to correct reprogramming at the local level.

We have not far to look to see why. Compare, for example, the party plenum of February 1964, a special meeting on agricultural policy, which turned out to be Khrushchev's last plenum, with that of March 1965, the first agricultural plenum of his successors. At the February plenum, Khrushchev spoke with satisfaction of the "unanimous understanding" shown by the speakers of the "importance of raising up agriculture and switching it in the direction of intensification." But not one of his Politburo colleagues spoke at that plenum, at any rate not on agricultural policy. In contrast, at the first Central Committee plenum *after* Khrushchev's fall, in March 1965, no fewer than eight Politburo members rose to speak on agriculture – none of them, needless to say, with any praise for Khrushchev. In his opening speech, Brezhnev drew up the bill of particulars: Khrushchev had ignored, said Brezhnev, the most elementary requirements of planned and balanced development. "But life," said Brezhnev, "severely punishes those who do not reckon with its laws." Khrushchev had set overambitious targets, Brezhnev charged, while cutting agricultural investment after 1958. He had ignored agronomy. His constant reorganizations had thrown the countryside into chaos. And he had pursued an unbalanced regional policy, systematically neglecting the non-black-earth zone in the northern half of the European USSR.[32]

Returning now to Khrushchev's speech at the February 1964 plenum with these later charges in mind, we can see clearly that his proclaimed "switch to the rails of intensification" (as he termed it) answered none of what the various Politburo members, as they sat listening, were presumably thinking. It was an all-too-familiar Khrushchevian performance: His new intensification policy, he claimed, was a logical continuation of the previous ten years; a decade of strengthening the technical and economic base of the collective and state farms now made it possible to attempt what would have been impossible before.[33] He called for all-out production of fertilizers, boasting that what had taken the capitalists decades the Soviets would achieve in seven years.[34] To his critics he made halfhearted concessions, which cannot have inspired much confidence, coming as they did from such a notoriously changeable man. On Lysenko, for example, who despite Khrushchev's protection was under growing and increasingly open attack in the Academy of Sciences: "I don't wish at all to say that there cannot be other opinions in science." But he insisted that Lysenko's methods had consistently proven themselves in practice, which amounted to saying that Lysenko continued to enjoy his favor.[35] The plenum delegates heard similar half-concessions on corn,[36] drainage in the non-black-earth zone,[37] and clean fallow in Kazakhstan.[38] These had been among the sorest issues of the previous few years, and Khrushchev was manifestly trying to placate his critics, but his conversion was too obviously forced to be convincing.

Khrushchev applied to his new investment policies the same campaign mentality that he had used his whole life. To mobilize enthusiasm for *khimizatsiia*, his plan to build overnight a modern chemical industry for agriculture, he reached for the model most familiar to him and his listeners: Lenin's *elektrifikatsiia*, the program to provide the entire country with electricity, the first of the major industrialization campaigns of the Soviet period.[39] But his rousing words only presaged more excess, more unbalance, and more bluster.

Khrushchev's conversion to modern agriculture, in sum, was incomplete, an uneasy mixture of old and new. Khrushchev argued for irrigation, but the word that recurred in every paragraph was corn.[40] He argued for reclamation but put off something so basic as rural roads.[41] Worst of all, Khrushchev retained his old faith in the magic virtues of reorganization. In 1962 he split the party apparatus into an agricultural half and an industrial half, throwing rural administration into chaos.[42] Some have interpreted these moves as Khrushchev's "second best," a frustrated reaction to his inability to gain more funds for agriculture.[43] But it seems more likely that to the end of his career he was convinced that pressure and proper organization were the methods of choice.[44] What Khrushchev's successors were reacting to was not the new in Khrushchev's program but the old, what they termed his "harebrained schemes."

The remarkable thing is that to the end Khrushchev retained impressive control of the traditional levers of power, such as personnel appointments and control over organizational structure, yet they could not save him. There is some uncertainty among Western experts about the extent to which he controlled personnel appointments directly, but he was apparently able, down to the end, to make the personnel changes he desired in agriculture, and he hired and fired with abandon as long as he was in the Kremlin.[45] But in his increasingly frantic efforts to exert power, Khrushchev alienated the government leadership, his fellow Politburo members and the Party apparatus below. His failure, then, was not that of failing to control the classical means of building power but to build and maintain authority, two things that in the traditional Western understanding of Soviet politics have always been virtually synonymous.[46] One of the chief lessons of the Khrushchev period, which Brezhnev seems to have turned into a fundamental principle of his government, is that they are in fact quite different, that in the absence of authority the manipulation of the traditional levers of power by the supposed leader of the Politburo can produce a revolt of the elite.

Even before Khrushchev's fall, then, much of the road had already been covered toward the agricultural policy of his successors. Khrushchev's negative example discredited the worst of the traditional approach, and his partial conversion after 1960 helped to lay the foundations for the post-1965 policy, without which the program would have gotten off much more slowly. There is no particular evidence for supposing that after 1960 the Soviet elite was opposed to the idea of a major new agricultural policy. On the contrary, by 1964 Khrushchev himself, because of his personal and political liabilities, had become the principal obstacle to its emergence.

*Building a new agricultural policy, 1964–1970*

It took five more years after March 1965 for Brezhnev to create a stable coalition for a large-scale program of investment in agriculture. Behind the leaders' apparent unity in 1965 there were three different views on which of the negative lessons of Khrushchev had been the most important – insufficient funding, excessive administrative pressure and disorganization, or excessive centralization.[47] Initially there was no need to choose among them, because there was so much to be done in all three directions. But in 1966 agreement ended.

The immediate cause of the fracture was that classic disaster of Soviet agricultural policy – a bumper crop. As it had so many times in the past, the abundance pouring from the fields smothered the case for greater agricultural investment. Funds were cut. Azerbaijan diverted agricultural funds to build a subway; Moldavia built railroads; and throughout the country agricultural construction teams were reassigned to urban industrial sites. Gosplan, as it had in every previous five-year plan, rerouted resources planned for agriculture to cover emergencies in industry. Twenty percent of the five-year allocation for agricultural construction and equipment was diverted to other sectors, and growth in fertilizer production was cut back.[48] The Politburo was openly divided. Whereas Brezhnev talked about a national crisis in agriculture, Kosygin insisted that the situation was basically sound and that further progress should come from better organization, higher productivity, and local initiative.[49]

What was at issue was not only investment priorities but the regime's entire approach to management. Kosygin backed reforms aimed at deconcentrating economic administration. He aimed to rely more on enterprise managers, using economic levers on the manager's profit motive to elicit more efficient performance. A liberal faction of agricultural experts, taking their cue from him, argued for the same in agriculture.[50] In their view, local farm chairmen should have incentives to use their own initiative, should specialize according to local conditions, and should make their own production decisions. To maintain overall control and correct imbalances, the state should manipulate prices instead of interfering by administrative means. Some of the experts' arguments, as the debate proceeded, began to sound a bit subversive; a few of them, in fact, held up as a model the pre-collectivization agricultural policies of the New Economic Policy of the 1920s. By implication, they were calling into question the fundamentals of the previous thirty-five years.

But this movement did not last long. Starting in 1968 the Politburo turned away from management reforms in agriculture and back toward a policy based primarily on centralized investment. Over the next three years a coalition took shape that held steady throughout the 1970s, surviving good harvests in 1973 and 1976–8 without weakening. Kosygin's public utterances on agriculture began to sound nearly identical to Brezhnev's. What caused this new and remarkably durable consensus, after such obvious discord at the outset?

Bad weather played an important part. The late 1960s and early 1970s produced a run of extremes: The record harvest of 1966 was followed by bad ones in 1967, 1969, 1972, and 1975. After each one, agricultural investment jumped. Severe meat shortages in 1969 and 1970 helped too. Advocates of agriculture and those of consumer goods finally found common ground, whereas in 1966 and 1967 they had competed with one another for investment resources.[51] In 1971 the Kremlin launched an ambitious program to expand and modernize animal husbandry, which from 1971 to 1975 absorbed 40 percent of the total agricultural investment budget.[52] In fact, protecting and expanding its growing livestock has become the most important single aim of the Brezhnev program.

The emergence of the post-1968 consensus presumably owes something as well to traditional power politics and the replacement of personnel in key positions, for the new agricultural policy and Brezhnev's power grew together. During the late 1960s Brezhnev's personal prestige was increasing rapidly, to judge from the recognition his colleagues and the press began to give him, and this reflected (at least in part) his growing control over the party apparatus. In 1965 and 1966 there was a flurry of replacements of *obkom* first secretaries and Central Committee department heads, and during the next five years thirty-two out of seventy-two Russian *obkom* first secretaryships changed hands.[53] All this clearly benefited Brezhnev. At the Twenty-fourth Party Congress in 1971, four men associated with him (Grishin, Shcherbitsky, Kunaev, and Kulakov) were appointed full members of the Politburo. Symbolic of the simultaneous consolidation of the agricultural policy and Brezhnev's political position was the rise of A. P. Kirilenko, a close Brezhnev associate, and the decline of G. I. Voronov, a Politburo member long associated with agriculture but consistently reserved about increased investment.[54] As Voronov slipped, his associates slipped also, as did their power to oppose Brezhnev's policies. Personnel changes in the top agricultural spots have been relatively infrequent, but they have come at crucial times. Perhaps the most obviously important one was the appointment in 1970 of a high party official, T. I. Sokolov, to the position of first deputy chairman for agriculture in Gosplan just at the moment when agriculture's share in the Ninth Five-Year Plan was being determined. Another key appointment was that of F. D. Kulakov in 1965 to the position of Central Committee secretary for agriculture, from which vantage point he supervised agricultural policy until his sudden death in 1978.

Yet traditional power politics did not play the same visible role in the development of Brezhnev's policy as under Khrushchev. Far more prominent, at least as far as foreign observers could tell, was the element of persuasion. Brezhnev campaigned tirelessly during those years for his conception of agricultural reform. Instead of jawboning in public with military and heavy-industrial ministries, as Khrushchev had, he enlisted them in the cause.[55] And when the weather happened to give a good crop, Brezhnev refrained from crowing victory and stressed, instead, that progress would take a long time. In every speech he called for investment and more investment.

A final point that undoubtedly helped Brezhnev's agricultural program is that it was conservative in design at a time when the tone of the whole regime was turning conservative. In the debate over agricultural management described earlier, Brezhnev had been on the conservative side from the start.[56] But already by 1967 the rest of the Politburo must have started lining up with him, for the debate among agricultural specialists suddenly altered in tone. The conservatives grew loud and abusive, whereas the liberals began withdrawing from print. Switching to a semi-market mechanism, the conservatives said, would cause instability and inflation. The government would lose control over agricultural output, and the result would be anarchy. This change in tone reflected developments throughout the economy, for everywhere the economic reform slowed down and soon halted. Official fashion shifted toward centralizing, "rationalizing," computerized methods of management[57] and in agriculture the essentials of the inherited system – the centralized management, the state procurement system, the administratively determined prices and cropping patterns – were no longer questioned even indirectly.

Within these conservative boundaries, however, there is virtually no major candidate for agricultural spending that has not found support. As the strength and stability of the agricultural consensus grew stronger and more stable after 1970, it engendered one major new program after another:

| | |
|---|---|
| 1965–6 | Expansion of reclamation, fertilizer production, mechanization; continuation of the Virgin Lands program |
| 1965–7 | Rural construction program |
| 1968 | Reestablishment of 1965-level funding for the three above programs |
| 1970 | Animal husbandry, rural electrification |
| 1971 | Livestock-raising complexes |
| 1972–3 | Water-pollution-control program |
| 1973–4 | Farm specialization, feed grains, agroindustrial complexes |
| 1974 | Non-black-earth program |
| 1975–80 | Growing discussion of major river diversions for southern agriculture |
| 1978–9 | Rural roads |

This mix of programs prompts two opposing thoughts. On the one hand, it is striking evidence of the extent to which the Soviet leadership has been converted to new views. Conservative as the Brezhnev program may be in its emphasis on central investment instead of reform of management or basic structures, it is next to revolutionary, at any rate when compared to traditional Soviet policy, in its apparent recognition of the need for balance, breadth, and a long view. Having accepted the need for a radical reconstruction and modernization of the countryside, the Kremlin also has evidently accepted the implications that such a major undertaking engenders a flood of related needs for off-farm production, basic infrastructure, development of new resources, scientific research, and much more. That they have accepted that fact and have launched such a wide array of large programs is the most extraordinary aspect of the Brezhnev policy.

But the very length of the list and the fact that all regions, all programs, and all crops were being pushed simultaneously also suggest that the Kremlin was reaching too far and too fast. During the 1970s the Brezhnev program became virtually open-ended, in high gear on all fronts at once. Apart from such general formulas as the creation of a "material and technical base" for agriculture and its "industrialization and scientific progress," it had no precise goals, no stated outer bounds, no clear cutoff point or limit. How far, then, do the leaders intend to go in view of the fact that the country's comparative advantage lies almost anywhere but in agriculture? The point of diminishing returns cannot be far off; indeed, some Western specialists believe it is already past.[58] One historic imbalance has been succeeded by another.

What accounts for this? Historically there has been a tendency toward excess built into the structure of power in the Kremlin, and that may be at work here. First, consider the side effects of the fact that consensus and coalition are formed together: Because agricultural policy was one of the issues on which Brezhnev based his claim to supreme leadership in the late 1960s, it is difficult for anyone in the Soviet elite to address the problem of how much is enough or how fast is too fast in agriculture without appearing to call into question the very basis of the ruling coalition. Then, once the bandwagon has started rolling, once institutional commitments are made and careers are on the line, the same features of Soviet politics that make it difficult to form a new consensus in the first place also make it difficult to challenge an established one; here one might list the absence of countervailing loci of power, the lack of access to influential media for independent criticism, and the resulting inability of losing players to regain advantage by widening the circle of conflict. Finally, precisely because the Brezhnev policy called for such major changes in long-established priorities, and because the ministries and state committees have a proven ability to subvert such changes, the Politburo presumably must lean with all its might to push its program through, knowing that anything less than total commitment on its part can precipitate a retreat like that of 1966-7. These features call to mind a machine that must run at top speed if it is to run at all, and which at top speed has such momentum that it cannot be stopped or maneuvered. There is the danger that for all the innovativeness and basic sensibleness of the Brezhnev agricultural policy, it has been accelerated into a self-defeating absurdity, a galloping *fuite vers l'avant* of the kind that in earlier generations covered the countryside with tree belts and corn, and from which it can be rescued only by the advent of some other competing crisis, such as the energy shortage, which shows signs of displacing agriculture as the chief domestic urgency of the 1980s.

Understanding this mixture of conservatism, conversion, and overconversion in the formation of the new agricultural policy is clearly vital for our understanding of the system's capacity for reform. We need to know where the leaders got new ideas and what they did with them, how the new programs originated, whether there are any effective sources of criticism to offset official enthusiasm – in other words, we need to know about the relationship of political power to technical expertise. The next section begins with a brief general discussion about the growing participation and apparent influence of agricultural specialists, as a prelude to the more detailed analysis in the four chapters to follow.

### Agricultural specialists under Brezhnev

Krushchev's fall in 1964 was a liberation not only for agriculture but also for agricultural specialists. The traditional approach to agriculture, described in the last chapter, had been fatal for science and sound technique. Leaders who listened respectfully to an airplane designer or a nuclear physicist had no hesitation in overriding or co-opting agronomists and plant scientists. The smallest points of agronomy could become political issues.[59] Sycophants and quacks held influential positions in the bureaucracies of biology and agriculture.[60] The agricultural sciences were depressed areas; of all the major natural sciences, they grew the most slowly during the 1950s and 1960s, both in overall numbers of specialists and in the share of postgraduate degrees among them.[61] Not until the late 1960s did they begin to gain secure and respected standing.

How could technical specialists in agriculture, under these circumstances, have played a significant role in shaping the emerging agricultural reform? Once again we must go back to Khrushchev.

Khrushchev treated agricultural specialists with his characteristically unpredictable blend of bonhomie, belligerence, and occasional vindictiveness. Specialists who agreed with his views of the moment he praised and protected. Those who did not he harassed. His successive agricultural favorites purged the clients of their predecessors and installed their own, and the cycle was repeated several times during Khrushev's rule.[62] New agronomic systems lasted only so long as the political influence of their promoters: Thus the "Orenburg" system of deep autumn plowing was the order of the day until the protector of its promoters, Politburo member G. Voronov, began to lose influence in early 1964.[63] The man who played the game best, Trofim Lysenko, the perennial arch-quack, enjoyed, thanks to Khrushchev, one last ride to the heights of influence.

Yet Khrushchev never succeeded (perhaps because he never really took the trouble) in completely suppressing dissenting views. He could, and did, order textbooks replaced and courses changed. He could expel specialists he didn't like from jobs and honorific positions, and he could protect his favorites from embarrassing investigations and direct criticism. This was serious enough, because it prevented the lasting and broad-based revival of the agricultural sciences that only a reform of teaching and full control over institutions could achieve. But even Lysenko's dead hand and Khrushchev's occasional harassment could not prevent agricultural scientists, geneticists, and others from doing research here and there, accumulating data, and even publishing books that argued positions considerably different from the official ones. This work, as we shall see, reached the political elite and was discreetly encouraged by them. Khrushchev's own thinking, in his last two or three years, was affected by it.

The most striking case is that of genetics. As early as 1955, the science division of the CPSU Central Committee encouraged work on hybrid corn, even though the underlying theory of the double cross was Mendelian and therefore officially taboo. One of the most supportive members of the Central Committee staff, A. M. Smirnov, was himself a plant physiologist by training. Another active sympathizer in the party apparatus was F. S. Goriachev, the first secretary of the Novosibirsk province committee, who supported the creation of a genetics research institute at Academic City.[64] The geneticist N. P. Dubinin, one of the pioneers of the revival, mentions the steady support he received from V. A. Kirillin, then head of the party Central Committee's science division, and from V. S. Emel'ianov, a former deputy head of the secret police who was then chairman of the Committee for the Use of Atomic Energy.[65] When one reads of such high-level, if discrete, support for genetics in the 1950s, one begins to understand why Lysenko's power vanished instantly as soon as Khrushchev was gone.

Another example of the curiously mixed treatment meted out to agricultural specialists in the Khrushchev years comes from the Virgin Lands, where debates raged among rival politicians and agricultural scientists over the right techniques to use in dealing with weeds, erosion, and early frost. Two local experts, A. I. Baraev and T. S. Mal'tsev, developed a system based on early and shallow plowing and ample clean fallow.[66] During the last four years of Khrushchev's rule their system became a political football. They were attacked first by Lysenko, who had his own system of late plowing and intertilling with corn.[67] Lysenko favored his own local scientists, who exchanged broadsides with Baraev and Mal'tsev in the local and specialized press. Khrushchev himself was frequently involved, chiefly in harassing those who favored clean fallow.[68] At one point, in characteristically pungent language, Khrushchev held up for Baraev's edification the example of a Kazakh kolkhoz chairman: "He will put a flea under your shirt, comrade Baraev, and this would not be inopportune, because it would wake you up and stop you dreaming."[69] Yet throughout this difficult period Baraev and Mal'tsev kept their jobs, continued their work, and published books (in Baraev's case) advocating the very system that Lysenko condemned.[70] At the worst of the pressure they had to trim their sails a bit in public – in 1962 Baraev was obliged to announce that he was correcting "shortcomings" at his institute and that he would give up clean fallow "in the next few years" – but nothing worse. They enjoyed support from the local party leadership and from Agriculture Minister Matskevich.[71] And these debates and disputes were amply reported in the press. This was typical of the peculiar two-handed treatment of agricultural scientists during Khrushchev's years in power.

Such mixed treatment helps to explain how in such a generally depressed field some excellent scientific and policy studies were published or made available to influential leaders even before Khrushchev's fall, later serving as the basis for new policies. Brezhnev writes in his memoirs that he was familiar with the work of Mal'tsev and Baraev as early as 1955. McCauley notes the work of P. M. Zemskii, who in the late 1950s carefully documented the case for giving greater priority to the European USSR and especially to the non-black-earth zone. Zemskii's book reads like a blueprint for the reclamation program now under way, especially the drainage and land-clearance programs of the northern half of the European USSR.[72]

After Khrushchev's fall the official treatment of agricultural specialists changed suddenly and markedly. At the March 1965 plenum of the Central Committee, Brezhnev denounced the failure to distinguish between technical and political authority:

> True science takes nothing on faith; it cannot be the monopoly of particular scientists, and still less of administrators, no matter how much prestige they may have. Unfortunately, we have recently had instances in which people incompetent in science at times took upon themselves the role of arbiters in disputes among scientists, and in so doing hampered their initiative and stood in the way of free, creative discussion of scientific topics.[73]

Brezhnev went on to call the role of agronomists and livestock experts "as important as that of engineers in industry."

Khrushchev's successors have kept to the policy set forth by the March plenum. Lysenko quickly fell into disgrace, and political bosses are now more restrained about interfering in the details of cropping practices.[74] Baraev and Mal'tsev became heroes and in 1972 Baraev was awarded the Order of Lenin.[75]

As the leaders debated with one another over agricultural policy, agricultural specialists played their part by sounding warnings of dire consequences if abuse of the land continued. Inventories showed Soviet soils to be badly damaged by erosion, salt, and improper acidity and moisture.[76] Prime cropland was being taken over by industries and cities at an alarming rate; many millions of hectares were flooded by hydropower reservoirs.[77] The implications for future food supply were ominous. A commission of the USSR Academy of Sciences and the State Committee on Science and Technology reported to the Council of Ministers in 1968 that production of eggs, meat, and grain would fall short of dietary targets by 1980. Other studies on the same subject were even more pessimistic.[78] And new studies by geographers showed the sharp outer limits imposed on Soviet agriculture by its northern latitude and continental climate, underscoring that the only hope lay in greatly improved efficiency.[79]

Note the timing of these warnings: They were clustered around 1968, when funding for agriculture faltered briefly. It is likely, therefore, that they can be considered supporting material for the battle then going on within the top leadership for agriculture over the priorities to be assigned during the Ninth Five-Year Plan.

Although less obviously political, technical debates in agriculture since then have been no less vigorous. Throughout the late 1960s and early 1970s, for example, specialists argued with one another in books and specialized journals over the wisdom of developing irrigation in the southern steppes as quickly and extensively as official policy called for. Some argued that the soil of the steppes was especially vulnerable to insalination and water-logging; therefore, it was unwise to expand irrigation there on a large scale without experienced personnel and careful preliminary observation. This strengthened the case of those who felt that top priority should not go to irrigation in the south but to drainage and liming in the northwest.[80] Similarly, specialists argued over whether fertilizers could to some extent substitute for irrigation;[81] whether it was sounder to build new reclamation networks or to remedy the deplorable state of older ones;[82] whether it was feasible to tap major northern rivers to supplement scarce water in the south;[83] and to what extent established water users should be forced to give way to the needs of agriculture and irrigation.

This brief sketch suggests that the role of agricultural experts was indeed an important part of the evolution of the Brezhnev policy, but what we have seen so far raises more questions than it answers. The one dominant fact about technical experts of all kinds in the Soviet Union is that their partici-pation and influence – indeed their very positions and the survival of their disciplines – are directly dependent on the receptiveness and goodwill of political authorities. How then can we speak of their influence or, rather, under what circumstances? To what extent are the new ideas and attitudes, the overall technocratic cast of the Brezhnev program or its tendency to over-optimism and excess, traceable to the experts or their agencies? Has there been any lasting change in their relationship to the political leaders, to such a degree that one might even speak of a reform in the way new policies are formed in the Kremlin? These questions are explored in the next four chapters.

What political lessons can we draw from the way the Brezhnev agricultural program was initiated and developed? As Western observers have tradi-tionally understood it, a collegial leadership like that of the Soviet Union, lacking stable rules of tenure and succession, should obey two general rules. First, because there is no formal and regular mechanism by which the outs replace the ins, and because decisions among the ins are reached by unanim-ity, policy changes in normal times are likely to come slowly and piecemeal. Major changes require great upheavals, such as a purge or a coup. Second, because the good things in Soviet life come from holding office, and there is no formal definition of powers or tenure, political life is insecure. Therefore power and policy are mixed to a greater degree in the Kremlin than in any Western system, and the builder of a coalition in the Kremlin must work at least as much on his colleagues' fears and ambitions as on their policy views. In fact, coercion and maneuver, in most Western writing on Soviet politics, are more important than information and persuasion.

The story of the new agriculture policy departs from this scheme substan-tially. A coup did indeed occur, but it did no more than facilitate the emergence of views that had been slowly developing among Khrushchev's colleagues for several years; and it took several more years after the coup for these views to mature into a stable consensus. The transformation of priorities that took place in the Politburo between 1954 and 1970 owed less to the accumulation of power through the traditional instruments than to the building of *authority* (or, in Khrushchev's case, the failure to build authority) through persuasion and debate, the pressure of events, the formation of alliances, and the identification of parallel policy interests.[84]

But this happened slowly. The new agricultural policy took fifteen years to evolve, and there were many wrong turns along the way, lurches to one side and the other down a path of slowly changing attitudes and assumptions. For years the political elite underestimated the seriousness of the agricultural problem, then underestimated the difficulty of dealing with it, trying to handle it instead by gimmicks and half measures. Only the sharpest goads – repeated crop failure, civil disturbances, the prospect of humiliating dependence on foreign sources – forced the learning process along.

The points do not contradict our conventional understanding of Soviet politics; instead, they merely modify our conception of what is cause and what is effect. In the view of many Kremlinologists, power politics based on coercion and maneuver are cause: Without such instruments, major policy changes cannot occur. The consolidation of power positions through personnel changes is also cause: It permits the evolution and consolidation of new policy. But in the present case, the line of causation also ran in the opposite direction: Failures in agricultural policy were one of the main causes of Khrushchev's overthrow, and the gradual formation of new consensus on agriculture was one of the contributing causes to Brezhnev's growing power in the late 1960s. Policy differences, not just power politics, can cause a succession; changes in policy viewpoints and values can create a successor. In an elite that is no longer moved primarily by fear or fervor, a leader must rely on other resources to build the authority that will allow him to grasp the levers of power. The examples of Brezhnev's rise and the consolidation of his agricultural policy suggest that persuasion and the gradual building of consensus have become more important political instruments than they once were.

The question is: Can a process of consensus building that requires a decade or more to produce a new policy meet the increasingly pressing needs of the Soviet economy? And once a new policy is formed, can the Kremlin fine-tune or curtail it as needed? We have noted that once the Brezhev coalition was formed, it locked the agricultural policy into high gear and drove the industrialization of the countryside faster than was sensible. Yet it may not be possible to scale it down or change its direction until the Brezhnev coalition itself comes to an end. Can such a slow mechanism of adjusting and altering major policies be adequate to deal with the crises of the next two decades? We shall return to this question in the concluding chapter.

# PART I
# ADVICE AND DISSENT IN THE SHAPING OF BREZHNEV'S AGRICULTURAL AND ENVIRONMENTAL PROGRAMS

If the formation of political coalitions in the Soviet elite depends more strongly today than in the past on consensus on policy, if the authority of the leader rests increasingly on his ability to persuade, build alliances, and show results, then the position of technical advisers and critics, and also that of their agencies, is bound to be altered. As we shall see in Part I of this book, the last fifteen years have been a time of growing official receptiveness to the ideas and recommendations of experts and specialists of a great many kinds. But does this imply a lasting alteration in the way policies are formed in the Kremlin? Does the increased participation of technical experts give them influence or even power? Have technical specialists really played an important role in shaping the Brezhnev policies? These are the questions raised in the next four chapters.

We first take up three cases of the participation of technical specialists in the expansion of the Brezhnev policy. The first case deals with the rise of environmental issues to political respectability and an official place in policy, culminating in a major clean-water program in the southern half of the Soviet Union, an essential long-term part of the southern strategy. The second is the story of the revival of an official price on capital and the role it played in displacing old dogma about resource use and in humbling one of agriculture's most important competitors. The third is a unique case of technology assessment: a lengthy public debate over proposals to reroute northern waters to southern basins to supply water to agriculture and industry. Each of these cases is an important aspect of the changing attitudes that underlay the Brezhnev program. And insofar as they determine the future availability of land and water, they will play an important part in the ultimate success or failure of the new agriculture. But most important, all three are examples of how new issues and new values gradually gain official recognition and take hold in state policy. All three examine the role of technical specialists in bringing new ideas and values to political leaders and translating them into new policy. Finally, a fourth chapter returns to the underlying theme of political power, examining the extent to which technical specialists and advisers have succeeded in overcoming the consequences of their dependence upon the State for funding, facilities, and access, and in developing a secure base for giving independent advice and playing influential roles.

# 3
# ENVIRONMENTAL ISSUES RISE TO OFFICIAL LEGITIMACY*

If agriculture was held in low regard prior to the late 1960s, environmental issues were hardly regarded at all. The successive public movements that tempered the effects of industrial and urban development in the West – sanitary engineering, conservation, and lately environmentalism – reached Russia as the feeble lapping of a remote wave. So completely did the goal of industrialization dominate all others that in the cities of southern USSR as recently as the mid-1960s and perhaps even later,[1] even the provision of drinking water for the urban population was commonly neglected if it competed with industrial needs. Yet in little more than a decade, starting from near-total political exclusion, environmental issues have gained an established (if far from high-priority) place in the Soviet system of planning and policy making.

This dramatic rise to political respectability is linked to the Brezhnev agricultural policy in several ways. First, an environmental program expands the supply of clean water available for irrigated agriculture, and consequently it is an essential part of the southern strategy. Second, environmental reform, like agricultural reform, was prompted in the first instance by the need to respond to an impending crisis: crop failure in the case of agriculture and a serious decline in commercial freshwater fishing, combined with an outbreak of cholera at a key moment, in that of the environment. This "remedial" aspect shared by the two reforms is a sort of long-overdue final chapter to the first two generations of the Soviet period, for in both cases some action was necessary to counter the side effects of unbalanced industrialization.

Both the agricultural and environmental reforms involve a reexamination of the past and an admission that serious mistakes were made. Soil was damaged, valuable land was flooded, water was untreated – all this is now frankly acknowledged. Thus both the agricultural and environmental reforms signal the spread of new attitudes toward air, land, and water, at least as essential raw materials for future economic growth, if not as values in

* The original version of this chapter appeared under the title "Environmental Conflict in the USSR," by Thane Gustafson, published in *Controversy: Politics of Technical Decisions* (Sage Focus Editions, Vol. 8), Dorothy Nelkin, Editor, copyright 1979, pp. 69–83, and is reprinted herewith by permission of the Publisher, Sage Publications (Beverly Hills/London).

themselves. In this sense the official establishment of environmental issues is a "third-generation" reform.

But at the same time we must be aware of a sentimental aspect of both agriculture and environment in Soviet society. A strong recent trend in Russian literature is the "village movement," a genre that depicts rural society as one of the great sources of Russian virtue and strength.[2] This sentiment for the countryside, widespread among many young people, is one of the acceptable outlets for rising Russian nationalism.[3] The same element is present in the environmental movement, as we shall see. When *Oktiabar'*, the conservative literary monthly, published an exposé on Lake Baikal; when Mikhail Sholokhov spoke out on environmental protection as *nashe krovnoe delo* (our vital task), the link to Russian pride was unmistakable, and it surely accounts for an important part of the receptiveness of the Russian elite to environmental issues.

These four common features have potential implications, ranging from the routine and the remedial to the potentially radical. Which ones in fact were uppermost in the rise of environmental issues to political legitimacy? What motivated the advice or protests of technical specialists, and how (if at all) did that advice affect the reactions of the political authorities? The evolution of the politics of the environment appears, at first sight, to be a case of especially influential and radical participation by concerned scientists. But, as we shall see, the final outcome has been channeled in conservative directions just as the overall agricultural policy has been. The story begins in Siberia, at Lake Baikal.

## Lake Baikal

The fight to save Lake Baikal has been a twenty-year cause célèbre unique in Soviet politics. The lake itself is perhaps the most remarkable natural site in Russia. Several hundred miles long and in some places nearly a mile deep, Lake Baikal holds one-fifth of the world's freshwater in a state so pure that one can see far into its depths. Through literature and folklore, every Russian from childhood knows its beauty and has learned in school of the unique animal species that live there.

In 1958 the Soviet paper and pulp industry was instructed to design a plant to produce a tough, durable rayon cord, suitable for reinforcing automobile and aircraft tires, perhaps for military bombers.[4] The project, in any event, was sizable, for the projected new plant was to produce more than half of the 400,000 tons of cord that the tire industry was expected to consume annually by 1971.[5] As industry planners cast about for a location for the plant, they had two major considerations in mind. First, water for the production of the so-called super-super grade of rayon required an expensive process of preliminary demineralization before it could be used. The purer the initial source, the lower the demineralization cost.[6] Second, the special varieties of softwood required for viscose could be found in the forests of the Buryat ASSR in eastern Siberia. So the planners settled on Lake Baikal.

The news that a large industrial enterprise would soon be built on the lake touched a nerve, particularly among scientists and journalists. Almost immediately, a wave of protest began to build. The first objections appeared in Siberia in 1960 and reached the pages of the Moscow press the following year.[7] In 1963 the conservative and nationalistic *Oktiabr'* published an exposé about the proposed Baikalsk plant,[8] and in 1964 several major newspapers joined the movement, notably *Literaturnaia Gazeta*, the widely read weekly of the Union of Soviet Writers. By 1966 Baikal had become a highly visible and high-level public issue. At the Twenty-third Party Congress that year the conservative novelist Mikhail Sholokhov (author of *And Quiet Flows the Don*) rose with an appeal. "Our descendants will not forgive us," he said, "if we do not preserve this glorious lake, this sacred Baikal."[9]

No precedent existed to suggest to the plant's designers the storm that lay ahead. The first ripple of trouble was a law that appeared in 1960, requiring that the Baikalsk design include facilities for waste treatment.[10] Accordingly, a research institute in the pulp and paper industry was commissioned to produce a treatment design, which was then tested in a pilot version near the Finnish border.[11] This in itself suggests that the project was under unusual behind-the-scenes pressure from the start, for at that time few builders of industrial facilities outside the two or three largest cities gave any particular thought to waste treatment. But it soon developed that the industry lacked the experience or the qualified manpower to handle the waste-treatment assignment, and it soon fell behind schedule. Even then, however, industry officials did not foresee major opposition and construction of the Baikalsk factory itself proceeded normally, with production slated to begin in 1966.

By 1964 the factory was more than half completed, but only one of three projected settling tanks had been dug, and no other work on the waste-treatment complex had been done. In response to protests, the State Lumber Committee took measures in late 1964 to accelerate the work on the treatment site.[12] But in 1965 workers at the site wrote a letter to *Literaturnaia Gazeta*, reporting that the builders were working round the clock to lead the main waste pipe directly to the lake, bypassing the site for the settling tanks altogether.[13] The famous waste-treatment plant had achieved no more than the "laborious purification of about forty gallons of water."[14] It was evident that if industry officials could not get the waste-treatment facility to work, they intended to begin without it.

At first it looked as though they would get away with it. In the preliminary skirmishing between 1962 and 1964 to obtain the endless interagency clearances and sign-offs that any Soviet construction project requires, pulp and paper officials won most of the early rounds.[15] But the project's opponents evidently found sympathetic ears in higher places. In 1962 the main Soviet agency for science policy, the State Committee for Scientific Research (a body with apparently important connections to the military[16]) called the industry's waste-treatment plan unsound.[17] The prestigious and well-connected Siberian Department of the Academy of Sciences, which had approved the plant designs in 1964, reversed itself one year later, using much the same arguments as the State Committee for Scientific Research.[18] As the Baikalsk plant – but not the waste-treatment facilities – neared completion in 1966, the protest against it reached the top. We have already noted Sholokhov's speech at the Twenty-third Party Congress. Shortly afterward, an open letter appeared in *Komsomol'skaia Pravda* recommending that the plant be dismantled. It was signed by an extraordinary collection of elite citizens: a vice-president of the USSR Academy of Sciences (B. P. Konstantinov), several Academicians, Heroes of Socialist Labor, a Lenin Prize laureate, and, interestingly, a section head of the Russian State Committee on Construction. In March 1966 Gosplan, presumably acting on instructions from the party leadership, called together a commission of experts and instructed them to make final recommendations within three months.[19]

The chairman of the commission was an inorganic chemist, N. M. Zhavoronkov, head of the chemistry section of the USSR Academy of Sciences. A recent *samizdat* ("underground") account charges that his commission was formed to preside over a whitewash,[20] and indeed it soon reported in favor of the Baikalsk project.[21] Shortly afterward, the commission's opinion was submitted to a highly unusual combined session of the top officials of Gosplan, the State Committee on Science and Technology, and the Presidium of the Academy of Sciences – striking evidence of the high-level attention the problem had gained by this time. This joint group approved the Zhavoronkov recommendations unanimously.[22]

The opponents of the plant were outraged, and said so publicly. An engineer who was present later wrote that the commission went against the opinion of most of the experts consulted, who had favored diverting the wastes through a pipeline instead.[23] Academician A. Trofimuk, a prominent opponent, wrote that the entire affair had been handled too hastily.[24] Some even charged that the pulp and paper industry had promised that wood pulp would be supplied to Baikalsk by rail alone and that no logs would be floated across the lake. But this promise was apparently made to secure the commission's approval and was not subsequently kept.

Nevertheless, to call the Zhavoronkov verdict a whitewash is to misunderstand the importance of what had happened. The remarkable thing was not that the commission returned the recommendation that it did. Under the circumstances, it was the conservative, "responsible" decision that one might expect of a similar blue-ribbon panel anywhere, even if we discount the high-level pressure that was probably brought to bear on it. Rather, what was remarkable was the *public* pressure and publicity that surrounded the committee from all the sides involved. In a conversation with the author ten years later, what Academician Zhavoronkov remembered most vividly was the constant din of the media, which prevented the commission, he said, from concentrating properly on the facts. In words that would bring a rueful smile to the face of many an American panel chairman, Zhavoronkov complained that the plant's opponents ignored difficult technical matters and that many of their objections were irresponsible.[25] But for the American chairman such public pressure would be routine; for Zhavoronkov it was unique – ten years later he was still indignant about it.

The battle did not end with the Zhavoronkov commission. Newspapermen and scientists were angered by what they regarded as the duplicity and the high-pressure tactics of the paper and pulp industry. First, it had refused even to show its designs to the Academy of Sciences until 1961.[26] Reporters complained that they were being surrounded by a fog of ministerial optimism, which didn't quite conceal the ministry's determination to have its way.[27] For example, in 1965 the chief engineer of the design agency offered assurances to a *Pravda* reporter that there would be no contamination of Baikal, thanks to the plant's elaborate treatment facilities.[28] Yet later that same year the same engineer stated: "The present design for the purification installations was developed not because of the danger of pollution to the lake, for that danger doesn't exist, but in order to quiet down the prolonged dispute between scientists and designers."[29] Meanwhile, the designers were careful to build the water intake for the factory three miles away from the waste pipe.[30]

Opponents began to charge that the paper and pulp industry had used fraud and pressure to secure approval for its designs. They reported that the committee had originally consulted a second-rank member of a fisheries institute for an advisory opinion, and then used his statements to mislead other state agencies into giving their approval, despite the fact that the expert subsequently disavowed his earlier assurances, and his institute disavowed *him*.[31] In an angry open letter a vice-president of the Academy of Sciences exclaimed:

> The State Committee thought it possible to fool the government by justifying its choice of a building site in a seismic zone, and claiming that it was impossible to get clean water anywhere else. They submitted inflated estimates of the available stocks of raw materials in the Baikal area, and understated the expenses of construction and operation.[32]

Drawing the moral of these events, a reporter from *Literaturnaia Gazeta* wrote: "The story of the dispute over Baikal shows convincingly that departmental zeal and willfulness are capable of drowning out the voices of even the most authoritative scientists."[33]

To follow what happened next, we should note than even before it was completed the Baikalsk plant had begun to lose much of its original justification, particularly its military significance. Rayon was already an obsolete fiber when the planning for the plant began. Specialists from the Soviet tire industry declared in the mid-1960s that they were already phasing out rayon and that by 1970 more than a third of all Soviet tires would be made with nylon cord. Indeed, according to the *samizdat* account mentioned earlier, production of nylon cord began in the Soviet Union in 1964, and as a result the Baikalsk plant now produces only about two-thirds of the 240,000 tons of rayon it was originally designed for.[34] As early as 1966, it had been partly converted to the production of kraft paper and turpentine.[35]

This may help to explain why, after 1966, the plant's critics began to make some headway. They did not manage to stop the plant itself, which began production in late 1966, but during the same year seven additional waste-treatment units were built. "The money for this," said *Literaturnaia Gazeta*, "more than 2.5 million rubles, was allocated without delay." When a reporter from *Literaturnaia Gazeta* visited the installations, he noted that the purified effluent had a slight yellowish tinge and a faintly musty odor, but a neutral taste.[36]

However, an official of the Ministry of Land Reclamation and Water Management, the agency responsible for oversight of water-quality requirements, reported that the full waste-treatment performance specified by the design had not been attained and that the sewage discharged into Lake Baikal contained an unacceptable quantity of sulfur compounds and mineral salts. A number of other problems remained unsolved as well, particularly the question of operating personnel for the waste-treatment facility. Living conditions at Baikalsk were rigorous, and pay was low, so that out of 240 specialists at the treatment complex, 100 left for other enterprises during the summer of 1967 alone.[37] Without permanent cadres, it was impossible to operate the new facilities smoothly.

More evidence accumulated during the following year that waste treatment at the Baikalsk plant was still not up to par. Concentrations of inorganic compounds in the vicinity of the outfall were already higher than forecast; those of suspended particles were more than twice as high; and those of organic compounds three times higher. *Pravda* reported that the number of plants and animals had decreased by one-third to one-half in the area where the plant's sewage was being discharged.[38]

In March 1968 the USSR Council of Ministers' State Committee on Science and Technology called together a new commission to decide what to do. This one deliberated for more than a year before producing a draft for a special resolution of the Council of Ministers. It adopted many of the proposals and the overall philosophy of the lake's most prominent defenders. In particular, (1) the Baikalsk plant was instructed to build, during the same year, still another unit, this time for the *utilization* of its wastes, and (2) all timber was to be transported by boat in the future. The Ministry of Forestry was instructed to clear the rivers of sunken logs and to clean all wood debris from the banks of rivers and the shores of the lake itself. Timber, rather than being dragged out of the cutting area, was to be hoisted out by special equipment. No logging was to take place on grades steeper than 25 degrees.[39]

But the 1969 decree soon turned out to be a dead letter.[40] It was followed by another in late 1971, this one issued jointly by the Council of Ministers and the Party Central Committee and presumably carrying more weight. Still more high-level paper followed: "temporary regulations" to implement the decree in 1974 and finally a comprehensive general plan in 1977, developed by the USSR Academy of Sciences. The latter was the work of yet another commision, which sat from 1975 to 1976.[41]

The flow of orders and regulations since 1971 has finally produced real results. In the view of American experts from the Environmental Protection

Agency who have visited the waste-treatment facilities at Baikalsk, they are among the most elaborate in the world (when they operate). The streams leading to the lake have been cleaned of sunken logs and debris. Transport of logs across the lake has been restricted and regulated. Logging in the nearby Buryat forests is so closely controlled that local party officials complain that the growth of the region is being seriously held up.[42] In short, the lake's defenders can boast of no mean achievement, for they raised a nationwide scandal, gained top-level attention for the lake for a span of more than fifteen years, and turned the lake's preservation into a Soviet showpiece that the government now eagerly displays to foreigners.

Yet the paradox of Baikal is that its defenders, for all their victories, are gradually losing the war. Large-scale economic development has now come to the entire region. The Baikal-Amur Mainline construction project, which passes to the north of the lake, is bringing in thousands of workers, and the railroad project is supplied partly over water across the lake. Industrial development continues throughout the Buryat republic, and if a recent *samizdat* account is to be believed, a major zinc and lead complex with military backing is being built on one of the streams leading to Baikal.[43] These threats to the lake are far more serious than the Baikalsk plant, and yet there has not been the same storm of protest that there was fifteen years ago.

What, then, is the lasting political significance of the Baikal affair? First, it revealed a widespread sympathy for an environmental issue among powerful figures within the Soviet political elite. That is the only way to explain the fact that the lake's defenders were able to get sustained media coverage and access to top policy-making circles for fifteen years. This receptiveness at the top gave the scientists who participated unusual freedom to fight for their views and newspaper reporters unusual latitude to publicize them. But it is important to point out that scientists' protests and newsmen's exposés by themselves could not stop the pressure tactics of the ministries; and they were effective only to the extent that they were able to gain access to top leaders and stimulate official action. This fact suggests the delicate and contingent nature of the influence of technical advocates and advisers – a theme to which we shall return.

The second significant point about Baikal is that it helped to establish the precedent that it is (sometimes) permissible to question an industrial project on environmental grounds. To be sure, that permissibility is fragile and hedged about with restrictions. Many details about pollution are subject to censorship regulations, and there have been brief bans on coverage of environmental problems in the media. But any reading of the Soviet press in the last few years shows that environmental issues are usually treated more openly than most other policy questions.

Nevertheless, it might have seemed that the Baikalsk fight was fated to be a unique event, an oddity without a sequel. The lake's fame, the gradual fading of any important justification for the project, the blunders of its designers – these were unique circumstances, not likely to be repeated. Moreover, the larger threats now facing the lake show the limits of ad hoc, sentimental opposition. But at the same moment another protest movement was building, this one larger and much more ambitious, to which we now turn.

### Opposition to hydropower

The European region of the USSR, the most industrialized and populous area of the country, is chronically short of energy. Until recently, the Soviet answer to this was hydropower. By the 1960s the map of the European USSR was dotted with dams and reservoirs, and millions of acres of productive agricultural land lay underwater. For thirty years the soundness of using land and water in this way was not publicly questioned. But in the 1960s, for the first time, Soviet scientists began studying and publicizing the damage. Within a few years their findings, appearing in hundreds of specialized publications and papers, described lost cropland, erosion, diminished water quality, declining commercial fishing, and many other severe effects.[44] During the second half of the 1960s, this work helped to defeat several large reservoir projects and to bring hydropower construction to a virtual end in the European USSR.

In the fervor of hydropower's opponents, the favorable publicity the press gave them, and their success in getting results, the crusade against hydropower resembles the Baikal affair. Indeed, it was more important than Baikal, because it was aimed at dozens of projects instead of just one, and it took on one of the most powerful institutions in the country. And like Baikal, the hydropower controversy was a step toward greater official acceptance of environmental issues as legitimate. But also like Baikal, the ultimate significance of the hydropower affair, as we shall see, is to show the limits of environmental reform and the fragile, highly contingent influence of scientists and participants in policy formation.

The most prominent figures in the movement against hydropower were geographers and hydrologists of the USSR Academy of Sciences (principally in the Institute of Geography and the Institute of Water Problems). The best-known and most interesting figure in this group is S. L. Vendrov, who came to the Academy of Sciences after an earlier career in river transportation. Vendrov launched a generation of graduate students into environmental studies. They traced in detail the effects of the Volga hydropower reservoirs on local climate, land, and hydrology[45] and later did field studies of a proposed diversion of the Pechora River to the south[46] and many other projects. In the early 1970s Vendrov's students were filled with a crusading spirit. They saw themselves as the frontline defense of the environment and had detailed knowledge of the work done by similar groups in the West.[47] Vendrov himself enjoys a prominent position as an adviser; he sits on advisory panels (*ekspertnye komissii*) of Gosplan and of the State Committee on Science and Technology. In his books he ranges more widely and expresses himself more forcefully than any other specialist in this field.

But he was not alone. Researchers in the Academy of Sciences were seconded by large numbers of hydrologists, icthyologists, soil scientists, and agronomists, working for water-using agencies like the Ministry of the Fishing Industry. Many of these agencies competed with hydropower for the use of scarce water in the relatively arid southern half of the country, and bad news for hydropower was, in a sense, good news for them. Researchers in the fishing industry, for example, showed the devastating effect of reservoir construction on commercial catches in the lower reaches of rivers like the Volga, pointing out that fish yields from the reservoirs themselves were much lower than hydropower designers had claimed they would be.[48] Acting under a mixture of professional conviction and institutional interest, these specialists helped to build the case against hydropower.

Perhaps the most important single contribution of their research was simply to document the damage done to agriculture by reservoir flooding: By the mid-1970s nearly 2.3 million hectares (roughly 5.7 million acres) of agricultural land had been flooded, about one-fifth of which consisted of highly productive plowland, mostly in the European USSR.[49] Much of this area was going underwater even as the surveys were being done; the area submerged by reservoirs doubled during the 1960s.[50]

As the 1960s progressed, these specialists and their agencies found official channels opening to them, through which they could bring their findings to bear on decisions involving the siting of new power plants. One example is the review procedure of Gosplan. Any project costing more than 50 million rubles must go before a Review Division (*otdel ekspertizy*), which nominates an ad hoc advisory commission (*ekspertnaia komissiia*) to perform the review. Most members of such commissions are specialists from the Academy and ministry institutes. But before this review even begins, the proposed project must run the gauntlet of sign-offs by other interested agencies.[51] Each of these stages provides the opportunity for technical specialists to express their views.

Gosplan's review committees gradually became receptive to antihydropower arguments in two stages. In the middle and late 1950s, as the Soviet Union rediscovered economics, economists began appearing on Gosplan's *ekspertnye komissii*, arguing that hydropower represented an inefficient use of capital – a view that Khrushchev himself began supporting at that time. Then, as the priority of agriculture began to rise in the 1960s, the ministries representing agriculture and reclamation acquired the clout to compete with the Ministry of Power. Until then, the objections of agencies affected by hydropower construction had gotten short shrift in the review process. Hydropower planners had been able to deal with the objections of agriculture and fisheries by providing for dikes, levees, development of new lands, and construction of artificial hatcheries to stock new reservoirs. Because the cost of these measures was assigned to the ministries concerned and not to the Ministry of Power (which had the resources), they were usually not carried out.[52] In sum, channels for review have long existed,[53] but it took a decline in the political priority of hydropower and a rise in that of its competitors to make the channels available for new arguments, creating a window through which geologists, hydrologists, and other technical advisers could make their objections felt.

Further channels of access to decision makers opened up during the 1960s. The Academy of Sciences created a Scientific Council on Water Resources Management (Nauchnyi Soviet po Vodnomu Khoziaistvu). In 1968 this council became a full-fledged institute of the academy. Similarly, the State Committee on Science and Technology organized a Scientific Council for Multiple-Purpose Use and Protection of Water.[54] The Ministry of Power itself, upon instructions from the State Committee on Science and Technology, organized an interdisciplinary research program on the environmental problems of reservoirs, which ran from 1966 through the mid-1970s.[55] This program brought together thirty research design institutes, representing all the affected agencies.

As the 1960s went on, technical experts and their agencies found they could gain access to the highest authorities: Arguments over agricultural compensation at the site of the Krasnoiarsk Dam in the 1960s were settled by the apparatus of the USSR Council of Ministers,[56] and disputes over the Cheboksar Dam on the Volga may have reached the Politburo itself.[57]

By the end of the decade, hydropower planners faced serious trouble. Projects proposed for the middle Ob',[58] the lower Volga,[59] the Amur,[60] the upper Kama,[61] the middle Enisei,[62] and the Pechora[63] were canceled or postponed after furious debate. Many more projects were redesigned, relocated, or seriously delayed by protests from technical experts and affected interests: The last three units of the Volga-Kama chain (at Saratov, Cheboksar, and the lower Kama[64]) were fought over at every stage; the Boguchansy reservoir on the lower Angara was moved upstream;[65] the use of Lake Sevan in Armenia as a source for hydropower was halted, and restoration of the severely depleted lake was begun.[66]

We might conclude from all this that scientists and technical advisers had showed considerable clout indeed, but the individuals involved did not think so. In interviews with the author in 1973, geographers and hydrologists of the academy institutes, and Vendrov in particular, observed that they would have had little success but for the intervention of powerful industrial ministries whose missions were threatened by the plans of the dam builders. This sort of intervention was not new. Even in the 1940s, the heyday of hydropower construction, the site of the Volgograd project was changed because it would have flooded valuable mineral resources. In the 1950s the discovery of metal-ore deposits caused postponement of the Abalakovskoe Dam on the middle Enisei. The same reasons account for several of the cancellations of the 1960s. For example, the coal-mining industry opposed the proposed diversion of the Pechora, and the petroleum industry fought the middle Ob' project.

But the chief new element of the 1960s was that hydropower now interfered with the leaders' new plans for expanded agricultural development in the European zone of the country – a fact that underscores the close link between the rise of environmental issues and the Brezhnev agricultural program. The result was a dramatic shift in priorities in water-resource development and use, which can be seen most graphically in the fact that after 1955 capital funding for hydropower collapsed, (Table 1) not to recover again until the

Table 1. *Capital investment in*
*hydropower, as a % of the 1955 level*

| Year | Percentage |
| --- | --- |
| 1955 | 100 |
| 1958 | 84 |
| 1960 | 70 |
| 1964 | 67 |
| 1970[a] | — |

[a]Though no data are given for the 1970s, the slowdown in construction continued to the time of writing (1970), according to Neporozhnii. *Source*: P. S. Neporozhnii, ed., *Gidroenergetika i kompleksnoe ispol'zovanie vodnykh resursov SSSR* (Moscow: Energiia, 1970), p. 56.

mid-1970s. At the same time reclamation prospered. In fourteen years its annual central allocations of capital increased more than tenfold.[67]

These developments amounted to a complete reversal of the previous priorities of hydropower and reclamation as claimants for capital funds and water. By 1968 reclamation was being funded at nearly four times the annual level of hydropower (2.4 million rubles for reclamation, 600 million rubles for hydropower.)[68] By the Ninth Five-Year Plan (1971–5), more capital was being allocated to reclamation than to *all* forms of electrical power generation.[69] In the light of these figures, it is not hard to see why the Ministry of Power began losing siting battles and why environmentally minded specialists found a receptive audience.

Does that mean that they had influence? If they did, it was limited. The response of hydropower builders was mainly to move east of the Urals, which they had already been planning to do. Because of the leaders' growing concern about energy in the late 1970s, hydropower has gained a new lease on life in Siberia, and in the Tenth Five-Year Plan it was scheduled to account for 20 percent of the country's net addition to electrical generating capacity.[70] Neither have environmentalists extended their success to other forms of energy generation that might be considered environmentally harmful, such as nuclear power. Despite some evidence of concern among scientists,[71] nuclear safety is not a legitimate public issue, at least not yet. Pollution from agricultural runoff (pesticides and fertilizers), though discussed in technical journals, has not become a public issue either.[72] In sum, the ability of technical specialists to raise a public issue and influence its course is highly channeled; if they succeed in raising one part of a large issue such as the environment, that clearly does not mean that their success will spill over into other parts. Such success as they do have is largely contingent upon larger political currents. Whether or not they realized it at the time, geographers and other scientists who went to war against hydropower in the 1960s turn out in retrospect to have been serving as one of the instruments of a transfer of political priorities in the European USSR from hydropower to agriculture.

During the Baikal and hydropower episodes, however, we observe an important change in the environmentalists: They began to form institutes and training programs, mobilize data, publish journals, and gain established channels of participation. In sum, the tangible expression of the rising legitimacy of environmental issues was the institutionalization, professionalization, and regularization of the people behind them. The next step in this evolution can be seen in the form that the environmental movement has taken in the 1970s, which is the subject of the next section.

### Soviet environmental policy in the 1970s

Despite the publicity surrounding the Baikal affair and the hydropower controversy during the 1960s, very little was being done elsewhere to protect public health or natural resources from the effects of pollution. In 1972–3, on the eve of the present expansion of the water-quality program, only one quarter of the industrial wastes and process water discharged into the Volga were given even the most cursory treatment, and the volume of effluent was increasing by 4 percent a year.[73] Elsewhere the picture was no better: Throughout the country only 16 percent of all municipal wastes were being treated in 1970, [74] and the volume of effluent increased by 19 percent from 1970 to 1974.[75] Unless the leaders reacted quickly, it was clear that they would soon face major threats to the health and future development of the entire southern half of the country.

But now things have rather suddenly changed. In the last eight years, the Soviet Union has launched a heavily funded environmental program, aimed chiefly at preserving clean water. In 1973, annual investment for water quality abruptly jumped fivefold, from 300 million to 1.5 billion rubles.[76] In the spring of 1976, General Secretary Brezhnev announced a five-year, 11-billion-ruble program of capital expenditure for environmental protection, most of it devoted to water.[77] For the Eleventh Five-Year Plan (1981–5), a further increase of more than 50 percent is being discussed.[78] It may be too soon to speak of the "ecology gap," but the Soviet Union may soon exceed, in money terms at least, the level of effort of the United States.

Along with the funding came a series of steps leading to a much more elaborate incorporation of environmental concerns into the formal structure of government. In 1970 a national water code came into effect, followed over the next three years by detailed water legislation for each of the fifteen union republics.[79] Special decrees singled out high-priority areas: the Volga-Ural, the Severskii Donets, the Caspian, Azov, and Baltic seas.[80] In 1972 enforcement responsibility for water quality was assigned to the USSR Ministry of Reclamation and Water Management (Ministerstvo Melioratsii i Vodnogo Khoziaistva – often known as Minvodkhoz), then one of the fastest-growing agencies in the country.[81] This gave the water-quality program a strong institutional defender. In 1974 environmental protection was incorporated into the national economic plan, and Gosplan now has a special division for the environment, with subdivisions for air and water quality.[82] Finally, at the beginning of 1978, the State Hydrometeorological Service was upgraded to the rank of a state committee, with the new name of State Committee for Hydrometeorology and Oversight of the Environment (Gosudarstvennyi Komitet po Gidrometeorologii i Kontroliu Prirodnoi Sredy). Its chairman, Iu. A. Izrael', is a member of the USSR Council of Ministers. In short, the environment, which fifteen years ago had practically no standing at all, is now present in every part of the government structure.[83]

The immediate impetus for the new program was an impending crisis in public health. Because of pollution, catches of freshwater fish plummeted in southern basins, including those of important earners of foreign exchange such as sturgeon. Massive kills occurred regularly in the spring. Cholera, caused by untreated sewage, broke out at the mouth of the Volga. These events coincided with a rapidly rising demand for clean water in the southern USSR, caused by the spread of irrigated agriculture under Brezhnev.

The design of the program shows clearly what the leaders are most concerned about. Moscow receives the greatest attention,[84] but outside the capital most of the pollution-control effort is directed at the eleven river basins of the country's southern zone, in which more than 80 percent of the country's agricultural and industrial production is concentrated.[85] In this group, top priority goes to the Volga and Ural basins. The Volga basin alone, which supports 25 percent of the country's population, industry, and agriculture, accounts for about one-third of the waste-treatment capacity added during the Ninth Five-Year Plan (1971-5).[86] Other areas and republics get less attention: Kazakhstan received only 56 million rubles for water-quality construction in 1974;[87] Georgia was allocated 29 million rubles for 1976;[88] Tadzhikistan got an average of just over 5 million rubles per year from 1971 to 1975.[89] In sum, this is not a program designed primarily to preserve wilderness or protect natural beauty but to protect public health and facilitate further economic growth (particularly of irrigated agriculture) in the most highly developed regions of the country.

This chapter develops three main themes. First, it argues that the influence of scientific advocates and advisers in securing recognition and legitimate status for environmental issues was fragile, contingent, and necessarily opportunistic. It depended on their ability to take advantage of the receptiveness that crisis or changing political priorities induced from time to time in political leaders. This is not pressure-group politics, but the politics of waiting for the open window. The window could not be forced open; the opponents of Baikalsk or hydropower could not force the hand of political leaders through courts, electoral campaigns, or any of the other instruments available to their counterparts in the West. But by taking advantage of openings created by interagency rivalries, the elite's pride and nationalistic sentiment, the concern of political leaders over agriculture, oil and coal deposits, public health, foreign-exchange balances, and so forth, environmental advocates were able to make their case. Many different open windows will do, apparently; the art of being a successful advocate in Soviet politics is to find them.

The second theme arising from this chapter is that official receptiveness was sufficiently strong and consistent to enable environmental advocates to consolidate their opportunities by developing an institutional and professional base, from which they now participate regularly (if not, as we shall see in Chapter 8, on fully equal terms) in the mechanism of policy formation. This institutionalization, professionalization, and official incorporation of a new issue is a key step, the visible symbol of its official recognition. Henceforth, environmental advocacy is no longer limited to ad hoc protest campaigns. But this recognized status was achieved, as with any establishment, at the price of a considerable channeling, in which the more radical themes of protest (of the sort that can be found in the environmental literature in *samizdat*) have been excluded. Just as in agricultural policy, where the course chosen is the most conservative one, so also in official environmental policy: The most conservative aspect, the policy most consonant with traditional aims, has been the policy most strongly pursued.

Do these first two themes mean that the influence of environmental scientists exists only when it corresponds to official desires and concerns? In that case, it would be no influence at all. But the third theme from this chapter is that the environmentalists succeeded in adding more than a little of their own. Official consciousness has been raised; protection of the environment is now part of the obligatory lip service of official speeches and May Day slogans; money and resources are being spent that would not have been otherwise; and, as we shall see in the coming chapters, the scope of official decision making has considerably broadened. At the top of the system, at least, attitudes toward resources and growth are becoming more balanced, and this evolution can be traced directly to the participation of scientific advocates and advisers. In the next chapter we shall see another example of the same themes, drawn this time from a famous issue in Soviet economics – the price of capital.

# 4
# DISPLACING STALINIST DOGMA ON THE PRICE OF CAPITAL

To rethink the premises of growth in the Soviet Union has meant, first of all, sweeping out the remaining intellectual cobwebs of Stalinist dogma on investment and resource use. This is a logical step: A system increasingly preoccupied with scarcity and efficiency must know how much things cost and what alternatives are being forgone or foreclosed by any proposed action. This is the domain of economics. But from the 1930s to the 1950s economics and economists had been systematically driven out of print, out of sight, and in many cases out of existence. Stalin's generation behaved as though they did not want to know how much their approach to industrialization was costing them; growth was guided by engineers and political administrators – and even today most Politburo members are both. Yet to deal with the problems of a developed economy the Soviet Union can no longer do without the sciences of scarcity, and the leaders know it. Indeed, economics began to revive soon after Stalin's death.

Much has been written in the West about this resurrection.[1] Western observers have followed especially closely the efforts of Soviet mathematical economists to gain a professional place in the sun against the resistance of the old-line political economy (the bastardized form in which the discipline was handed down to the 1950s), to develop a scientific basis for prices in a command economy, and to win acceptance for decision-making tools like cost-benefit studies and input-output analysis.[2] Soviet economists have succeeded so well that for twenty-five years they have been the fastest-growing scientific specialty in the country. During the last half of the 1960s, the growth of the economic profession reached a breathtaking average of 15.2 percent a year.[3]

For all the rapid growth of the profession, its revival was in other respects slow and difficult, because of the deadweight of established beliefs that could not be tackled directly. One of the thorniest of these was the "price" of capital in planning and project design, what economists call the capital-intensity problem. It was thorny ideologically because it resembled the capitalist concept of interest, which had been taboo in Stalin's time. But it was no easier politically, because the prospect of a higher valuation on capital threatened the interests of some of the most powerful ministries. Thus, at the very moment that the economics profession was beginning its timid return to official life, those working on the capital-intensity problem found themselves faced with two rough jobs simultaneously: On the one hand, they had the delicate task of cleaning off thirty years of Stalinist dogma from the concepts themselves; on the other, they found themselves drawn into a political battle to cut back the agencies specializing in the great capital-intensive monuments of the Stalin era. But in this twin danger there was also opportunity. The leadership was receptive, the issues were ready at hand, and consequently economists had a chance to make a contribution to greater efficiency in the use of scarce resources.

Standing against them as the embodiment of Stalinist values were the powerful engineering agencies that carried out the spectacular investment programs of the 1930s through the 1960s. For arrogance and seemingly unassailable political strength few could equal Gidroproekt, the hydropower engineering agency. Hydropower construction was intimately associated with the Gulag system, because for a generation it relied on convict labor for every major dam, canal, or reservoir built in the USSR. The top officials of Gidroproekt – particularly Academician S. Ia. Zhuk, whose name the institute now bears – were general officers of the KGB, and as late as the 1950s the agency itself may have been a branch of the secret police. Working out of a modern high-rise building that dominates the Leningradskoe Highway in northwestern Moscow, Gidroproekt in the 1960s maintained ten regional offices and employed thirty thousand to fifty thousand employees in engineering and design alone – a number comparable to the Civil Works Directorate of the U.S. Army Corps of Engineers. At its peak in the mid-1960s, Gidroproekt was at work on more than four hundred projects at any one time, and was unquestionably the dominant force in water-resource planning and development for the entire country.[4]

In the 1950s, after Stalin's death, hydropower's ties with the secret police were severed and Gidroproekt was incorporated into the Ministry of Power and Electrification (Minenergo). The result was a sudden comedown for hydropower at the hands of the thermal-power officials who dominated Minenergo. Something of a purge apparently occurred, for many prominent hydropower personalities retired or moved between 1957 and 1962. A cost-cutting campaign, launched by a speech by Khrushchev at the inauguration of the Volgograd hydropower station in 1957, served notice to hydropower designers that the halcyon days were over. "Beginning in 1958," writes a high official of Gidroproekt, "preference was given to the construction of thermal-power stations, both in the European portion of the USSR and on Siberian rivers."[5] Hydropower construction entered a dark period from which it did not recover until the mid-1970s.

It is apparent from this brief account that there were several issues involved in the humbling of hydropower, including the massive settling of old scores that we call de-Stalinization. But it is significant that one of the instruments enlisted for the purpose was economic analysis. This was partly tactical opportunism: Any stigma will do to beat a dogma. But we should not underestimate the genuineness of many Soviet statements, then and since, that hydropower and the other capital-intensive monuments of the Stalin period had been a shocking waste of resources, and that it was high time to create a more rational basis for the allocation of capital. It was this mixture of motives that gave the economists their opportunity as well as their limits and that constitutes for us the real interest of this conflict.

Did the economists succeed in influencing official policy on the allocation and evaluation of capital? This question is related to the larger ones under discussion in two ways. First, the decline of hydropower was an important precondition for any meaningful reallocation of water and land use toward agriculture in the European zone of the USSR. Therefore, to the extent that economists had a hand in it, they helped to clear the way for the expansion of the Brezhnev policy. Second, the systematic use of interest norms on capital in product design and evaluation is potentially the kind of curb on official enthusiasm needed to keep agricultural investment within reasonable bounds. Whether it has never been used or even seen as such is an important clue to the capacity of Soviet technical experts and political leaders to ask, "How much is enough?"

### The capital-intensity problem: repression and rebirth

How is one to decide how to allocate capital? The controversiality of the capital-intensity problem in the Soviet Union lies in the difficulty of finding a theoretical basis for interest. Interest can be interpreted either as a cost associated with time preference (that is, the relative preference expressed by society for economic returns in different time periods) or as an opportunity cost. Neither of these interpretations, however, is compatible with Marxian theory[6] or Soviet planning practice. The opportunity-cost interpretation, in particular, cannot be easily reconciled either with the labor theory of value or with the Soviet price system. A decision on allocation of capital is essentially end-oriented; it must have as its foundation a meaningful indicator of demand that will provide information about ends. However, the labor theory of value does not reflect demand, and therefore it provides no guide to ends. Likewise, the Soviet price system, despite periodic reforms, does not supply a consistent or meaningful guide to objectives.[7] As a result of these problems, the questions of capital allocation and capital intensity have been controversial since the beginning of the Soviet period, and they were hotly debated in Soviet economic journals throughout the 1920s.

Abruptly, in 1930 and 1931 the economic staffs of government departments were purged and the capital-intensity problem disappeared as a subject of public discussion. As Gregory Grossman put it, "The economic literature disappeared with the economists themselves."[8] At the same time, a reaction against the supposed association of interest with capitalism caused the official "price" of capital to be reduced to zero. Credit reforms in the early 1930s virtually eliminated interest in the financing of capital in industry, and the official line emphasized the greatest possible application of technology to the high-priority sectors of the economy, brooking no discussion of what the economic limits of such "maximum mechanization" might be.[9]

As both economists and the interest rate vanished from the public scene, the theoretical link between the decision of "what to produce" and the decision of "how to produce" was severed; the former became the preserve of the political leadership, and the latter, that of engineers. Contributing to this separation was an administrative division between the centers in which the two decisions were made: "What to produce" was classified conceptually as "planning" (*planirovanie*); "how to produce," as part of "project making" (*proektirovanie*), and the two were handled in different offices.

This created an awkward problem. The orders the Soviet project maker received from the planner carried an implicit interest rate of zero.[10] But a zero interest rate was an absurdity. It made the most capital-intensive projects seem cheaper than the least capital-intensive ones, if only the former had lower current costs. Thus, for example, every hydropower plant would become preferable to every thermal one. Such a bias not only offended common sense but was in total contradiction with a very real scarcity of the capital each ministry actually had at its disposal. This problem was especially acute in capital-intensive industries such as electrical power generation. The resulting dilemma is acknowledged frankly by present-day Soviet economists:

> The characteristic feature of the power industry is that the necessity of co-measuring capital and current costs penetrates literally every technical-economic step in design and every calculation . . . To apply the criterion of minimization of current costs would have led to a clearly irrational use of the limited supply of investment capital . . . Life itself, and the direct requirements of design practice in the field of electrical power, rendered essential a broad application of the principles of [economic effectiveness used in] GOELRO.[11]

The designers' answer was subterfuge. Hydropower economists write today that in hydropower project evaluation the interest rate was never really abandoned.[12] Gregory Grossman's findings indicate the same thing: An interestlike criterion was used sub rosa in hydropower design and in several other capital-intensive sectors throughout the Stalinist period.[13] However, the essential feature of the capital-intensity criterion as it was used during this period is that it was the work of engineers, not economists.[14] The same was true of publications on the subject, for engineers did not confine themselves to pricing capital in project evaluations; they also discussed the question in their journals, resorting to a variety of euphemisms to camouflage its resemblance to interest. The discussion was especially vigorous in the power industry, where the problem of capital intensity could not be ducked. In fact, when eventually the engineers' policies on capital intensity began to draw fire from ideologists late in the Stalinist period, causing engineers in other fields to retreat from print – even then, the discussion in the technical journals of the power industry did not stop.[15]

With Stalin's death the situation changed sharply. Within a short time a series of actions by his successors showed they were seriously concerned about the scarcity of capital. In the field of water-resource development, one could mention the interruption of construction on the Volga-Baltic Canal, reduced allocations to hydropower after 1955, cost-cutting pressure on hydropower designers after 1957, and a series of decisions favoring thermal power over hydropower in 1958.[16]

During the same period Soviet economics returned to life and Soviet economists returned to the question of capital intensity. In 1957 the Institute of Economics of the USSR Academy of Sciences convened an All-Union Conference on Questions of Capital Effectiveness, which adopted several of the principles long in covert use among hydropower designers.[17] In 1960 the academy published a *Tipovaia metodika*[18] (Model methodology), which set forth officially, for the first time since the 1920s, prescribed procedures for calculating the "effectiveness" of capital investments in Soviet industry. Thus the 1957 conference and the 1960 methodology mark the beginning of the end of the peculiar situation that had prevailed since the early 1930s. But that was not the end of the controversy. The 1960 methodology, as we shall see, left most of the important questions unsettled, including the political ones involving resource use in the European USSR.

But before we go on to discuss what happened next, we should observe that the capital-intensity problem is an early example of the kind of third-generation problem described in the first chapter of this book, for its overt use in project design was a response to the inadequacy of thumblike administrative means for fine-tuned decision making. Capital can be apportioned administratively among major sectors or among major projects by a rough system of "priority awareness," that is, by sniffing the air and reading *Pravda* carefully. But what prevents this in technological and design choices for individual projects, especially in a highly technical and capital-intensive field like hydropower, is that (as Beschinskii observed in the passage quoted earlier) "the necessity of co-measuring capital and current costs penetrates literally every . . . calculation." This is what made it essential to have an explicit criterion, even at the Stalinist nadir.

### The evolution of the capital-intensity debate since 1960

The 1957 conference on capital intensity released a flood of debate, proposals, and counterproposals, which has not yet abated. Because of the discussion, both the definition and the level of the "capital-effectiveness criterion" have evolved considerably, resulting on the whole in a higher official "price" on capital (in terms of current savings in costs) in project design. This seriously threatened the economic attractiveness of hydropower, and hydropower economists and officials soon became prominently involved in the debate.

Let us examine, first of all, the basic formula prescribed by the 1960 methodology. In traditional practice, Soviet project makers are assigned a fixed output target, say, so many kilowatt-hours of electricity. Their task is to design a project to meet it at the least total cost. The 1960 methodology provides that, given alternative projects producing the same output, the more capital-intensive one should be chosen if it produces savings in current costs (excluding interest) equal to, or greater than, a certain percentage of the additional capital outlay required. That percentage is called the capital-effectiveness norm:

$$\frac{I_2 - I_1}{K_1 - K_2} \geq E_n$$

where $I_1$ and $I_2$ = annual current costs (including operation, maintenance, and replacement of each project); $K_1$ and $K_2$ = capital costs of each project; and $E_n$ = capital-effectiveness norm.

To permit a ranking of more than two alternatives, the following formula is used:

$$I + E_n K = \min$$

In other words, project makers must choose the project with the lowest combination of current annual costs and discounted capital.

Three points, however, were left unclear. First, the formulas were based on the assumption that the construction and "gestation" times of the alternatives compared would be the same and that both output and current costs would be constant over time once the projects reached full output. How were designers to proceed if these assumptions did not hold? Second, the formulas assumed that the alternative projects would meet identical output targets. But what to do in the case of alternatives with outputs of different mix and reliability? Finally, and most important, the methodology did not specify how high the norm itself should be. These questions were loaded with consequence for hydropower designers. Hydropower projects take longer to build and to bring into full operation than thermal plants. Once they are operating, their greater reliability is offset by fluctuations in output caused by variable streamflow. Hydropower projects have always served a greater variety of purposes than thermal plants, and these were not reflected in the standard capital-effectiveness formula. But the most threatening feature of all was that a high-capital-effectiveness norm would destroy the economic justifiability of several hundred projects then on hydropower designers' drawing boards. Throughout the 1960s, hydropower planners and economists fought a rearguard battle to defuse the capital-effectiveness norm. After losing the early rounds, they were in the main successful by the late 1960s in staving off the worst. After a rapid review of the issues, we shall explore why.

*How high a norm?*
Since the appearance of the 1960 methodology, the trend has been toward a higher "price tag" on capital. One source refers to a "gradual" rise from 4 to 10 percent up to 1969.[19] Another mentions a range of from 7 to 10 percent for the decade of the 1960s.[20] Since the late 1960s the rate in use has reportedly remained at 10 percent, about twice the unofficial values used from the 1920s through the 1950s.[21]

However, there was considerable pressure during the 1960s to apply to hydropower projects even higher norms. In 1966 the State Committee on

Science and Technology (GKNT) issued a methodology calling for a rate of 15 percent,[22] whereas Gidroproekt's own methodology, issued at the same time, held out for 10 percent. Hydropower officials reacted sharply to the proposed higher figure. Seventy-five percent of the hydropower capacity then on the drawing boards or under construction, they argued, would have the appearance of being economically unjustified.[23] The most famous hydropower projects of the 1960s and 1970s, including the giants at Bratsk, Krasnoiarsk, Saiano-Shushensk, and Ust'-Ilimsk, would fall below the required capital-effectiveness norm.[24]

The move by GKNT to raise the norm was perceived as a direct attack on hydropower. A Gidroproekt engineer later commented:

> The process of developing and perfecting the methodology for the economic justification of hydropower projects in the last five years has been characterized by a struggle between the supporters and defenders of hydropower. In 1966 GKNT developed a methodology for the determination of the effectiveness of capital investments, which if put into effect would have led in essence to the liquidation of further hydropower construction.[25]

Gidroproekt and other hydropower institutes responded with research programs to underscore the dire long-term consequences of such high norms for various sectors of the economy and to develop alternative principles as a basis for lower norms. Much of the latter work was directed at assessing the historical performance of hydropower relative to thermal power. There followed a war of expert studies, pitting Gidroproekt against the Power Division of GKNT.[26] Gidroproekt's studies, not surprisingly, showed hydropower in a favorable light, concluding that the ratio of profit to total capital invested for Soviet hydropower as a whole in 1970 was 12.3 percent, as opposed to 10.9 percent for thermal power.[27] These figures, representing average rather than marginal rates of profitability (and probably calculated before interest charges), were irrelevant to the issue at hand and should be viewed mainly as propaganda. Nevertheless, Gidroproekt's hard work paid off. The GKNT's proposed methodology was rejected,[28] and a compromise value of the norm was adopted instead. The methodology currently in force prescribes a figure of 12 percent, and provides in addition that in special cases still lower norms may be authorized by Gosplan. Hydropower apparently benefits from this provision, for it continues to operate under a norm of 10 percent[29] – five points lower than GKNT had wanted.

In their fight Gidroproekt found important allies among both economists and ministry officials. The Council on Productive Forces, a long-term planning group in Gosplan, supported the hydropower position, as did the Institute of Economics of the Academy of Sciences.[30] And as the 1960s went on, Gidroproekt was joined by the increasingly powerful Ministry of Reclamation. The latter's position is not hard to explain. Reclamation, compared to hydropower, is equally capital intensive and has a longer period of maturation and a higher uncertainty of output; and reclamation economists were presumably just as concerned as their colleagues in hydropower to prevent unfavorable definitions and values of capital-effectiveness methodology. As the 1960s went on and the priority of agricultural investment began to rise, support for stiffer capital-effectiveness norms faded.

*One value or many?*

Much the same story occurred over the question – equally arcane in appearances but equally loaded with political consequence – whether there should be a single value for the capital-effectiveness norm, applicable throughout the economy, or several. Broadly speaking, opinion among economists evolved in the direction of a qualified single value. Hydropower officials favored multiple values instead; and ultimately a compromise was reached that adopts the principle of a single norm but allows exceptions in special cases. However, the interesting feature of the debate in this case was the diversity of views all around. So far the reader may have gained the impression that special-interest economists supported only their organizations' "line." This particular debate shows otherwise.

In practice, a wide range of capital-effectiveness norms could be found in the Soviet Union in the 1960s. In industry, the norms issued in 1962 by Gosplan and the Academy of Sciences went from a low of 10 percent for electrical power and transportation to 25 percent for consumer and food-processing industries, and 33 percent for chemistry and machine building.[31] In various sectors of water-resource development, norms varied from 10 to 33 percent. In fact, a similar range existed within the Ministry of Reclamation alone.[32]

The issue was not whether there should be a completely uniform rate, but rather how much departure from uniformity was desirable. Under the opportunity-cost interpretation of capital intensity, if you wish to allocate resources efficiently you must set the value of the capital-effectiveness norm equal throughout the economy, *provided* that the other price parameters are also meaningful for the purpose of maximization[33] and that calculations upon which the norm is based include all relevant benefits and costs. But since that is far from the case in the Soviet Union (or anywhere else for that matter), Soviet economists will agree that some departures from a uniform rate may be warranted, although they still support the general principle of uniformity. Academician T. S. Khachaturov, one of the best-known authorities on the question of capital effectiveness, invoked the arguments that (1) certain sectors of the economy have more potential than others for promoting mechanization and automation of production; (2) the objectives of investment are not only to produce maximum profit and "economic effect" but also to promote purposes that are "essential for society, for the state"; (3) the question of how to produce cannot be decided separately from the question of *what* to produce (this apparently implies that, though strictly speaking the capital-effectiveness norm applies only to the decision of *how* to produce, state policy can use it as a means of influencing the composition of the bill of goods by allowing more liberal investment criteria in some branches than in others.[34]) Consequently, Khachaturov was against a single value.

Khachaturov's colleague at the Institute of Economics, M. N. Loiter, argued much the same position in the mid-1970s, adding that the special importance of the capital-effectiveness norm for policy making is that it is the most "concentrated management instrument" available. Loiter recommended lowering the norm – that is, making it more permissive – by 15 to 30 percent in especially important, capital-intensive programs, such as "branches of significance for defense."[35]

What both men were defending was not exactly multiple rates but the principle of a uniform rate tempered by exceptions. This was eventually the official position also. The 1966 methodology of the GKNT advocated a single value, and so does the official 1969 Model Methodology, of which Academician Khachaturov was one of the principal authors.

Hydropower and other power organizations in *their* proposed methodology supported multiple norms. Individual specialists, however, seem to have been divided. One article supported nonuniform levels, arguing that the power industry was on the threshold of a major technological jump (into nuclear and magnetohydrodynamic technology), which would inevitably cause a temporary drop in the return on capital and should be taken into account in the value of the norms.[36]

On the other hand, other power specialists favored a single level and explicitly rejected Khachaturov's arguments. For example, one article stated: "[The capital effectiveness norm] serves as an indicator of *how* to produce, not of *what* to produce, and for that reason it does not depend on the economic significance of this or that type of output for the economy."[37] Another recent article by hydropower specialists, also in favor of a single value, expanded on this point:

> The minimum allowable capital-effectiveness norm must have, as a rule, a single value for all branches, since from the standpoint of the economy as a whole it does not matter where the economic effect sought through additional capital outlays is attained . . . The problem of whether to encourage a more rapid growth of some branches relative to others is a question of "economic proportions" and cannot be decided by means of different levels of the capital-effectiveness norm, since the latter serves only as an instrument for making the most economic choices *within* a given branch.[38]

This diversity of views may simply mean that by the early 1970s the essential compromises over policy had been achieved and that the political heat had gone out of the issue. Hydropower's more modest status had become an established fact, and organizations traditionally devoted to hydropower were being switched to other tasks. Gidroproekt, for example, made up for the decline in conventional hydropower assignments by turning to nuclear power, pumped storage, and even to an important role in the development of the Kama River truck complex.[39] Consequently, whereas hydropower officials still sought to shape design rules around the most favorable interpretations of the capital-effectiveness criterion, the explosive connection between fine points of economic theory and policy outcomes was apparently gone. Then, after the mid-1970s, when official support for hydropower construction began to increase again, the "window" for debating the fine points of the norm narrowed again.

*The issue of the time factor*

One last point of contention in the capital-intensity debate was the use of a so-called time factor. The basic capital-effectiveness formula of the 1960 Model Methodology had been written for the simplest possible world: It assumed instantaneous construction, one-shot capital investment, immediate attainment of planned output levels, and constant current costs. To remove these assumptions meant bringing into the picture two additional costs of capital: Capital tied up in construction (or "frozen," as the Russians say) and the "gestation" costs associated with incomplete use of capital while the project is being brought up to full output. These costs are reflected in Soviet design through the use of a second norm, called a time factor.

However, the time factor is a relatively recent innovation. As late as the 1960s the costs of frozen capital and of project gestation were not directly taken into account at all in project design and evaluation.[40] Such a convention implicitly favored hydropower, with its longer construction and gestation time, over alternative power projects. To take these additional costs into account the 1960 Methodology provided that when two alternative projects differed in construction time or in their schedule for capital outlays, designers should make them comparable by discounting each year's capital outlays for each project to a common "basis" year. The discount factor to be used for this purpose was called the time factor.[41] But the brevity of these directions gives the impression that considerable latitude was deliberately left to individual ministries to define the time factor as they thought best (or perhaps even not to use it at all). No formula for it was given and the value of the factor was not specified. Yet depending on how it was defined and applied, the time factor could increase or decrease the economic attractiveness of capital-intensive projects, and it stimulated a decade of animated discussion among hydropower designers and economists, as well as some interagency skirmishing.

The first controversial question concerned the definition of the time factor itself: Why was there any need, asked some specialists, for a separate time factor? And why should it have a different value from the capital-effectiveness norm? According to Beschinskii, the argument was often heard during the 1950s that a separate time factor was unneccessary because the productive "immobilization" of capital during construction could be reflected in the value of the capital-effectiveness norm.[42] Such opinions reflected a view among many economists at that time that the time factor, because it expressed the opportunity costs of "frozen" and "gestating" capital, was in essence no different from the capital-effectiveness criterion, which also expressed opportunity cost – that of capital diverted from other uses. As the time factor and the capital-effectiveness norm together expressed the full opportunity cost of capital, why not simply use a single norm? However, during the 1960s most Soviet writers on this question came around to the view that there was indeed an important conceptual difference between the two norms and that position is the one most of them accept today.[43]

But what should the value of the time factor be? In 1966 the State Committee on Science and Technology took a hard line, advocating that both the capital-effectiveness norm and the time factor be set at a high value of 15 percent. Gidroproekt responded with a counter-methodology, holding out for a time factor of 5 percent.[44] Hydropower designers, in fact, used the 5 percent figure throughout the 1960s.[45]

A lower value of the time factor had the effect of understating the opportunity costs of long construction times and gestation periods – a difference of some advantage to hydropower. But their justification for it had little to do with fancy theory. Instead, they represented the lower time factor as something of a trade or more exactly as a concession owed to hydropower in exchange for the discriminatory effect of existing methods of computing depreciation charges in project design. The background to hydropower's claim is this: Gosplan regulations since 1961 have required that depreciation charges (included in current costs for the purposes of project evaluation) be computed according to what is called in the United States the straight-line method. This method assumes that the funds deducted for depreciation do not earn interest during the lifetime of the project:

$$I = \frac{K}{t}$$

where $I$ = annual depreciation norm, $K$ = total capital costs, and $t$ = useful life of project. Soviet hydropower officials have long argued that the straight-line method unjustifiably favors the less capital-intensive variant – that is, thermal power. They advocate instead the use of what Americans call the sinking-fund method of calculating depreciation charges, which credits all the competing projects under consideration with interest earned by the accumulated depreciation fund during the project's lifetime and hence tends to favor the more capital-intensive one:

$$I = \frac{rk}{(1+r)t - 1}$$

where $r$ = time factor.[46]

The State Committee on Science and Technology (GKNT), in its proposed 1966 methodology, responded to the logic of this position by recommending *both* identical values for the time factor and the capital-effectiveness norm *and* the adoption of the sinking-fund method.[47]

In the end, however, the essence of the hydropower position prevailed. The 1969 Model Methodology – the one in effect today – prescribes a time factor equal to two-thirds of the capital-effectiveness norm (8 and 12 percent, respectively) and retains the straight-line method of computing depreciation charges. According to one Soviet expert, the combination of unequal norms and straight-line depreciation produces much the same results in project evaluation as the combination of equal norms and sinking-fund depreciation.[48]

To sum up the economists' achievements of the 1960s: They succeeded in reviving and expanding a vital economic concept that had been driven underground under Stalin; they participated in a decade-long process of debate and analysis that saw the capital-effectiveness norm more than double in value; and they expanded its meaning to allow for the complexity and uncertainty of real-life investment situations, rather than the highly abstracted analysis practiced covertly up to the 1960s. But how do we know that all this had any actual impact on design practice? It is not possible to see the details of the connection between the economists' debates and actual design and planning decisions. But all of the information on which this account is based comes from the specialized journals whose contributors were intimately involved in problems of design and planning and in addressing fellow specialists. These were no abstract academic debates, but inquiries engaged in by people who were wrestling with concrete problems. By the end of the 1960s the application of capital-effectiveness criteria had become established practice in Soviet design and planning, with far-reaching consequences, one might have expected, for the efficient use of capital.

Yet in the next section we shall see that the influence of economists was more apparent than real and depended on the confluence of their opinions with the political trends of the moment. Since the late 1960s the canons of capital effectiveness in the water-resources field have been observed mainly in the breach, and the concept itself still suffers from restrictions that limit its practical applicability as a lever for policy.

*The ineffectiveness of the capital-effectiveness criterion*

By the late 1960s, proponents of the strict application of capital-effectiveness criteria appeared to have reached some sort of outer boundary, beyond which they could not progress. New political priorities arose: The liquidation of the police empire and the redistribution and trimming of its component parts were followed, in the water-resources field, by new investment policies under Brezhnev. The first tide had favored a close look at capital effectiveness; the second, as we shall see, favored the opposite. In addition, the first official flush of enthusiasm over economics passed as it became clear that the questions raised by economists infringe on the priority-setting prerogatives of planners and politicians.[49] Whether the issue was prices, or input-output analysis, or incentives, or capital-effectiveness evaluation, the story was essentially the same. Consequently, the economists were constrained in their latitude to push questions to their logical conclusions. These two things taken together provide a plausible explanation as to why the economists appeared to lose ground.

Let us take first the matter of changing investment priorities. As the Brezhnev agricultural coalition moved into high gear in 1970, with reclamation as its leading program, the Soviet economist M. N. Loiter wrote acidly that "almost any irrigation or drainage project looks profitable at the present time and can be included in the list of projects to be built."[50] The Volga-Ural Canal, for example, was approved for construction despite a projected capital effectiveness of only 7 percent.[51] Hydropower, too, as it moved east of the Urals during the 1960s, managed to secure advantageous compromises and some special allowances besides.

Moreover, because of the way capital-effectiveness norms are defined and calculated, it has not been difficult to make a project look capital effective. One way this is done is through judicius assignment of costs. Hydropower and its relationship to reclamation is once again the classic example. Since World War II, all large water-resource projects have been officially designed to satisfy several purposes simultaneously; hydropower, transportation by water, and reclamation are usually the three most important ones. However, the traditional method of financing multiple-purpose projects was to assign nearly all projects costs to the leading purpose, which in most cases until very recently was hydropower.[52] As a result, it was estimated in the late 1960s that the Ministry of Power had carried over 80 percent of the total capital expenditures for multiple-purpose reservoirs and canals involving hydropower.[53] For some parts of the country the figures were even higher. For example, for the major series of dams in the European USSR, hydropower's share was 85 percent.[54]

This arrangement was not a problem for hydropower organizations so long as the priority of hydropower was high and the "price" of capital low. As these conditions changed, the assignment of costs among purposes became a source of bitter conflict among the major agencies involved.

There are two direct reasons for this: First, standard procedure calls for establishing the capital effectiveness of each purpose in a multiple-purpose project separately, based on the costs officially assigned to each purpose in the "financial estimate" (*smeta*) accompanying the project report. In other words, if hydropower designers can persuade the Ministry of the River Fleet to shoulder a portion of the costs of a dam in exchange for the added channel depths created by the resulting reservoir, then the costs assigned to hydropower will be correspondingly lower, and this in turn may determine whether the hydropower component of the project meets the capital-effectiveness norm and whether it can be economically justified. This is no idle consideration, as can be seen from Table 2, which compares the share of project costs assigned to hydropower with the "break-even" share beyond which the hydropower component becomes non–capital effective.

Table 2. *Comparison of hydropower project costs*

| Project | Percentage of project costs assigned to hydro in project report | Percentage beyond which the hydro component becomes non–capital effective |
|---|---|---|
| Lower Kama | 69 | 66 |
| Saratov (Volga) | 92 | 88 |
| Kiev (Dnieper) | 76 | 62 |
| Pechora | 52 | 58 |
| Cheboksar (Volga) | 82 | 84 |
| Volgograd | 80 | 100 |
| Mogilev-Podol' (Dniester) | 61 | 76 |

*Source*: L. G. Goruleva et al., "Nekotorye voprosy raspredeleniia zatrat," *Trudy Gidroproekta* 29 (1973): 198.

In the first group of projects, the share assigned to hydropower was so large that the hydropower component as a whole failed the capital-effectiveness test. (Note, however, that all these projects were built anyway.)[55] For the second group, a relatively small shift in hydropower's share could have the same result. Only the Volgograd project could have carried the entire cost of the multiple-purpose project and still retained its "justifiability." The same process also works in reverse: In some cases, hydropower projects that intitially failed the capital-effectiveness test have been approved once a portion of the costs were reassigned to other purposes.[56] In recent years, because of the rising priority of purposes such as reclamation and flood control, a number of projects have been authorized with less than two-thirds or even less than half of the costs assigned to hydropower. This is one of the reasons why hydropower has gained a new lease on life east of the Urals. The entire procedure, however, has little to do with economics. Soviet sources agree that cost shares in multiple-purpose projects are not based on economic return accruing to each purpose but rather on inter-agency bargaining, which on occasion can be prolonged and bitter. The lead agency is encouraged to drag in as many side purposes as possible, so as to lessen its own load; whereas the organizations representing those purposes, on the contrary, have an incentive to hang back in the hope that project benefits will accrue to them for nothing. The role of the economist, in such cases, is to help massage the numbers for his employers.

The sharp-eyed reader will have noticed that one of the reasons why cost allocation causes such conflict is that each agency must do its own capital-effectiveness calculations separately, based on what *its* investment alterna-tives are for meeting assigned output targets. There is no *economic* in-strument for evaluating the relative capital effectiveness of investment across agency boundaries; the norm applies only to the question of *how* to produce within each agency, not to the question of *what* to produce across all agencies.

Economists have not shied away from tackling this problem. There does exist a form of the capital-effectiveness criterion, called the general effec-tiveness method, that can serve, at least in principle, for comparisons across agencies, because it is based on profitability. It is defined as the profit (*pribyl'*), or net return (*chistyi dokhod*), per unit of capital expenditure.

As one compares the 1960 and 1969 methodologies, one finds that the official importance of the general-effectiveness norm has greatly increased since 1960. In 1960 no actual formulas for the general-effectiveness norm were given; in 1969 there were several. In 1960 the general-effectiveness method was to be used only for the purpose of establishing ex post facto the effectiveness of *past* investments; and it was to be used at the highest planning levels and in individual enterprises, but not, apparently, at any level in between. Thus in the 1960 version the general-effectiveness method appears to have been intended primarily as a method of checking the results of past decisions, rather than as a direct criterion for present choices. In the 1969 version, in contrast, the general-effectiveness method is prescribed for forward planning as well as ex-post assessment.

The implication of this was potentially quite important: Project makers who previously only made decisions on *how* to produce, subject to assigned output targets, were seemingly now being invited to participate in decisions on *what* to produce, traditionally the preserve of the planners and their "method of material balances." It is interesting to note in this connection that whereas the 1960 methodology contained references to the method of material balances as the basis for decisions on what to produce, the 1969 methodology did not mention material balances at all.

Some writers in the field of water-resource development carried this implication quite far. For example, A. A. Makeev, a hydropower specialist, wrote in Gidroproekt's technical journal:

> The calculation of general effectiveness enables us to answer a wider circle of questions: Do we need this output at all? What should we produce? In what proportions and in what sequence?[57]

Interestingly, the journal's editors felt obliged to sound a note of caution at the end of Makeev's article by pointing out that his interpretation was broader than the 1969 methodology intended. Most water-resource specialists continued to maintain a position considerably short of Makeev's, stressing instead the importance of the method of material balances and the inadvisability of basing capital-allocation decisions on profitability.[58] For hydropower specialists, this was partly a matter of their agencies' interest. The general-effectiveness method reportedly often biases design decisions against the more capital-intensive alternative, yielding results contrary to those produced by the comparative-effectiveness method.[59]

But the main trouble with the general-effectiveness norm is that it is dependent on the vagaries of the price system. This poses acute problems in reclamation planning, for profitability in project design is calculated on the basis of state purchasing prices, which are set so as to produce more or less equal income to all firms, that is, not to approximate the scarcity value of the product. This has produced some peculiar consequences, described by the reclamation economist B. G. Kovalenko:

> No one has any doubts about the absolute necessity to irrigate pastures and hayfields to create a stable feed base for livestock, yet profitability indicators...in some cases appear to show that such measures are not capital-effective.

> Grain crops on irrigated land in the majority of cases show a loss and come out non-capital-effective. Even one of the most valuable crops – cotton – likewise comes out non-capital-effective in such new irrigation areas as the Golodnaia Steppe, the Karakum Canal, and the Amy-Dar'ia basin and others.

> In practice, when such clear contradictions appear, [designers] resort to a search for every possible additional factor...and sometimes simply doctor the figures, so as to make an essential project come out "capital-effective."[60]

The author concluded by strongly opposing the general-effectiveness method.

The seeming invitation to economists to put their skills to work at the external margin – that is, on the question of *what* to produce – coincided with the economic reforms of the middle and late 1960s, which were intended to raise efficiency by increasing the importance of economic incentives and economic indexes of performance – notably profitability – as opposed to the traditional emphasis on physical outputs. Thus, one of the important functions of the general-effectiveness norm was to serve as a gauge of profitability in capital investment as the new system spread. But in the 1970s the economic reform was curtailed, partly because of technical obstacles of the kind just described. In the water-resources field, several types of agencies never did go over to the new system, no single methodology was ever adopted for evaluating multiple-purpose projects, and consequently there is no agreed-upon *economic* instrument for allocating investment priorities for this scarce resource. Despite twenty years of debate, voluminous writing, countless draft methodologies and proposals, it is hard to see how much practical difference the economists have made.

Despite the revival and full institutionalization and professionalization of Soviet economics since the mid-1950s, the economic issues involved in capital investment and resource use have been only partially rethought and do not yet constitute a major contribution to the more efficient use of natural resources. Suffice it to mention that after two decades of debate there is still no agreement on the way to assign value to water or land, even though Soviet economists agree that capital-effectiveness calculations lose most of their meaning if such basic quantities are left out of the balance.

The obstacles are not so much ideological as they are technical and political. In the present-day Soviet literature there is little of the concern of the 1930s to avoid all analogies to the capitalist concept of interest. It has become common, in fact, for Soviet economists to refer to the capital-effectiveness norm as *protsenty*, that is, interest, and to the application of the time factor as *diskontirovanie* (discounting). There was, to be sure, a lively tiff for several years over whether the time factor should be simple or compound, and here the point was sometimes made that it was important to avoid capitalist practice. But on the whole that fear has lost its force. And for that reason, economists discussing the capital-intensity problem have had little need of mathematical disguises, unlike their optimizing colleagues who were obliged to sneak in marginal pricing as a concept in mathematical programming. During the Stalinist period, to be sure, engineers preoccupied with co-measuring capital and current costs disguised the interest rate by using its reciprocal instead and calling it the payout period, but today Soviet economists dismiss that kind of subterfuge with something like a wry shrug.

The political problem of capital-effectiveness economists is that their most promising political window – the economic campaign against hydropower – soon squeezed shut, and what others remained were too narrow to allow large issues to pass. Thus the question of what to produce remains, as before, the province of planners and political leaders, and the discussion of capital effectiveness remains confined to *how* to produce. The influence of the economists on these questions was further conditioned by the fact that most of them in this case were insiders, working (or having formerly worked) for the agencies concerned. Thus there was no cloud of outsider opponents buzzing around a cause célèbre, as at Baikal.

In the end, we are left with a picture of partial success and circumscribed influence, just as in the case of environmental protest. Official consciousness has been raised, no doubt, at least to the extent that capital effectiveness, like environmental quality, is now part of the obligatory rhetoric at congresses and parades. The specialists dealing with these questions occupy well-established institutional bases and have regular channels of access to decision makers. But in both cases one observes that their actual impact depends totally on changes in official receptiveness, giving the specialists and would-be advisers occasional opportunities but frequent frustrations.

We turn now to one last illustrative case, the participation of technical specialists in a long-standing debate to end chronic water shortages in the south by massive diversion of water from the north.

# 5
# TECHNOLOGY ASSESSMENT
# SOVIET STYLE*

In the mid-1960s, an American engineering firm achieved notoriety with a plan to divert more than 130 cubic kilometers of water annually from Alaska and northwestern Canada to the United States and Mexico via a network of canals and reservoirs that included an 800-kilometer trench reservoir in the Rocky Mountains.[1] Now, after fifteen years of environmental legislation and litigation, such a project could sooner be built on the far side of the moon than in the western United States (to say nothing of the participation of the Canadians). But something like it may soon be built in the Soviet Union. Soviet planners and engineers are talking seriously of rerouting the flow of several northern rivers to support irrigated agriculture in the southern half of the country, arrest the decline of the Caspian and Aral seas, alleviate their pollution problems with clean northern water – in short, to remove at one bound the most important obstacles to the further development of the southern half of the country. The idea has recently gained important official backing and is moving rapidly toward advanced engineering and economic studies. Construction could conceivably begin within the next five years.

Conceivably, but not inevitably. The idea of such a titanic engineering venture has stirred up a highly emotional public argument in the Soviet Union, among competing regions, institutions, and technical specialists. As a result, the diversion projects offer the fascinating spectacle of a full-fledged and relatively open "technology assessment" (to use the term fashionable in Washington) of a project that an earlier Soviet generation would have undertaken without public debate. But what has been the effect of that debate on the course of policy? That is the subject of this chapter.

That the diversion idea is being taken seriously at all is due, first of all, to the high priority of agriculture and conservation under Brezhnev, and especially of what I have called the southern strategy. The south has sunlight and a long growing season, and the Brezhnev agricultural program bets heavily on the southern regions. But without more water that strategy will fail.

---

* The original version of this chapter appeared in *Science*, Vol. 208, pp. 1344–48, June 20, 1980. Copyright 1980 by the American Association for the Advancement of Science.

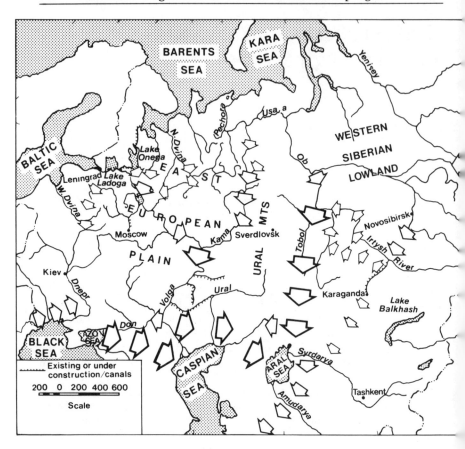

Current European and Siberian diversion proposals in the USSR. Redrawn from Philip P. Micklin, "Soviet Plans to Reverse the Flow of Rivers: the Kama–Pechora–Vychegda Project," *Canadian Geographer* 18, No. 3 (1969).

What can be done? There are three possibilities. The first is to make additional water available by using present supplies more efficiently. This would require a much more efficient reclamation program,[2] better regulation of streamflow, a large and effective investment in pollution control,[3] and the rapid reallocation of water from established users to agriculture. This is the so-called "intensification strategy," which amounts to wagering that the water liberated through efficient and rationalized use will be sufficient to support the growth of the south and west at least through the end of the century. This strategy has been discussed in the opening chapter. Suffice it to say here that the efficiency of the new agriculture and related programs has become one of the chief issues within the leadership in the past two years.[4] The leaders are apparently shaken in their faith that "intensification" alone will solve the problem.

The second possibility is to cut back the southern half of the agricultural program in favor of a northern strategy. There has long been a rival current of opinion among Soviet specialists that top priority should go to drainage and liming in the wet and acid areas of the Moscow region and the European northwest. Indeed, in 1974 the leadership began an ambitious program to develop the region known as the non-black-earth zone (*nechernozem'e*). It calls for 10 million hectares of new drainage projects by 1980, and great publicity is being given to the fact that important parts of it are being directed by Central Asian reclamation teams working in the north as contractors.[5] Yet the southern programs continue at the same rapid pace as before, and there is no sign that the southern strategy has lost first place.

The third possibility is to bring more water into the region from outside. The basic idea is to block the path of some of the country's largest northward-flowing rivers, back up their flow over the low divide that separates the country's northern and southern faces, and run the water to the south.[6] Such north-south transfers could ultimately cost considerably more than 100 billion rubles and would represent one of the largest engineering projects ever undertaken by any civilization.

No wonder that the Soviet leadership has shrunk until now from a project of such cost and scope. Even now some top leaders, notably Kosygin, clearly prefer the first alternative, at any rate for the foreseeable future.[7] But recent events, as we shall see, have caused the diversion idea to be moved up toward more active consideration. In October 1976 a resolution of the Central Committee of the CPSU on the targets of the Tenth Five-Year Plan authorized preliminary economic and engineering studies for the two main diversion projects. In December 1978 the Party Central Committee and the USSR Council of Ministers issued a joint decree setting specific deadlines for the completion of full engineering and economic justifications for the diversion projects.[8] In two years the leadership has come a long way toward committing the country to the diversions. Even so, they have taken twenty years to reach this point, and that lengthy reserve, that very lack of commitment had a very important consequence: It gave technical specialists and advisers an open window to study, criticize, and even alter the diversion proposals. However, as the leadership (however unwillingly) now moves closer to a commitment, will the window abruptly close? With what effects? We shall return to these questions after a review of the proposals themselves.

*Background of the diversion projects: institutional forces*

The river-diversion debate has had a long and tumultuous history. The first serious design proposal was advanced in 1954 by the Leningrad office of Gidroproekt, the Soviet hydropower design agency. It was a hydropower project typical of the Stalin era: The plans called for a single large dam across the Pechora River in north Russia, which would have flooded more than 1.5 million hectares and would have completely cut off the lower reach of the river.[9] The original design would have diverted approximately 40 cubic kilometers a year from the Pechora and Vychegda rivers to the Kama-Volga basin, primarily to supply additional water to the hydropower projects there.[10] In other words, the initial motivation was energy, not water.

But even as this first design was being developed, the political priority of hydropower collapsed, and the Pechora project was one of the major casualties.[11] The initial design aroused opposition because it would have submerged oil and gas deposits (the Komi oil fields are currently the only ones in the European USSR whose output is increasing) and cut out a major part of the food resources of the Komi region in the far north. To meet opponents' objections and to push the project through, Gidroproekt engineers redesigned it several times. One of the later versions shows how much national priorities were shifting away from the big hydroprojects of Stalin's time and toward greater regard for the scarcity of agricultural land: It would have flooded 6,000 square kilometers less, but would have required 500 megawatts of electrical capacity annually to pump the water over a divide so as to make it flow south – a trade-off that would have been unthinkable in Stalin's time (and may become unthinkable again in the energy-scarce 1980s). Despite these changes, the Pechora project, which had come close to adoption in the 1960s, gradually lost ground.[12] As hydropower agencies weakened politically, they began to have trouble from upstart competitors, especially after 1965, once Brezhnev's expanded agricultural program got under way. The Ministry of Reclamation began taking over tasks that had previously been the province of Gidroproekt and luring away Gidroproekt personnel to work in its own research-and-design network. In 1971 the Ministry of Reclamation was named the lead agency for the major river-diversion projects, and the hydropower planners found themselves faced with a strong rival agency.[13]

Reclamation designers, as they gained influence, had their own ideas about major river-basin diversions. Around 1969 the ministry's principal institute for long-term planning, Soiuzvodproekt, developed an alternative scheme, which called for drawing water from the western lakes and rivers of north Russia instead of the Pechora. By 1973 Soiuzvodproekt had refined the western-lakes project, given it a lower price tag, and was advertising it as superior to the Pechora scheme.[14] Among its claimed advantages are several that are very much in tune with current Soviet policies: The western-lakes proposal would not require any reservoirs, would flood fifteen to twenty times less land than the Pechora project, would supply water to the most polluted stretches of the Volga (thus indirectly helping Moscow), and would require less time to build and less capital.[15]

Gidroproekt's Pechora project is far from dead, however. Indeed, even Soiuzvodproekt recommends building both, and the fact that the Pechora and the western-lakes versions complement one another makes such an alliance possible. Still at issue, however, is which of the two versions shall come first,[16] and at this writing no official decision has yet been made.[17] In the most recent party-state decree on the subject, Soiuzvodproekt and Gidroproekt share responsibility jointly.[18]

We see then that the shifting political fortunes of rival agencies have been an important element in the shaping of the European diversion proposals over the years, reflecting the changing times and the changing priorities of the political leadership. The brute-force approach that Gidroproekt proposed to employ in the 1950s has become unfashionable today, so much so that the design, location, and even the principal justification of the Pechora project are completely different now from what they were twenty years ago. But the chief catalysts in this process we have not yet introduced: the scientists and technical specialists who acted as spokesmen and defenders for the affected regions and interests.

### The European diversion project: protest from the north

The early version of the European project, as we have seen, would have flooded large areas of lowland in the part of northern Russia known as the Komi Autonomous Republic. In 1967 geographers and economists in the Komi ASSR began attacking the project.[19] They found allies in the oil and gas industry, for the diversion project also threatened to inundate valuable oil fields, greatly raising the costs of extraction. According to local calculations, these costs, if reckoned into Gidroproekt's economic analysis, would have added 2.5 billion rubles to the total costs of the project over the period 1970-2000.[20] The Komi scientists also objected to the anticipated loss of agricultural land, for the Pechora project would have flooded the area's major sources of food, forcing shipments from other parts of the country to feed the region's growing labor force. In addition, the proposed compensation dam originally included in the project would have collided with plans to build thermal-power plants based on cheap Pechora basin coal.[21] As the Pechora project was redesigned during the 1960s, these same specialists kept a watchful eye on it.[22] Their findings appeared for the most part in local journals with very small circulations, but they were subsequently picked up by fellow geographers in Moscow and given wide currency in national journals. The result was a sizable campaign against the Pechora project.

The Komi geographers continue their watch today. In their view, even the present Gidroproekt version is undesirable, for it would still cut off virtually the entire flow of the Pechora River, wipe out the migration of anadromous fish, diminish the fertility of floodplains, and cut down the agriculture of the region.[23] But in the last year or two a new note has crept into their writing: The Komi scientists are beginning to sound as though some sort of major diversion project is now inevitable:

> No one doubts nowadays the necessity of diverting a portion of the flow of northern rivers to the south of the country ... Yes, the north must help the south; that was talked about at the 25th Party Congress ... [But] it is no secret that many design decisions in our water-resources projects amount to purely engineering grounds: how to obtain the necessary quantity of water. The ecology is often simply forgotten about.[24]

Clearly, the Komi scientists' suspicion of Gidroproekt has not relaxed a bit. But the explanation for their changed tone is most likely that since the Twenty-fifth Party Congress the diversions have become the declared policy of the leadership, and therefore they can no longer be opposed in principle. Whether under such conditions the project's critics can retain their influence, we shall discuss in a moment. First we must turn to a third diversion proposal, potentially the most significant of the lot.

### The Central Asian diversion project

In the last four years the complexion of the entire diversion issue has been unexpectedly transformed by the emergence of a far larger and ambitious proposal, to divert Siberian waters to Central Asia. That proposal is not exactly new – the basic concept goes back to the nineteenth century – but what has changed in the last couple of years is that, for reasons we shall look into in a moment, it is suddenly being taken seriously as a project for the 1980s.

The water supply of Central Asia depends largely on two rivers, the Amu-Dar'ia and the Syr-Dar'ia, that flow into the Aral Sea. The two rivers, fed by snowmelt from the Pamir mountains to the southeast, support a thriving cotton economy and a booming population in one of the world's most arid regions. But both rivers are now being used to their maximum, and the level of the Aral Sea is falling. A crisis looms, no more than ten or fifteen years away. The idea behind the Central Asian transfer scheme is to divert a portion of the Ob' River in western Siberia southward over the Turgai Gate, which separates western Siberia from Central Asia, to the Aral Sea basin.[25] Whereas the various European proposals make use for the most part of existing river basins, the Central Asian proposal would require constructing a canal some 1,500 kilometers long. The problems involved in laying an artificial river across established roads, power lines, railroads, and so on, while controlling seepage and evaporation, put the Central Asian project on an entirely different scale from the European diversions, in terms of expense, time, and possible side effects.[26]

As recently as two or three years ago, the Central Asian scheme was spoken of, even by its promoters, as a project for the next century.[27] Weighing against it, first of all, were the vastly greater complexity and expense of the project itself. Very preliminary estimates put the cost of just the first stage of the Central Asian project at more than 30 billion rubles (including associated agricultural development),[28] a figure that, if experience anywhere in the world is any guide, is only a first installment. Second, until recently, the thrust of the Brezhnev agricultural program pointed away from Central Asia toward the European USSR, and it seemed highly improbable that a project of such magnitude could be adopted for that region, especially since the mid-1970s when the growth rate of agricultural investment began to taper off. Still another count against the Central Asian project was that it would inevitably cause damage in western Siberia. In the 1960s an alliance of geographers and the oil and gas industry defeated a Gidroproekt plan to build a major reservoir on the middle Ob' River,[29] not far downstream from the proposed diversion point, and that episode is unlikely to have been forgotten. Finally, early versions of the Central Asian project alarmed geographers and climatologists, who warned that withdrawing such large quantities of relatively warm water from the inflow to the Arctic Ocean might change climates the world over.[30] For all these reasons, Soviet sources until recently spoke of the Central Asian diversion scheme as a long-range prospect, and there was no doubt in anyone's mind that the European project came first.

What has apparently changed all that is the vigorous lobbying of southern party leaders and a growing awareness in Moscow of the grave problem of runaway population growth in Central Asia.[31] The role of party officials as lobbyists for their regions was evident in the way the diversions issue was handled at the Twenty-fifth Party Congress. Two members of the Politburo – Kunaev of Kazakhstan and Rashidov of Uzbekistan – spoke out strongly in favor of transferring water to the Aral Sea basin. Kunaev's argument stressed economic benefits for the entire country: "[Diversions] will provide explosive industrial and agricultural development of new and exceptionally promising areas, in the interests of the entire Soviet nation."[32] His speech was seconded in the same terms by Rashidov, who spoke of the "immense importance to the state" of the Central Asian diversion scheme,[33] as did First Party Secretary Gapurov of Turkmenistan.[34]

Two officials from the southern part of the European USSR defended the European diversion projects: Bondarenko of Rostov province and Medunov of Krasnodar province, both of whom stressed the importance of diversions for irrigated grain production in the north Caucasus. But curiously, though more water in the Volga would benefit other regions as well, such as Saratov province and the Tatar ASSR, the representatives of those regions had nothing to say on the subject.

It is possible that the intervention of the southern party leaders actually swayed the Politburo. In his opening report to the Congress, Brezhnev had not mentioned the diversion proposals. The spirit of his words, in fact, was entirely in the opposite direction: He stressed efficiency and intensification, the discouragement of new projects, and the rapid completion of old ones.[35]

But in Kosygin's speech the following day,[36] detailed studies of both the European and the Central Asian diversion projects were included in the list of "Basic Directions," adopted by the Congress as the foundation of the Tenth Five-Year Plan.[37] To be sure, before mentioning the diversions, Kosygin stressed the importance of saving water and using it more efficiently, which was the course the leadership had consistently favored until then. At any rate, the main thing is that the diversions reached the official agenda, and the strong lobbying of the southern party leaders may have played a role in that.

One need not look far for plausible reasons. In the last four years the link between Central Asian population growth and water shortages has been mentioned more and more prominently in the Soviet press. The preliminary results of the 1979 census show that during the period 1970–9 the populations of the Turkmen, Uzbek, and Tadzhik republics grew by 28, 30, and 31 percent, respectively, compared with 6 percent for the Russian republic.[38] In the last few years the more alarming implications of the differential growth rates have been addressed directly and publicly by Soviet experts themselves.[39] The first article explicitly connecting Central Asian population growth to the need for large-scale diversions from Siberia appeared, to my knowledge, in 1975,[40] but the demographic problem has since become one of the strongest justifications used by the project's promoters.[41] Though it is not possible to trace in detail the link between the demographic problem and the need for additional water, one can only note that as the public treatment of the former has grown franker, official support for the latter has grown stronger.

During the spring of 1978 the Central Asian project cleared a major hurdle when it was approved by a review commission (*ekspertnaia komissiia*) of Gosplan, the powerful State Planning Committee. What this means is that a very preliminary plan for the Turgai Gate design has now gained official sanction and will serve as the basis for subsequent engineering and economic studies.[42] The most recent official action on the diversion proposals is a decree of the party Central Committee and the USSR Council of Ministers, which takes the first step into actual engineering and economic studies of both the European and the Central Asian diversion proposals. In this decree, dated 21 December 1978, the European and the Central Asian projects are given virtually equal billing: The economic and engineering justifications (*tekhniko-ekonomicheskie obosnovaniia*) for the European project were due in 1979, and those for the Central Asian project were due in 1980.[43] What is especially striking about the decree is that it contains detailed instructions to various supporting ministries to prepare working models of the new construction equipment and materials that will be needed for the job and to draw up plans for mass production. Clearly, all of the preparatory steps are being taken to make it possible to begin construction sometime during the decade of the 1980s.

Yet the government has not yet committed itself. A project so expensive would mean a major shift in investment priorities and a degree of commitment to the development of Central Asia that the Soviet regime has never made before. The two diversion projects together would be the ultimate expression of the southern strategy of development, which leaves many people in the northern regions less than enthusiastic, especially those who favor competing programs in the Ukraine, the non-black-earth zone, and western Siberia. The military and their seven supporting industrial ministries presumably have their own opinions about the diversion of so much money, and investment capital in the 1980s will be extremely tight. Prime Minister Kosygin, in a recent article on the upcoming Eleventh Five-Year Plan (1981–5), repeated his views of two years before that the diversions are expensive, insufficiently studied, and premature.[44] As for the approval of the Gosplan review commission, it means little more than a preliminary technical approval. Many a project has been approved at that level but has never been heard from again. The real fight will begin when the engineering and economic studies now under preparation finally give the authorities something concrete to argue about.

But the two projects have now moved close enough to official endorsement that the stakes of the game are becoming very high. Will the assessment of the projects be distorted by rising political pressures? Will the projects' critics lose the window through which they have been able to debate and influence the issues? To gain some idea of the answers, we turn now to a closer look at the participation of the various scientists and technical specialists.

## The role of the technical specialists and scientific advisers

The party-state decree of December 1978 calls for a full assessment of the environmental, as well as the social and economic, effects of the proposed diversion projects, and recent Soviet articles report an extraordinary mobilization of specialists to study them. More than 120 research institutions and design organizations are involved,[45] and one often reads in the Soviet press the claim that such elaborate technological assessment has never been seen anywhere else in the world. The question is, what is this elaborate technological assessment likely to achieve?

The specialists involved until now can be divided into three broad groups. First, there are engineers and related specialists working for the design institutes attached to the major ministries: Gidroproekt for hydropower, Soiuzvodproekt and Soiuzgiprovodkhoz for reclamation. They have not been blind advocates: In the official journal of Gidroproekt in the early 1970s, for example, one found articles discussing the environmental impact of large diversion projects[46] and even questioning the need for any such projects at all.[47] But the role of these specialists, on balance, is that of boosters for the large projects that are part of their mission.

The second group of specialists consists of locally based scientists working in regional institutes of the various Academies of Sciences. To this group belong the spokesmen for the interests of the Komi ASSR and western Siberia, who oppose the projects, and also the Central Asians and the south Russians, who favor them.

Finally, the third and perhaps most influential group of specialists consists of geographers and biological scientists located at institutes of the USSR Academy of Sciences in Moscow, especially the Institute of Water Problems and the Institute of Geography. Neither of these institutes keeps to a single "line" on the diversions issue. In the Institute of Geography, for example, M. I. L'vovich, a well-known authority on the world's water resources, mentions the generally beneficial effects of the Siberian diversion project on the environment of western Siberia.[48] His equally distinguished colleague at the Institute of Water Problems, S. L. Vendrov, an authority on the environmental impact of large reservoirs, takes the opposite view. The Institute of Water Problems (IVP) is staffed to a large extent by hydrologists, many of them with career experience in hydropower and, to a lesser extent, in reclamation (S. L. Vendrov, for example, worked in inland-waterway transportation institutes for twenty-five years).[49] The Institute of Geography, in contrast, is staffed primarily by professional geographers. If there is a difference in outlook between the two institutes, it is that the IVP is basically well-disposed toward large engineering projects. The decree of December 1978 gives IVP the job of lead agency and prime contractor for all research bearing on the size and order of execution (*ob"emy i ocherednost'*) of the diversion projects. The Institute of Geography is better known as an environmental defender. Its specialists have fought battles against large projects in the past and have had a hand in several victories.[50]

In sum, the specialists involved in the evaluation of the diversion projects are a highly varied group, and as time goes on they are becoming more so. We must add the demographers and economists working on Central Asian population problems, geologists specializing in oil and gas deposits in western Siberia and northern Russia, climatologists and soil scientists, and even the occasional Americanist, who may contribute an article about American diversion schemes. Their concern over the costs and dangers of the diversions has led to an explosion of environmental research.[51] But the danger is that a growing share of the research funding is being channeled through the two main agencies designing the projects, Gidroproekt and Soiuzvodproekt, the prime contractors for most of the research effort. If pressure grows to produce results supporting diversions, will critics still manage to be heard?

The position of the geographers is especially delicate, for though they fear ill effects from the diversions, they are as yet unable to document them, and they are divided among themselves. The matter of possible climatic effects from the diversions is a case in point: Soiuzvodproekt now proposes to divert such a relatively small quantity of water during the first phase of the Central Asian project that it seems most unlikely that it could have any effect on the temperature balance or the climate of the Arctic Circle. When a sufficient number of specialists were willing to say so before the review commission of Gosplan in the spring of 1978, the commission dismissed the climatic issue as groundless.[52] However, even those who go along with the Gosplan decision write that the data on which it was based were "quite modest."[53] Similarly, expert opinion is divided over whether the Central Asian project will be favorable or unfavorable to western Siberia.[54]

Geographers and their academic colleagues are now apprehensive that in the rush to get on with the next stage of project making, the environmental aspects will get lost. They point out that most of the scientific and technical organizations mobilized to study the diversions projects are located in Moscow and Leningrad, not on location.[55] The information currently available is not enough to support basic choices.[56] There is some awareness, for example, that the threat of damage to western Siberia must be weighed against the possibility of the disappearance of the Aral Sea (with the consequent possibility of dust and salt storms in surrounding regions), but little knowledge is available on either.[57] Research institutes in Siberia, according to critics, have been especially slow to get organized. The powerful Siberian Division of the USSR Academy of Sciences has organized a Scientific Council on Water Transfer Problems, a device commonly used by the academy to deal with practical policy problems, but so far the creation of the council has not led to the next step, which would be the organization of laboratories or divisions within existing institutes to do research on the effects of the transfer.[58] One reason may simply be that it takes a year or two to make significant alterations in a Soviet institute's research plan, and the scientists may have been caught flat-footed by the speed with which a formerly long-range project has suddenly begun to move.[59] Another reason may be found in the language of the December 1978 decree, which does not provide for specific funding but leaves general responsibility for financing the necessary research to the major organizations involved. Such vague instructions, on past form, may well lead to underfunding of research on environmental impact.

In sum, the latitude enjoyed by technical specialists to criticize or oppose the diversion appears to be a hostage to the project's political priority. So long as the major institutional backers were competing against one another and the political leadership favored the intensive strategy anyway, specialists of all kinds could criticize the projects freely and hope to have an impact. But now we see the western Siberians and the northern Russians moderating their criticism in print, institute directors like IVP's Voropaev supporting with the step-wise approach now proposed by the project's backers, and the leadership of research passing into the hands of the prime contractors, that is, the very agencies in charge of developing the project designs. Meanwhile, the researchers who are not committed to any institutional or regional viewpoint find themselves at a disadvantage because their own research will take a long time to reach the stage at which they can back up their disquiet with hard facts. Consequently, whereas at earlier stages the advice of specialists manifestly played a part in altering the initial project designs, the window for effective influence may now be narrowing. Perhaps the greatest single force keeping it open is the overall tightness of investment capital, which makes a full-scale commitment by the leadership unlikely in the near term.


The river diversion issue is perhaps the most remarkable example of a phenomenon to which Western observers of Soviet politics have been calling attention for some time: that policy debate in the Soviet Union is remarkably open under some circumstances and can actually affect official policy. Yet what this case also demonstrates is that when the political stakes begin to rise, scientists are not in a strong position to maintain their influence.

A second remarkable feature of the diversion case is that events have gradually persuaded the political leadership, over the course of a decade, to consider a course of action it initially thought of as far over the horizon. How did that happen? Two separate forces appear to account for the recent stepping-up of the diversion projects. First, the implementation of "intensive" water-saving measures in the southern half of the country is proceeding much more slowly than the leaders' goals for the region require. Though these programs have been vigorously pursued, they have so far cost more and achieved less than the leadership evidently hoped for. But as the "intensive" strategy loses ground, the "extensive" strategy – bringing in more water from outside – grows more and more attractive.

The second force, which accounts particularly for the strong advance of the Central Asian diversion project, is the growing alarm reflected in the Soviet press and official speeches over the population boom in Central Asia and the limits to growth imposed by scarce water. Although additional water alone will not resolve the dilemmas of employment in Central Asia,[60] the lack of water sets the ceiling beyond which no growth can take place, and hence it is emerging as one of the most serious problems confronting Moscow. What seems to have swayed the political leadership is not so much the power of groups or regions as the force of circumstances, which impels the leaders to take steps to defend their own top priorities.

The contribution of technical advisers has been to document and publicize problems of existing resource and population policies and to call attention to the possible consequences of alternatives courses. In this particular case their participation has been, at least until now, as vigorous and public as it might have been in the United States. But it was due to an exceptional political conjunction, which created a window for specialists to voice their views and find allies. As the window threatens to close, we observe the increasingly constrained position of the experts, for they have no independent bases of power or means of publicity once the political leadership commits itself and is no longer receptive to debate on every side of the question.

The issue is not yet closed, however. The importance of foreseeing the long-term consequences of major technological undertakings is as well understood in the Soviet Union today as it is in the United States, and whether by the name of technology assessment or of *kompleksnaia otsenka*, the concept has become part of the official language of both countries. But the crucial test of technology assessment is whether it can stand up against a strong head of political steam. The outcome of the river-diversions debate in the Soviet Union will tell us a great deal about the authority of scientific advice in Soviet policy making and the capacity of technical experts to adopt and maintain independent political positions.

# 6
# BRINGING NEW IDEAS INTO SOVIET POLITICS

The common theme of the last several chapters has been the role of technical specialists and advisers in the evolution of some of the key aspects of the Brezhnev programs for land and water. Unfortunately, the cases we have just considered give us no single picture, because the findings point in two directions at once. On the one hand, it is clear that technical specialists have helped to create an "atmosphere" of new ideas about natural resources, capital, and the environment and an official rhetoric that is quite different from that of a generation ago. Official treatment of several formerly despised fields, and of specialists in them, has also changed a good deal. In several instances, their participation has been vigorous and seemingly influential, both in drawing official attention to a new issue and in shaping the leaders' response to it.

On the other hand, we have found that advisers and protesters alike have lacked the independent leverage to force a new idea into official currency unless at least a part of the leadership had already been made receptive to it by policy needs. For technical experts to muster facts and publicize them required the support (however covert) of allies and sympathizers in strong, established positions. Finally, new ideas, in the course of being converted into new policy, have been channeled in conservative directions.

What do these ambiguous findings mean? Do they point to any fundamental change in the relationship of knowledge and power in the formation of new policies, or is the relationship essentially the same as before? It has become a commonplace in Western literature to say that the growing complexity of "postindustrial" societies has turned technical expertise into a political resource; but the conventional teaching about Soviet politics has been that technical expertise is "not deployable on the plains of politics" to the same extent in the Soviet Union as it is in the Western political systems, because of the Soviet technical experts' dependence on the state and their lack of external leverage. Is that "non-deployability" now changing, as the Soviet political system begins to grapple with the problems of a third-generation society and economy? If technical expertise is becoming a resource for power, then in whose hands? And with what consequences for the capacity of the Soviet political elite to develop new policies and muster consensus around them?

The plan of this chapter is to address these questions by taking up a wider range of cases, drawing from several other studies available in the Western literature. In addition to agronomy, enviromental sciences, economics, and geography, discussed in the last four chapters, there exist Western analyses of Soviet demography,[1] genetics,[2] sociology,[3] other branches of economics,[4] and management[5] (including science policy and the management of technological innovation). On the basis of this broader sample, what can we say in answer to the questions raised above?

First, many Western scholars have noted changes in the *extent* to which technical experts participate in policy making. Two especially important Western studies are Franklyn Griffiths' analysis of the role of academic "Americanists" in the evolution of official Soviet perceptions of the United States and Peter Solomon's study of the contribution of criminologists to Soviet criminal justice.[6]

Peter Solomon argues that the increased participation and influence of specialist-advisers in the formation of policy has been one of the most significant features of Soviet politics since Stalin. He concludes with the overall judgment that "in the realm of criminal policy, at least, there seemed to be no grounds for suspicion that the scope or quality of specialist participation in the USSR made it less significant than specialist participation in the West."[7]

In Solomon's view, the key event that has made criminologists effective participants in policy making is the *institutionalization* of their counsel, that is, the creation of regular channels through which their knowledge and advice reach decision makers *as a matter of routine*. What brings this about? One of the reasons such channels become available is the discovery by ministry heads that the specialists are useful to them in arguing for the positions of their agencies. But for Solomon the growing participation of specialists is due to more than the choices of administrators and politicians; it is part of the overall evolution of Soviet society and economy. Even if the Brezhnev leadership had wished to prevent this evolution, he writes, it might not have been able to.[8]

Franklyn Griffiths's findings complement Solomon's: In his study of "Americanology" in the Soviet Union, he stresses the importance of *professionalization* of knowledge and advice about the United States – in other words, acceptance by the leadership of the fact that knowledge about the United States requires the development of professional experts, institutes to house them, access to Western sources, and freedom to travel. Griffiths argues that professionalization quickly leads to semi-independent advocacy, a process that is difficult to arrest without active intervention on the part of the leadership. Professionalization is the first step toward institutionalized participation. Griffiths, like Solomon, believes that this process is due to long-term causes: He calls them "objective policy requirements" and "functional differentiation in Soviet society."[9]

The result of professionalization and institutionalization, in Solomon's view, is an increase in the *scope* and *quality* of the specialists' participation. By scope Solomon means the extent to which the specialists' advice engages more than narrow technical issues; by quality he means the timeliness of participation and the availability of channels to important policy makers. Solomon finds that the advice of criminologists reaches high-placed officials early enough in decision making to have a real impact on the policies adopted; that the specialists do not simply carry out and legitimize policies adopted higher up, but that they advocate new policies to political leaders and actually contribute to educating them.

This book finds the same thing. First, the scope of participation of specialists in the expansion of the Brezhnev program has been impressively broad. We have seen specialists balancing Central Asian cotton or Baikal rayon against synthetic fiber from petrochemicals; electrical peaking power versus water for irrigation; southern grain versus northern forage; environmental damage to western Siberia or the Komi ASSR against further deterioriation of the Caspian and Aral seas; the pros and cons of out-migration from Central Asia against those of increasing investment within the region, and many others. These would be considered political questions of major scope anywhere in the world.

The quality of technical advice, in the sense defined by Solomon, is likewise high in the cases we have seen in this book. The views of technical specialists on reclamation, potential food shortages, environmental damage, interbasin diversions, and demographic problems in Central Asia reached political leaders before major decisions were taken. In some cases, the response of technical specialists, though late, contributed to reversing or modifying decisions that had already been made. And throughout the period in which the Brezhnev programs were evolving, the specialists' institutional bases and their channels of access to policy makers expanded steadily through the use of consultants to the Central Committee staff, the growing number of advisory bodies to the State Committee on Science and Technology, and the like.

At the same time, there are definite limits to the specialists' scope – at least, their public scope. The capital-effectiveness criterion is not used to determine *what* to produce, only *how* to produce. The soundness of the basic approach of the Brezhnev agricultural program cannot be called into question, any more than the well-foundedness of giving priority to the development of eastern Siberia or to military projects, however damaging to the environment. The best illustration of these limits is Lake Baikal, which could be defended – barely – against the paper and pulp industry but not against the military or the broader threats arising from the development of the entire region. Nevertheless, despite these limits the scope of advice and the quality of debate on technical questions, compared to even the Khrushchev era, has broadened considerably.

What are the political implications? Solomon considers this question carefully: What the specialists have gained, he concludes, is a certain influence, which stems chiefly from their usefulness to the needs of political leaders and high-ranking bureaucrats. In recent criminal legislation, the policies finally adopted have corresponded to the specialists' recommendations more often than not, and this fact, added to the increased scope and quality of the specialists' participation, leads Solomon to view Soviet criminologists and legal scholars as increasingly effective advocates.

But might this not simply mean that specialist-advisers have become skillful politicians themselves, able to trim their public views quickly to the official wind? Solomon thinks not. He sees the direction of influence as primarily one-way, from the specialists to the policy maker. But for Griffiths, the advice of specialists is strongly affected by the known prejudices of the leaders and the policy needs of the moment.[10] He sees a two-way process of mutual influence, which produces a shared perception compounded partly of tactical considerations and partly of the experts' professional opinions. This Griffiths calls a "transactional perception."[11]

Solomon and Griffiths may have reached different conclusions on this point because they happened to study different cases. Solomon's criminologists may have been in a stronger tactical position than Griffiths's Americanists because they dealt with domestic policy instead of foreign; their issues were less visible and sensitive; and they quietly advanced the political interests of their ministries (thus gaining stable protection and leverage), rather than serve in the more delicate and exposed position of staff to the Central Committee.

What emerges from both authors' findings, however, is how fragile the influence of specialist-advisers is. They depend on the pleasure and the need of the sovereign, not only for their access, but also for their funding, their ability to publish, and even their standing as legitimate professionals. What, we should ask, prevents political leaders from ignoring what they do not wish to hear or shutting down lines of inquiry they do not like? Why won't the trends of recent years be reversed and the progress undone? To say that a lasting change has occurred in the relationship of political power and technical knowledge in the Soviet Union, it is necessary to show what will stay the leaders' hand when conflict arises. In other words, the question of the influence of Soviet specialists cannot be separated from that of their independence.

Moreover, such independence, however embryonic, touches upon the most fundamental powers of the traditional political system. Power, after all, has two faces: *positive* power to raise issues, to overcome opposition and win political battles, to set the public agenda, and to launch policies and implement them. *Negative* power prevents issues from being raised, limits public debate and the scope of policy making to the issues that the leadership regards as legitimate,[12] and confines the flow of information to those who have an official "need to know." The monopoly of negative power has been, since the 1930s, one of the fundamental bases of the political system. How can such a monopoly accommodate *independent* participation on the part of the specialists?

One of the most important instruments of negative power is secrecy. Officials in one agency, more often than not, cannot find out what those in neighboring agencies are doing, what data they are using, or even what statutes they are governed by. Anything touching on military matters, of course, is particularly restricted. It is not so long ago, for example, that

American negotiators at the SALT I talks discovered that their civilian opposite numbers were not cleared to receive information about their own strategic force levels.[13] In contrast, American negotiators at the summit were struck by how much better informed Gromyko soon appeared to be about Soviet military matters *after* he became a member of the Politburo in 1973. To take a more everyday example, Soviet environmental officials insisted to the world that the Soviet Union produced no polychlorinated biphenyls (though the Swedes detected them at the mouth of the Neman), only to discover that their own military had been making them for years.[14] And the principle of "official need to know" is not limited by any means to the military. It is enough to say that some 85 percent of the decrees of the USSR Council of Ministers are not published and are circulated only within interested agencies.[15]

To be sure, there have always been zones within which negative power has been partially suspended, whenever the leaders' need for new ideas outweighed the political or ideological dangers they might carry. And over the years, as the country and its leaders have become less obsessed about enemies without and within, and as the ideology has become more obviously unable to provide useful detailed guidance on policy, the zones of suspended negative power have widened. Though the fundamentals of the system are out of bounds, the range of what can be debated in public as "technical" has grown; and political leaders now refrain from making *ex cathedra* pronouncements in fields that are officially recognized as scientific and respectable.

Secrecy too has declined slightly. Many issues that were formerly limited to small audiences are now discussed more openly. Twenty years ago, a position paper by P. L. Kapitsa on the alarming lag of the Soviet Union in low-temperature physics could only circulate internally.[16] Today, frank criticism of an equally sensitive subject, the state of the Soviet computer industry, appears in the national newspapers,[17] and acknowledgment of the U.S. lead in computer technology can be found in specialized (but nevertheless publicly available) books and journals;[18] and Kapitsa himself is able to rise at a plenary session of the Academy of Sciences to warn about the dangers of nuclear power,[19] a warning that was recently echoed by the man most closely associated with the early years of the Soviet nuclear power program.[20]

In some cases this suspension of negative power has gone quite far, and the leaders have shown some tolerance for what inevitably happens next: The airing of an issue that is initially "scientific" soon brings forward issues of basic values and priorities. Discussion of Soviet birthrates, Central Asian migration patterns, and irrigation of cotton leads by inference to questions about priorities among regions,[21] nationalism, and racial prejudice. Yet the Soviet literature on these problems has been remarkably frank and unrestrained.[22] In this book we have seen other examples of the same thing, in the rise of environmental issues and the open discussion of interbasin diversions, the politics of hydropower, and agricultural policies.

But does suspension of negative power mean the beginnings of fundamental independence on the part of specialists? All the instruments of negative power remain in place: the ubiquitous system of censorship and controls maintained by the State Committee for the Press and the Propaganda Department of the Central Committee; the supervision of teaching and research by the Science and Education Department of the Central Committee, not to mention similar roles played by other organs such as the KGB; and above all, the monopoly by the central leadership of means of support, access, or appeal for specialists' ideas. The apparent independence of technical specialists can last only so long as these instruments are used with indulgence.

Moreover, the experience of recent years seems to show that the suspension of negative power alone is not enough to ensure growth and participation in policy making for a new (or reborn) discipline or line of inquiry. It must receive not merely toleration but *active support* from above, first to gain stable professional and institutional existence and then to maintain lines of access to policy makers. In other words, Soviet specialists are dependent on politicians twice over, first, for toleration, second, for interest. To test this question, let us look at some famous cases.

In his memoirs, the geneticist N. P. Dubinin describes how, despite the continuing repression of Mendelian genetics in the 1950s, the military's need for real knowledge about the genetic effects of radiation caused research to revive strongly in that area, ten years ahead of the final overthrow of Lysenko and the official revival of genuine genetics.[23] Because of Khrushchev's interest in hybrid corn, that corner of genetics also revived early.[24] Similarly, the first official support for sociology was stimulated by the practical need of the leadership to find out why volunteers in the Virgin Lands program were streaming back to the European USSR and subsequently by the desire of the local party organs and government agencies to investigate problems of labor discipline and turnover.[25] The rapid adoption of cybernetics in the Soviet Union was due in large measure to the promise of its more down-to-earth components (systems analysis, input–output analysis, and computer science) to suggest rational solutions to pressing problems in planning – in fact, to rescue the very system of centralized planning from the dead end it appeared to have reached by the late 1950s.[26] Ten years later the same factors contributed to the Soviet enthusiasm for American methods of business management and administration.[27] And similarly, renewed support for demography was stimulated by declining birthrates in Russian cities.[28]

These examples suggest two points: First, official interest in new ideas and the willingness to suspend official prohibitions arise out of specific practical problems for which previous policy or dogma has no solution or definite prescription. The initial success of specialists in responding to specific policy needs may give them an entering wedge by which to advance the field as a whole, thus widening the initial window provided to them. Dubinin, for example, was soon in business at the head of a laboratory for radiation genetics, and shortly after that he was gathering the scattered survivors of his field into a full-fledged Institute of Genetics at Academic City in Novosibirsk. Thus new fields and ideas may require an opening; but once they get it they are not slow in taking advantage of it.

One reason this is so is that the pioneers of new fields have been able to form profitable alliances with politically influential figures, who stand to benefit from what the specialists have to offer. A vital element in the revival of criminology, according to Solomon, was the fact that criminologists and jurists specializing in criminal law were useful to the heads of law-enforcement agencies, once the latter were called upon to propose new policies.[29] In agronomy, advocates of clean fallow in the Virgin Lands, like Mal'tsev and Baraev, found support from local officials who were overwhelmed by weeds, wind erosion, and drought. Genetics and economics benefited in the same way: Research on radiation genetics in the mid-1950s enjoyed active support from the State Committee on Use of Atomic Energy. Major figures in the Soviet nuclear-weapons and space programs, like Kurchatov, Keldysh, and Solov'ev, helped create a laboratory for radiation genetics in the academy; and Dubinin became accustomed to having his books published by *Atomizdat*, the publishing house of the State Committee on Atomic Energy. The same thing happened in economics: One of the first laboratories for mathematical economics, the Scientific Economic Research Institute, was created in Gosplan,[30] and there existed also a group working on mathematical economics under V. S. Nemchinov in Gosplan's Council for the Study of Productive Forces (SOPS).[31] Sociological research centers sprang up like mushrooms under the sponsorship of the Ministry of Higher Education, the Academies of Medical and Pedagogical Sciences, the State Construction Committee, and several others, but most important of all, in the Ministry of Defense, the KGB, and in the provincial party apparatus.[32]

These early alliances, and the speed with which they grew as soon as an opportunity appeared, suggest that prior seeds lay under the ground, waiting for the warm breeze of opportunity. Every new field and new idea, it seems, goes through an early, semi-covert period, and during this first *sub rosa* stage, the quiet assistance of sympathic protectors is vital. Genetics is once again the prime example. To bypass the dominance of Lysenko and his allies in biology, genetics found a more-or-less covert home in institutes of physics and chemistry.[33] Physicists and chemists sponsored public talks by molecular biologists on the stunning developments then taking place in their field, such as the identification of the structure of DNA.[34] The base provided by chemists and physicists was so effective that when Soviet geneticists finally published their own journal, *Genetika*, most of the articles in the first five years were original Soviet research, the bulk of it contributed by scientists in institutes created during the 1950s.[35] Similarly, new currents in economics enjoyed important early support from non-economists in the USSR Academy, particularly from mathematicians. Soviet sociology likewise began as a *sektor* for Concrete Sociological Research in the USSR Academy's Institute of Philosophy. Every new field has had its early period of underground germination, but not without quiet help from established people.

The role of influential allies in establishing new institutions is crucial in the Soviet Union because resources are so centralized. At the earliest stages new ideas cannot get started unless institute directors or other allies are willing to volunteer funds and facilities in modest amounts. Thus even under Stalin the economist Novozhilov managed to continue his work under the auspices of Leningrad Polytechnical Institute.[36] Dubinin began his radiation-genetics laboratory in a shack in the academy's Botanical Garden.[37] Early sociologists worked as volunteers in ad hoc task forces formed by local party officials.[38] The presence of such small, concentrated hives of activity – many of them located away from Moscow – helps to explain why new ideas buzz forth surprisingly quickly as soon as they are given official encouragement.

It helps, of course, if the sympathizers have some extra money to spare, and in this respect the 1960s may have been more favorable than the 1970s, for the former was a time of rapid growth of scientific personnel and institutions, whereas during the latter decade there was a virtual halt in some areas. A vivid and perhaps unique illustration is the role of the Siberian Division of the Academy of Sciences in the late 1950s and 1960s. Academician Lavrent'ev, the founder and longtime patriarch of Academic City in Novosibirsk, enjoyed ample resources, direct support from Khrushchev, and unique authority. He was able to give a start to many new disciplines, including genetics, mathematical economics, sociology of work, mathematical linguistics, systems analysis, and many others. During those years, the academy enjoyed relatively greater latitude than it does today, and it is possible that the combination of tighter resources and a less open political atmosphere may hinder the development of new lines of research.

How much of the early, informal phase of development is actually unknown to higher authority, and how much of it requires at least tacit support or tolerance? The answer undoubtedly depends on the sensitivity of the subject. Research on a topic like optical memory systems, for example, presumably requires lower-level clearance than sociological analysis of popular responses to party propaganda. A lot depends on whether the leadership has taken an official position or not. Nevertheless, even a nonsensitive line of inquiry cannot remain informal for long, because the creation of a new research area (known as a *napravlenie*) requires the approval of higher authority. In sociology, for example, the establishment of a *sektor* for empirical sociological research in the Institute of Philosophy seems to have required Khrushchev's personal approval.[39] In genetics, Dubinin mentions the help of individuals in the science division of the Central Committee staff and of the *oblast'* party officials in Novosibirsk.[40] In both of these fields, then, the staff of the top political leadership was involved from the beginning, and this may be increasingly true in the future, because of the growing practice of mobilizing specialists as "consultants" to the Central Committee. For example, the Americanist G. A. Arbatov served on the staff of the Central Committee even before the creation of the USA Institute in the Academy of Sciences. It seems unlikely, from the cases we have any knowledge of, that politically sensitive lines of research could enjoy much more than a sporelike existence without tacit high-level toleration.

Such sympathy and support from above are even more important for the next step: Formal institutionalization implies a real commitment on the part of at least *someone* in authority, because it is no easy matter to create a new institute or a new curriculum in the Soviet Union. It is often a zero-sum game that requires, first of all, repudiating or at any rate lowering the prestige of whatever traditional group the new specialty has been competing with. The founding of the Central Econometric Institute (TsEMI) was a rebuff to traditional economists in the Institute of Economics. The establishment of the sociologists came at some cost to the philosophers. Converting a research institute like the academy's Institute of Electrometry and Automatic Systems in Academic City to digital electronics required the death of its previous director, an invasion from a neighboring institute by a new leader and his followers, and a purge of the old guard.[41] Inozemtsev's appointment as director of the Institute of the World Economy and International Relations (IMEMO) produced a shake-up in favor of international relations at the expense of international economics. Space is short; equipment is scarce; budgets are tight – consequently, one must view the formal establishment of a new field as the expression of considerable political support, the outcome of long years of negotiation and struggle.[42]

Formal establishment, then, is a crucial step. Armed with official sanction and an institutional base, a new field progressess rapidly. An institute, a journal, and a place in established curricula soon produce students, a full-fledged program, publicity, state prizes, data in support of one's arguments, a seat on advisory groups, a regular share of the budget – in short, all the weapons needed to consolidate one's professional place.

Once a discipline or subdiscipline has reached the status of a recognized and institutionalized discipline its existence becomes more secure. We should not forget, however, how much that security depends on suspended negative power. The example of sociology suggests how fragile the independence of a newly institutionalized discipline can be. Sociology initially appeared safe enough for even Suslov to give it a cautious blessing, for at a meeting in the Central Committee headquarters in 1955, he reportedly went so far as to say that historical materialism was in effect "Marxist sociology."[43] But by 1971, three years after the formal creation of the Institute for Concrete Sociological Research, the party leadership had become so alarmed by the ideological implications of the new discipline that it purged the institute, and those who remained active sought cover in abstract methodologies and mathematical treatments of narrow topics.[44]

In another sense, however, the example of sociology is the exception that underscores the recent pattern: It is not too hard to avoid provoking the Kremlin's thunderbolt, provided one observes a few simple rules. The most important is that the old must not be confronted on a broad front but rather sidestepped at particular points of need. Thus Mal'tsev and Baraev's ideas for steppeland farming (Chapter 2) did not challenge the Virgin Lands program; the protest over Baikal (Chapter 3) did not challenge the primacy of industrial development; nor did research into Russian women's one-child families confront the "socialist law of reproduction." In none of these cases was it necessary to confront received truth in order to respond to practical needs.

Moreover, an unsafe discipline may still prosper if it has a safe cover, and the very best is mathematics. No discipline illustrates this better than economics. Economists even managed the remarkable feat of sneaking into legitimate currency the notion of shadow prices, finessing traditional Soviet political economy by deriving them from a mathematical-programing matrix and calling them by the neutral-sounding name of "evaluations" (*otsenki*). Likewise, they have tried to sap the traditional Soviet method of incremental material balances as a basis for planning by championing input–output analysis, a method whose subversive implications are cloaked in mathematical discretion.

Once a discipline is established as an institution and as a profession, it gains a security that, if not quite independence, is at least not the same acute dependence on official tolerance and goodwill that seems to dominate earlier stages. The same is not necessarily true, however, of specialists' participation in policy making, even after professionalization and institutionalization have taken place. Channels of access to policy making, such as project review committees (*ekspertnye komissii*), scientific councils (*nauchnye sovety*), and consultant positions are more ad hoc and informal and therefore more dependent on the goodwill of higher-ups than an established institute or university *kafedra*. The members serve because they are acceptable and necessary to the leadership, not because they represent a professional group that can raise its spears if their man is dismissed. Their very composition tends to reflect movements of interest and receptiveness at the top, thus the appearance of economists on Gosplan's review committees in the late 1950s. Finally, their slowness and timidity when the issues are at all thorny suggest how cautious they are about appearing to prompt or preempt the political leadership. For example, the *ekspertnye komissii* of Gosplan were unable to reach an opinion on several of the more controversial hydropower projects of the 1960s. They blocked the European diversion project for years so long as the leadership was not behind it; but they approved the much larger and more controversial Central Asian project once it appeared to have high-level backing. Special commissions of the Academy of Sciences wavered repeatedly on the issue of Baikal. However solidly established the specialists' institutions may be, their participation in policy making remains wholly dependent on the leaders' acceptance of them and their advice.

It is perhaps not surprising, therefore, that every politically effective new field seems to be led by accomplished political animals: Dubinin, as we have seen, in genetics; A. G. Aganbegian and N. P. Fedorenko in economics and operations research; G. M. Gvishiani and V. M. Glushkov in cybernetics and management, G. A. Voropaev in reclamation and water management, G. A. Arbatov in American studies, and E. M. Primakov in Oriental studies – one can go on. The specialist-entrepreneur has become one of the most visible political types in the Soviet Union today; and these men symbolize better than anything else both the opportunities and constraints bearing on the leader of new fields and the would-be participant in policy making.

To sum up the argument so far: There is evidence from many different fields that the scope and quality of specialists' advice to policy makers (both central leaders and ministry-level institutions) have increased. There has also been a gradual suspension of negative power in numerous areas, one of the visible results of which is a greater freedom of public debate over technical questions that have policy implications, sometimes quite important ones. Another major result is the revival of several previously repressed or neglected fields. However, the evidence summarized in this chapter does not enable us to say that there has been any fundamental change in the essentially dependent state of Soviet specialists. The change amounts to this: A new group of specialists in social and biological sciences has been granted the same (or nearly the same) recognized scientific standing that the physical and engineering sciences have long enjoyed. Thanks to their newly established status, specialists in the biological and some of the social sciences now enjoy the same heavily qualified privilege of establishment opposition that their colleagues in nuclear physics, mathematics, or airplane design had even in the late Stalin period.[45] But their professionalization, institutionalization, and subsequent participation depend not only on the relative suspension of negative controls but also on active support and receptiveness from political figures. So long as this remains the case, we cannot say that there has been a fundamental change in the relations of power and knowledge in Soviet politics.

But isn't it true in any country of the world that the specialist's access and influence depend on the leaders' receptiveness and support? Yes, to be sure. Yet the differences are fundamental. In the federal government of the United States, for example, channels of participation by specialists, particularly in the natural sciences but increasingly in the social sciences as well, are anchored in statutes as well as in well-entrenched and vigilant professional groups.[46] In the National Institutes of Health, for example, the composition of advisory committees is a matter of law, not of the executive's prerogative, and the political leader who attempts to tamper with them or bypass them does so at his peril. The existence of constitutionally separate branches of government and Congress's constant and zealous pursuit of its right to know make the executive's periodic assertions of its privilege seem like vain protests against the ocean's tide. Even the chief executive cannot ignore or try to co-opt his most confidential advisers without worrying about leaks that will land the administration's officers before a congressional committee or a judge. The administration's need to forge alliances with professional interest groups means in practice that most executive appointments in the federal government must be cleared with a constituency of professionals whose displeasure can be noisy and painful; and the hand of many a specialist-appointee has no sooner lifted from the Bible after the oath of office than he becomes his constituency's man inside the administration. Although politicians everywhere are professionals of power and usually have an edge at their own game, the relationship of the American specialist-adviser to the politician is essentially different from that of his Soviet colleague. In the United States the specialist-adviser, because he often has independent leverage, can frequently *make* the politician listen. Can he do so in the Soviet Union?

One of the consequences of this difference is that once the Soviet leaders have made up their minds and chosen a course, dissenting viewpoints may not get a hearing. Open discussion of the interbasin diversions, for example, appears to be narrowing as the leaders approach a decision, as has environmental debate, once the government defined its policy. It seems likely that the same thing will happen again when the leadership has decided on the best way to cope with the problem of Central Asian manpower. When that happens, channels of access close down, institutes and journals become more circumspect, and sensitive subjects vanish from the press. The leaders' control over access and debate is still the leaders' most important and pervasive monopoly.

It is tempting to speculate how this monopoly affects the leaders' ability to deal with third-generation problems. Two broad possible consequences come to mind. First, negative power denies to specialists and officials, short of the very top, the facts and background necessary to form intelligent opinions on broad, complex problems. Breadth is further inhibited by the fact that Soviet technical curricula are narrow, research institutions are highly specialized, and technical experts are wary of venturing opinions outside their specialty that cannot be defended as scientific and objective. Truly informed, sophisticated, global overviews of policy problems in all their complexity and interrelatedness can take place only (if anywhere) at the top of the system, at the level, say, of consultants and staff of the Central Committee or of the *referentura* of the Council of Ministers. These are people who have "arrived," and presumably they are the ones least likely to be critical of fundamentals or to be hospitable to unorthodox views. Below the top, skills and data that should be in contact with one another are separated by organizational and disciplinary bulkheads as well as barriers of censorship, making rapid and informed responses impossible in any but the narrowest situations. True, there has been some effort to create councils of executive and technical people under the auspices of the local party apparatus, but judging from the tone of Soviet writings on the subject, they are either still largely symbolic or aimed at specific narrow problems.[47] By and large, despite the increased involvement of all kinds of specialists in policy formation, and the existence of "forum" media like *Literaturnaia Gazeta* and *EKO*, the Soviet Union still lacks the kind of broad public discussion and debate that loosens old thinking and breaks up encrusted outlooks, tests new ideas against the perspective of several fields simultaneously, and causes the consciousness of an entire society to evolve. Moscow, because of the possibility of informal social contact, is less affected than the provinces, which helps to account for another phenomenon described in this book: Moscow forges ahead with new policies; the provinces lag behind and continue to implement the old.[48] But the difference is only relative. Tunnel vision is a problem nationwide.

Another by-product of negative power, paradoxically enough, is the periodic national fad. Because new ideas on policy flow only when the leadership is receptive or undecided, when the official window does open, they come in a flood, unrefined, unintegrated, and untested. If the leaders listen and are convinced, they then venture too far and too fast. This clearly happened in computers and computerized management, in several areas of agricultural policy, and perhaps also in advanced forms of energy, like magnetohydrodynamics and fusion. At such times, there is little *independent* counterexpertise from other branches of knowledge and little opportunity to force the relevant issues into public view, so as to ask, "How much is enough?" Or "How fast is too fast?" or even, "Is the emperor wearing any clothes?" When disillusionment follows, the result can only be renewed suspicion of new ideas and a further reinforcement of negative power.

"The definition of the alternatives," says one of the classics of American political science, "is the supreme instrument of power."[49] This chapter shows that the Soviet leaders have managed to get the advice they need for new policies without losing control of that supreme instrument, but the future holds a dilemma for their successors: If the leaders relax further their exercise of negative power, they expose themselves to public criticism and challenge, even opposition. However, if they do not, they deny themselves the exposure to alternatives and the clarification of difficult issues that only more open information, communication, and discussion can bring. They also expose themselves to manipulation if they allow information flows to become so highly channeled that they become, in effect, the monopoly of government ministries. Military development and procurement may be a harbinger, for political leaders appear to have no alternative sources of expertise in weapons technology other than that supplied by the military and their associated industrial ministries. In either case, the leaders run the danger of losing control over the power to define alternatives. Which horn of the dilemma will they choose?

# PART II

# IMPLEMENTATION OF THE BREZHNEV PROGRAMS

The first half of this book was concerned with the sources of the Brezhnev program; the second deals with its progress. In the next three chapters, we examine three aspects of the implementation of the southern strategy: the transfer of power over water use from previously dominant users to agriculture and the implementation of the new environmental and irrigation programs. All three are at the core of the "intensification" approach favored by official policy, which aims at covering the future growth of the southern half of the country, particularly the development of irrigated agriculture, through the existing water resources. But for the intensification approach to succeed, a major transfer of power, skills, and resources must take place, from established economic interests to new ones. Each of the chapters in this section is a separate facet of the same challenge: Unless power over water use can be successfully transferred, unless industrial and municipal pollution is curtailed, and unless the reclamation program can produce higher and more stable yields without overusing water, then the southern strategy will not be able to supply the desired buffer for Soviet agriculture at anything like an acceptable cost or in a reasonable time. The leadership would then face an unpleasant choice:to trim its hopes for the southern strategy or to venture the additional resources to bring in more water.

What is at issue is political power: If the Kremlin proves unable to bring about the necessary transfer of resources from old purposes to new, or succeeds only at the price of much more delay and expense than the leaders foresaw, then what shall we conclude about their power and that of the various institutions involved? If the leaders are not able to get their way when they promote complex new programs, then what is the future of reform in Soviet politics? These questions are the subject of the concluding two chapters.

# 7
# LOOSENING THE GRIP OF OLD PRIORITIES: THE LONG STRUGGLE AGAINST HYDROPOWER

Far from Moscow, in the arid steppes of the south of the European USSR, carrying out the Brezhnev program means wresting water from established users and transferring it to irrigation. The government's new priorities clash with the old in many places but particularly in the operation of the dozens of power stations located astride the major rivers of the European USSR. These stations control the timing, amount, and reliability of streamflow for all users. The issue here is no longer the reallocation of capital in Moscow but the much more complicated and delicate matter of overseeing a partial transfer of power among competing agencies at a multitude of local points. Power officials have shown themselves resourceful at resisting change. As a result, the leaders' new priorities have been only partly translated into real changes in the field, and the reclamation program, for all its high priority in Moscow, is weakened where it ultimately counts.

Wherever water is scarce, hydropower and reclamation are natural competitors. Irrigators want water in summer; power-grid operators want it in winter to run through their turbines when demand for electricity is at a maximum.[1] This means power-grid operators try to keep reservoirs as full as possible at the very time when irrigators want them drawn down. Unavoidably then, reallocating priorities at this local level means trading electricity against irrigation water. Moreover, hydropower stations supply a special kind of electricity. Because they can be stopped and started easily (unlike steam generators, which develop stresses and cracks if they are heated and cooled too often and too quickly), they are the ideal way to cover daily and weekly peaks in demand, as well as unforeseen needs in between. This kind of "peaking power" is especially scarce in the southern half of the European USSR,[2] and so power-grid operators have a special interest in operating dams their own way.

Nevertheless, at first sight nothing could be simpler than to cut back the priority of power production by lowering the stations' targets for annual output of power and particularly their firm capacity in winter. Indeed, this is precisely what has been done in recent years, and the cuts are directly traceable to anticipated increases in demand for irrigation. In the Dnieper basin of the Ukraine, for example, consumptive withdrawals of water for irrigation are forecast to reach 5.6 million acre-feet by 1985 and 11.6 by the year 2000[3] (compared with 1.05 million in 1960).[4] Accordingly, the output of the Dnieper power stations is being curtailed, eventually by 20 percent or possibly more.[5]

Similar changes are in store for the Volga. If irrigation expands according to plan, consumptive withdrawals from the Volga for irrigation will amount to 10 percent of its average annual flow by 1980.[6] By the end of the century, the firm winter capacity of the Volga power stations could be curtailed by as much as half and channel depths reduced to 9 feet, to satisfy the needs of irrigation.[7] The cuts, in fact, have already begun. Reductions of 600 megawatts were planned for 1975 and 1,200 megawatts may be cut "in the future" (possibly in 1985).[8] The same story is repeated in many other places where irrigation and hydropower are in competition.[9] These changes are especially striking when one considers that the major dams of the Dnieper and the Volga are less than a generation old – some of them, in fact, were completed only in the 1970s – and cutting back their power output means swallowing major losses. This is a major change of direction indeed.

Yet cuts in yearly or even seasonal output are not enough by themselves to execute the needed transfer of resources, for conflict between the interests of irrigators and power-grid operators runs deeper. First, like everyone else in the Soviet Union, power-grid personnel have an interest (because of the structure of the bonus system) in *over*filling their plan if they can. Second, the operators must cope with more serious uncertainties than the irrigators, because in addition to natural variations in water supply, power stations are subject to unpredictable variations in demand from the larger grids to which they belong. Consequently, the operators are tempted to cheat and such "spot cheating" is extremely hard to control.

Why then is the Ministry of Power and Electrification allowed to retain control over the day-to-day allocation of water in the southern European USSR ? The ministry commands the key "switching points" in the field, such as dispatchers' control rooms at power stations, locks, and so on. And it also retains a commanding position in the formulation of the operating rules. When fights break out among competing agencies because of the high-handedness of the power-grid operators, local political authorities still rule on the side of electricity, for they cannot help but value scarce peaking power as much as they do scarce irrigation water, and choosing between them at the margin is no easy matter, as we shall see. The result is a considerable dilution of the leaders' new priorities and a successful defense of the established users' interests, which is bound to grow even stronger as peak-coverage power becomes scarcer in the 1980s.

### Control of key points in the field

In contrast to the situation in the United States, where the operation of hydropower stations may be in the hands of many different groups, all hydropower installations in the Soviet Union (with the exception of an insignificant number of small stations used for rural power supply) are operated by the personnel of the Ministry of Power, through a hierarchy of distribution organizations that culminates in a single Unified Grid covering the entire European USSR. This is true even when hydropower is not the "leading purpose" (*vedushchii komponent*) of the project.[10] How much influence this gives the ministry depends on what time frame we consider: (1) Annual patterns of operation are easily encompassed by central regulations, and the latitude traditionally enjoyed by the Ministry of Power has been sharply curtailed in recent years, to the benefit of irrigation; (2) seasonal and short-term patterns, in contrast, are more difficult for an outside agency to regulate in detail. This fact gives the Ministry of Power considerable leverage over responses to short-term, unforeseen changes in streamflow – in other words, the allocation of short-term uncertainty. In emergencies, the Ministry of Power's physical control of the power station enables it to override the requirements of other users and operate the station (for brief periods) to ensure the smallest possible loss of power to itself – in effect, passing on the costs of uncertainty to others. A few examples will make this point easier to see.

### The uses of "forcing"

One way in which the Ministry of Power puts its control over operation to good use is by filling the reservoir higher than its normal head, a procedure called forcing (*forsirovka*). There are two kinds of forcing, permanent and temporary, with very different political implications.

Permanent forcing.
Permanent forcing means making a long-term increase in the height of the column of water above at the station's turbines, which is of interest to the operators because it increases the turbines' speed. It requires authorization from the central authorities, and thus it represents an explicit decision on competing priorities, for to grant permission for forcing means greater power output at the cost of more flooded land. Thus the history of permanent forcing in Soviet hydropower is also a capsule history of the overall evolution of priorities in the Soviet Union over the last fifty years.

The most dramatic example occurred as a result of the sudden demotion of agriculture after the beginning of the First Five-Year Plan (1928–32). Symbolic of the new values was the Volkhov River project, the first hydropower plant of the Soviet era. Begun at the height of the Civil War to supply power to Leningrad, the project's reservoir had been carefully planned so as not to harm other interests upstream on the Volkhov River and Lake Ilmen', including the fertile meadows of the floodplain.[11] Completed in 1926, the power station was operated in the same careful way until 1929, when, to increase the power supply for industrial growth in Leningrad, "the operating personnel proposed and carried out" a 20 percent increase in the head by building a wooden parapet above the dam.[12] For an average gain of 100 million to 150 million kilowatt-hours per year, 250,000 acres of floodplain meadow and fodder land were put underwater – a striking illustration of the priorities of that period.[13] The area affected (the southern portion of the Volkhov River floodplain) suffered a loss of about one-third of its agricultural income.[14] The forcing level was then maintained for nearly thirty years, until 1958.[15] Increases of this type also took place at many power stations throughout the USSR until the mid-1960s.[16] Although formally an increase in the rated head came at the initiative of the station's operators, it seems that this initiative was systematically encouraged from above.[17] The impression that forcing was the established policy of the Ministry of Power until the end of the 1950s is strengthened by the fact that power-station operators were encouraged to consult with the local offices of Gidroproekt about the best ways to take advantage of the available margin of safety in the thickness of the dam to increase the normal head. For example, one source relates that in 1960 the normal rated head of the Kama station was raised by 10 percent, "after hard and long work by Permenergo [the distributing organization of the area] and after approval by the Ministry of Power." The increase in head resulted in a gain of 50 million kilowatt-hours per year, and considerable benefit to waterway navigation. But the source notes that in the documents relating to the change there was "not a single word" about the harmful consequences of increased heads for nearby agriculture and other interests,[18] and no additional funds were allocated to compensate agriculture or other users for the losses entailed.[19]

In the last fifteen years permanent forcing as a semiofficial policy has been brought to an end,[20] even though instances of it still occurred at least as late as the mid-1960s.[21] A symbolic turning point came in 1961 when the request of the Gor'kii power-grid operators for an increase in the head of the Gor'kii Dam was turned down by the newly created Republican Organs for Water Management on the grounds that the proposed raise did not take sufficient account of the requirements of other interested users.[22] As the Republican Organs (since incorporated into the Ministry of Reclamation) had little political power of their own (see note 5, Chapter 8), their ability to refuse the "request" of the Gor'kii operators testifies to a broader change of priorities in the country.

Temporary forcing.
A different and still very controversial matter is temporary forcing, which consists of raising the water level above its design level temporarily, to absorb part of the peak of the spring flood – a perfectly legitimate move, which is permitted by official regulations as an emergency measure.[23] The problem is that power-station operators then maintain reservoirs at this "temporary" high level for longer periods, without official clearance, to overfulfill the annual plan for output of firm power. This practice still seems widespread.[24]

The resulting gains in power output make the game worthwhile. For example, an increase of less than a foot in the reservoir levels at the Kuibyshev and the Volgograd dams on the Volga in 1959, 1960, and 1961 yielded an additional 200 million to 280 million kilowatt-hours of energy per year.[25] Similarly, at the Tsimliansk Dam on the Don River, temporary forcing in seven out of eleven years from 1953 to 1964 produced an average gain of 100 million kilowatt-hours annually, or about 22 percent above average output.[26]

But how damaging is this practice to agriculture and other interests? In the case of the Don River, just cited, it was claimed that total damage to agriculture over eleven years was 650 million rubles. Other sources claim in addition that temporary forcing erodes the banks of the reservoirs at an accelerated rate and so contributes to silting up the reservoir and shorting its useful life.[27] Many hydropower specialists, however, do not agree. The damage to agriculture, they say, consists mainly of a small delay in the beginning of spring sowing on the land affected, as well as some damage to the shoreline of the reservoir, but in return the higher reservoir levels aid the reproduction of fish and benefit river transport.[28] Needless to say, there is a lively controversy among the agencies concerned over their respective losses.

The interest of the forcing question lies in what it can tell us about decision-making procedures and the incentive systems influencing the behavior of power-station operators. Some Soviet sources say that the blame for unauthorized forcing lies with the operators of the power stations,[29] whose bonus system encourages them to attempt to overfulfill the output plan, and who do not bear the costs that forcing may impose. The decision procedure involved in temporary forcing is not as formal as in the case of permanent forcing, because temporary forcing arises, as we have seen, through a loophole in the regulations. Thus, whereas the permission of the Ministry of Power is required for permanent forcing, temporary forcing appears to be the result of decisions taken farther down in the hierarchy. Soviet sources suggest that temporary forcing is either the result of unilateral initiative on the part of the "operating organization" or occurs with the tacit permission of the administrative level immediately above it.[30] This fact makes the problem more difficult to control.

*Hydropower operation: control and controversy*
The use of hydropower to cover peaks in demand has a major impact on other river users. For example, all hydropower operations are sharply reduced at night, and some power stations, such as the Rybinsk on the Volga, shut down entirely.[31] This causes a heavy wave that travels downstream and produces major changes in channel depths, interfering with river navigation. The wave also increases the deposit of silt in river channels and forces additional expenditures for dredging.[32] When the bulk of Soviet industry converted to a five-day week after the early 1960s and hydropower units slowed to one-third to one-half their normal activity on weekends, shipping ran aground below the Gor'kii and the Rybinsk dams on the Volga.[33] River-transport officials began to demand relief. In 1963 new rules were issued for the operation of Gor'kii Dam, specifying minimum channel depths downstream,[34] but it seems that this has not yet solved the problem

to the satisfaction of the Ministry of the River Fleet. Similar complaints by agricultural, reclamation, and fishing interests can be found in numerous articles in the Soviet literature.

In each of the three foregoing examples of the Power Ministry's control over local points, the evolution of its powers in recent years has been the same: Annual and seasonal patterns of allocation have changed in favor of other users, but the latitude of the dispatchers to respond flexibly to short-term variations in streamflow and power demand has in most cases not been challenged. Indeed, it is not easy to alter the present system, because of the difficulty of controlling the day-to-day actions of the power-station operators from a distance. There are really only two ways to prevent the Ministry of Power from passing on the costs of short-term uncertainty to its neighbors, and neither one is very satisfactory: The first would be to remove hydropower stations from the control of the Ministry of Power altogether, a move that would make it difficult to operate a unified power grid; the second would be to develop even more detailed operating rules and appoint a strong regulator to enforce them. In the next section we take a look at the prospects for this second path.

## The politics of operating rules

When hydropower ruled Soviet rivers, its engineers wrote the operating rules. In most cases they were not subject to review by other agencies. In fact, formal rules to allow for the needs of other water users were often dispensed with altogether,[35] and where rules existed, they were often drawn up by administrative fiat without regard to local conditions.[36]

The removal of formal rule-making authority from the hands of power officials was one of the most important consequences of the decline of hydropower's hegemony. In 1960 a party-state decree created a network of Republican Organs for the Use and Protection of Water Resources and vested in them the authority to draw up binding operating rules for reservoirs. Since 1966, these agencies have been organized into a system of basin inspectorates under the Ministry of Reclamation,[37] and any proposed rules for reservoirs must be cleared by that ministry at either the republic or the Moscow level, depending on the importance of the reservoir.[38]

But despite these changes, the present system of operating rules still works to the advantage of hydropower. By the mid-1970s, the basin inspectorates had done little to change them. Where actual changes have occurred, it is because of vigorous lobbying by individual agencies. The Ministry of the River Fleet, for example, was able to win special operating rules in the late 1960s on the Volga, the Don, and the Ob' (although the power-grid operators have apparently routinely disregarded them).[39] Though the State Committee on Science and Technology sponsored a detailed review of the whole question of operating rules from the mid-1960s to the mid-1970s, contracting with more than thirty research institutes from the major ministries concerned, they have yet to produce detailed new rules.[40] In fact, writing comprehensive new rules may turn out to be impossible. Such regulations necessarily codify power relations among the various users and these, as we have seen, are unsettled. They also embody conventions on uncertainty and economic measurement, and these too are delicate issues among the users, as well as inherently difficult questions in themselves. The more detailed the operating rules, the greater the danger of freezing the allocation of water into inflexible patterns that allow no quick response to changing hydrological or economic conditions. Yet the looser the rules, the more latitude is given to whoever sits in the control room.

Consider, for example, the problem of allowing for uncertainties in streamflow. This is normally done by a so-called rule curve (*dispetcherskii grafik*). The basic idea is to regulate the operation of the dam not only on the basis of the water already in the reservoir but also on the basis of the water *forecast* to be in the reservoir within the next few days. The use of short-term forecasts, however, raises controversial problems in uncertainty reduction. The characteristic feature of such forecasts is an unavoidable trade-off between their timeliness and their accuracy. Consequently, power-station operators have generally been conservative in their use of them. To protect their own interests they reserve the right to cut off other users in case of need. In effect, the operators pass the risk on. For example, at the Rybinsk Dam on the Volga, a type of "fail-safe" procedure is used: Until the annual forecasts are received, the reservoir is drawn down at a rate that meets the optimim requirements of river transport. Then, as the forecasts are received, the rate of drawdown is gradually adjusted by interagency consultation. But when the forecasts are late or inaccurate, the power-grid operators act to protect themselves and river transport suffers a heavy loss. In 1960, 1963, and 1964, the forecasts were late at Rybinsk, and by the time they were received the reservoir had already been drawn down below the fail-safe mark. The power-station operators abruptly closed the dam, and river transport did not have its "guaranteed" channel depths in those years.[41]

In some cases power-station operators disregard both the forecasts *and* the interests of other purposes. This has happened notably at the Kakhov Dam on the Dnieper, where operators make deep pre-spring drawdowns regardless of the forecasts, so that by the beginning of the navigation season the reservoir is not filled enough to allow the passage of fully loaded ships through the locks of the canals.[42] In the case of the Dnieper dams, such episodes may be due to the very severe shortage of peaking power in the Southern Unified Power Grid.[43]

The complexity of these conflicts suggests that the eventual solution will not be comprehensive rules but a series of ad hoc, year-by-year allocations for each basin. On the lower Volga a rough-and-ready system of that kind has been in effect for more than fifteen years and may be a prototype of things to come. Downstream from the powerful Kuibyshev and Volgograd dams lies the Akhtuba valley, a fertile floodplain that owes its high productivity to annual spring flooding by the Volga.[44] Before the completion of the Volgograd Dam in 1958, the spring flood lasted an average of 112 days a year.[45] In the same area there also exists a highly developed zone of commercial fishing, an industry that likewise depends upon the annual flooding of the Volga to ensure spawning. As soon as the Volgograd power station began operation these activities were threatened.

Accordingly, every year since 1959, the Council of Ministers of the Russian Federation has ordered the release of part of the spring flood (instead of storing it in the reservoir until the fall) to provide the lower basin with a spring discharge that allows fishing and floodplain agriculture to survive. Over the years from 1960 to 1968 (the most recent year for which I have figures), these spills cost a total of 10.5 billion kilowatt-hours of electrical energy, an amount almost equal to one year's average output from the Volgograd station.[46]

Yet no one is satisfied. It is not enough simply to spill a certain volume of water through the dam in order to guarantee a proper flood downstream. Effective spawning conditions and proper soil moisture in the floodplain depend on such variables as the length of discharge, the rate of increase and decrease of flow, and the size of the flood peak. The first special spills did little or no good, despite the fact that a large quantity of water (73 million acre-feet) was released. Agricultural and fishing interests reacted by demanding a tightly regulated pattern of spills that would meet their needs.

However, despite important concessions to fishing and agriculture, the RSFSR Council of Ministers has apparently been unwilling or unable to dictate to the Ministry of Power the pattern that downstream interests demand. The Ministry of Power reserves the right to interrupt the spills if it appears that it will be left at the end of the spring flood with a depleted reservoir. In effect, it passes on the costs of uncertainty to agriculture and fishing, for it makes very conservative use of streamflow forecasts to reduce losses to itself. In two years when there were ominous variations in streamflow, which seemed to augur a lower spring flood than was forecast, the operators quickly interrupted the required pattern of spills. In two other years, when it appeared as though actual streamflow would be greater than forecast, power-station operators waited until they were quite sure before increasing the flow through the spillway. The increased spills, when they came, were too late to be effective. In still another year, when an unusually large demand for power the previous winter had left the reservoir level very low at the beginning of the spring flood, the operators made sure their reservoirs were filled up to their normal head before making any spills at all.[47] Once again we see the difficulty of reducing the Ministry of Power's latitude in responding to short-term uncertainty. Annual "dispatching" plans for the spring spills are drawn up in the third quarter of the preceding year. At that time streamflow forecasts are, of course, not yet available, and therefore the plan is prepared on the basis of main streamflow figures drawn from the historical record.[48] The most that the ministry has agreed to, under pressure, is to draw the Volga reservoirs below their normal working head, in years of low flow, by as much as 14 million acre-feet if fishing and agriculture have not received "a sufficient amount" in that year.[49]

The system of special spills on the Volga has caused a great deal of grumbling on the part of hydropower spokesmen, for they feel that they have been forced to make major concessions and that the other users have failed to keep their part of the bargain. The plans upon which the Kuibyshev and Volgograd projects were originally based would have created irrigation and modern hatcheries downstream, and this would have eliminated the need for spills. The Ministries of Agriculture and of the Fishing Industry, however, did not execute their part of the plan, and power officials now find themselves forced to sacrifice valuable power to keep outmoded economic activities in business. In addition, initial plans called for a long dike to be built near the mouth of the Volga, which would divide the delta in two and redirect most of its flow toward the eastern portion of the estuary, traditionally the most valuable for commercial fishing.[50] For some reason, however, construction of the "water divider" was not begun until several years after the completion of the Volgograd Dam, and construction went slowly. By the time it was completed, consumptive withdrawals from the Volga had increased so much that the spills had to continue.


If power-grid operators are able to retain control of key points in the field, it is not in any sense because they own them. But they have the expertise required to operate power stations as part of an integrated power system, and that expertise gives them an opening to pursue their own interests. Over periods of a season or a year, they do not have much latitude; but intervention becomes progressively more difficult as one moves toward periods of one week or a few days. Yet in arbitrating between power and irrigation, the shorter time periods are often the ones that count, and consequently the end result is an advantage to hydropower.

The problem is not that the government lacks the will or the muscle to enforce the implementation of its priorities. Rather, what it does lack is any efficient or flexible way of enforcing, by administrative intervention, the day-to-day "terms of trade" between power and irrigation in a situation filled with uncertainty. What will happen when irrigation projects in the southern regions of the European USSR reach full operation, and the issue is truly joined? It looks as though the authorities will be obliged to resort to something like the Volga "sterile spills" on other rivers as well, an arrangement that causes renewed conflict each spring and represents a kind of inefficient improvisation on the part of the central authorities. An alternative possibility, used in the United States, is to turn the operation of some power stations over to the Ministry of Reclamation, which could give the latter an incentive to develop its own internal trade-off between power and water. So far, I am not aware of any Soviet discussion of that possibility. Yet so long as power and irrigation remain the separate provinces of two competing ministries, there is no possibility of achieving reallocation except by constant conflict and administrative intervention.

What is the consequence? Threatened with a cut in their water supplies or with a loss of control over its use, established users have reacted by using whatever latitude was available, appealing to political authority for variances and exceptions, and complaining loudly at every turn. When granted a reprieve – whether by government temporizing or the slowness of irrigators to grow into their share – established users fail to take the positive steps required to diminish their dependence. The Ministry of the River Fleet has been developing oceangoing river shipping that requires even deeper channel depths (and hence more water).[51] The Ministry of the Fishing Industry does not develop hatcheries. Industries do not reduce their water consumption. All these independent and uncoordinated actions reduce the water eventually available for irrigation. Because the vertically integrated system of specialized ministries produces little community of interest in the field, there is no alternative to an inefficient and ineffective administrative intervention. And as we shall see in Chapter 9, the policies of the irrigators themselves do not improve matters. The contending agencies in the south of the European USSR find it easy to agree on only one thing: that more water must be brought in from outside.

# 8

# THE NEW ENVIRONMENTAL PROGRAM: DO THE SOVIETS REALLY MEAN BUSINESS?*

In the southern USSR, an expanding agriculture competes for scarce water not only with hydropower, as we saw in the last chapter, but also with industry and municipalities. These have long been accustomed to using water as a free good to dilute and evacuate their wastes. The only way to liberate additional water for irrigated agriculture is to make industry and municipalities use less and clean what they use. Therefore, the implementation of the southern strategy in the Brezhnev plan depends in part on whether the clean-water program launched in the early 1970s can actually be made to work. That will not be easy. Until quite recently, as we saw in Chapter 3, the Soviet Union had no environmental program worthy of the name (at any rate outside the two or three largest cities). Starting virtually from scratch, a skeptical industry and a newly formed enforcement bureaucracy are being asked to develop a major program in a hurry.

How well is it working? According to Soviet sources, water quality has already improved slightly in the areas of highest priority. The deterioration of the Volga has been halted.[1] In Moscow, water quality has improved "somewhat" in the last ten years.[2] Some sources claim that waste-treatment capacity is already catching up with the growing volume of industrial wastes nationwide.[3] It is hard to tell, however, which claims are real and which are inflated or overoptimistic.[4] And if we cannot establish that, how can we judge the real priority and prospects of the water-quality program? Fortunately, we can get a better answer by looking at the system of planning, implementation, and enforcement. The logic of this is that under Soviet conditions budgetary quantities by themselves mean little. Unless the plan provides also for human and material resources, funds for environmental protection will be returned to the state unspent, as happened routinely in the 1960s and still occurs occasionally. There must exist a specialized network for waste-treatment research, design, and construction. And in a system that is notorious for subverting plan targets from below by surreptitious "reprograming" of personnel and resources, there must be an effec-

* Portions of this chapter appeared under the title "The New Soviet Environmental Program" in *Public Policy*, Summer 1978. Copyright 1978 by the President and Fellows of Harvard College. Reprinted by permission of John Wiley & Sons.; and under the title "Environmental Policy under Brezhnev" in *Soviet Politics in the Brezhnev Era*, edited by Donald R. Kelley. Copyright 1980 by Praeger Publishers. Reprinted and adapted by permission of Praeger Publishers.

tive monitoring and enforcement system at the local level. Therefore, to determine the real priority and the likely future of the water-quality program, we must find out how strong these new mechanisms are.

### The enforcement system

The center of the enforcement system is the network of basin inspectorates subordinated to Minvodkhoz.[5] They are growing rapidly: Their staff has doubled since 1972 and now include more than five thousand engineers, inspectors, and scientists. Yet, as fast as the basin inspectorates have grown, their work load has grown even faster. They are responsible in principle for every factory, farm, and municipality using more than 100 cubic meters per day of water.[6] At each location they must execute a bewildering array of tasks.[7]

But the enforcement powers of the inspectorates are as formidable as their responsibilities, at least on paper. They are of two principle types: sanctions and power to withhold approval. I shall first discuss these powers as they exist in theory and then examine how effective they are in practice.

### Sanctions available in theory

The basin inspectorates have a graduated arsenal of punishments at their disposal. Executives of polluting enterprises[8] can be fined up to 50 rubles on the recommendation of the basin inspector, and the fine can be repeated at intervals of three months. Harsher penalties apply in the case of offenses considered to be criminal, such as a deliberate discharge resulting in a major fish kill. The next step up has real bite: The basin inspectorates can also deprive individuals of their bonuses.[9] This is a sizable threat to an enterprise manager, for bonuses may amount to half his total income. Cancellation, according to the inspectors, requires no more than a letter from the basin inspectorate to the state bank. Finally, as a last resort, an enterprise, or part of it, can be shut down, or the enterprise's access to the sewage system can be closed down or its water supply shut off.

In addition to sanctions, the basin inspectorates have a potentially important weapon in the fact that their "agreement" (*soglasovanie*) is required at several key points in the planning, design and construction of new enterprises and new waste-treatment facilities, in decisions on their use of water, and in their final commissioning on completion. In principle, this means that the basin inspectorates can prevent an enterprise from being located in an unsuitable place or from starting production if its waste-treatment facilities are inadequate. Thus, on paper at least, the basin inspectorates have veto power at each of the key stages of water consumption and treatment.

Of this imposing array of formal responsibilities and powers, how many are real? To get a realistic picture, we should first inquire what resources and political support the basin inspectorates actually have.

*Resources of the basin inspectorates: two examples*

The Moscow and Oka Basin Inspectorate is probably the best in the country. It is responsible for the city of Moscow and the six provinces surrounding it. But to cover a jurisdiction that includes 6,500 water-using entities and 21 million people, it has a staff of only 360 people and an annual budget of 1 million rubles, which pays mainly for salaries, operations, and upkeep of facilities.

To this writer, during a visit in 1976, the Moscow-Oka inspectorate looked like a semi-amateur organization. Most of the inspectors were retired military officers, as were both the chief inspector and his chief engineer. Most of the scientists and technicians employed in the inspectorate's laboratories were women (unfortunately, in Soviet science this is a sign of low status). Inspectors earned 130 rubles a month, barely average for the Soviet Union at the time,[10] and in the inspectorate's central laboratory in Moscow salaries were equally modest: A biological engineer earned 135 rubles per month, and the director of the laboratory earned only 170 rubles.[11] In an interview, the chief inspector acknowledged that with such salaries it was difficult to attract qualified personnel. Indeed, many of the everyday functions of the basin inspectorates were carried out by volunteers.

The basin inspectorates of the Ukraine looked much the same. In 1976 about one thousand people worked in the eleven basin inspectorates of this republic, serving a region of 55 million people.[12] Their annual budget was 3 million rubles, and their transportation, equipment, and laboratories were similar to those of the Moscow-Oka inspectorate. They too had some difficulty in attracting qualified personnel. According to Ukrainian inspectorate officials, only in the western Ukraine, where job opportunities are fewer and people want to stay in their home region, would young people work for the basin inspectorate. Elsewhere, in places like Moscow and the Don basin, competing job opportunities made it more difficult to attract qualified young professionals, and volunteers or retired military personnel were employed instead. The basin inspectorates, in other words, are not very attractive employers, and this fact suggests low status.

Compared with the Moscow-Oka and the upper Dnieper organizations, inspectorates in lower-priority regions like Kazakhstan are even less well staffed and equipped: In 1975 only fifty-nine people were employed in the basin inspectorates there, with responsibility for more than 200,000 kilometers of streams.[13]

In sum, unless there have been major changes since 1976, the personnel and the resources of the basin inspectorates are inadequate to cover their vast array of responsibilities. If their duties were limited to water-quality monitoring alone, a task they share with the Hydrometeorological Service, they might perform adequately,[14] at least in the high-priority areas. But when one adds their enforcement and reporting tasks, they cannot be effective in covering them all, and one wonders whether they are even expected to. To this observer, the personnel of the inspectorates seemed relaxed and unhurried; the central laboratory in Moscow could actually be described as sleepy. The inspectors and their superiors definitely did not give the impression of a harried crew struggling desperately to cope with impossible demands.

Thus the overall impression one gains of the basin inspectorates is that, though they may be evolving toward real influence and real professionalism, they are still low-priority organizations. This impression is strengthened when one considers their enforcement record.

### Enforcement in practice

Enforcement is undoubtedly growing tougher. Whereas fines were a relative rarity in the 1960s,[15] in 1973 about 5,000 enterprise officials were either fined or deprived of their bonuses in the Volga and Ural basins alone.[16] More than 6,000 enterprise officials were fined in the Russian Federation in 1974, and parts of 349 enterprises were shut down.[17] In Moscow, 32 enterprises were fully or partially shut down for brief periods in 1975, by order of the basin inspectorate.[18] In the Ukraine, basin inspectors claim they canceled bonuses for more than 9,000 management personnel during the Ninth Five-Year Plan (1971–5).[19] The basin inspectorates withheld approval on more than half of the 4,361 waste-treatment facilities completed and presented for certification in 1971.[20]

Through the figures on enforcement one can discern the same priorities among regions that we have already noted. Enforcement in Kazakhstan, for example, seems much less vigorous than in the Ukraine and the RSFSR: In 1975 only about 200 fines were levied there.[21] In Armenia only 17 managers were fined in 1974, and there were no closings.[22] The Ukraine ranks lower than Moscow: In contrast to the thirty-two closing in Moscow in 1975, the deputy minister in charge of water resources in the Ukraine reported only two or three closings per year in the entire republic.[23] One can also discern enforcement priorities in the relative attention given to different industries. In enforcing the Volga-Ural decree the basin inspectorates have focused especially on the chemical industry.[24] The petroleum-refining and petrochemicals industries are also prominently mentioned, both as the main causes of problems and the sources of some of the greatest strides.[25]

Shutting down a plant requires approval from higher authority. When plants are closed, it is usually for only two or three days and rarely more than a week. Most are older enterprises with obsolete technology, and the specific examples mentioned in interviews all concerned light industry: leather tanning, wool washing, sugar refining, and so on. Minvodkhoz officials insist that the purpose of closing an enterprise is to give a healthy shock to its parent organization (now called production association). In most cases the enterprise is allowed to reopen after the association has given suitable promises that action will be taken to remedy the problem. For example, *Pravda* reported recently the case of the Kirovakan chemical plant in Armenia, an antiquated facility and a serious health hazard. Trying to shut down the worst of the plant's shops, the republican Ministry of Public Health passed a special resolution. But in vain: The chemical industry had only to give assurances that something would be done, and the shop remained open. A year later, there had been no improvement, and the Armenian sanitary inspectorate took the last step remaining to it: It brought criminal charges against the enterprise director, a move that everyone recognized was aimed at the wrong target.[26]

Shutting down an enterprise is clearly a measure of last resort, undertaken with great reluctance. Many cases are mentioned in which enterprise directors are fined repeatedly for the same violation, yet the enterprise continues to operate. The enormity of closure can be judged from the language of a recent article about the Tagil River in the Urals:

> If you had told Doctor Samogol'tsev, fifteen years ago, that he would be putting a padlock on the gates and stopping a working plant, he would have thought you were a madman. That's right! The Plan, after all, is untouchable. And for him, as a native of the Urals, a factory is something sacred . . . Yet, today he put lead seals on a factory shop and halted production.

The account goes on to describe a shouting match with the enterprise director. The following morning, all the parties concerned were summoned from Nizhnii Tagil to Sverdlovsk, a distance of more than seventy-five miles, where the decision of the inspector was upheld. Clearly, water-quality inspectorates pick their targets carefully. In this case the inspector took the precaution of coming equipped with a document signed by a deputy minister.[27]

Enforcement of pollution control is not allowed to interfere with the fulfillment of high-priority output targets or with local employment. Minvodkhoz will not support its basin inspectors if they try to close a high-priority operation. In Moscow, for example, the inspectorate had repeated difficulty with two copper-refining and electrolysis enterprises.[28] The Moscow-Oka chief inspector tried on five different occasions to have them temporarily shut down but was overruled each time, he said, by the Minister of Reclamation himself.[29]

All in all, the basin inspectorates and other enforcement agencies do not appear very powerful. Soviet newspapers often report cases in which the protests of the basin inspectors are overridden or in which they are actually denied admittance to the plant's premises. As the chief of the Moscow-Oka inspectorate emphasized in an interview, the job of the inspectors is "difficult, conflict-ridden, and filled with tension."[30]

This weakness is partly explained by the fact that the basin inspectorates lack sufficient power and partly by the fact that the power they have is aimed at the wrong place. Their sanctions apply mainly to the local enterprise directors, such as the hapless chief of the Kirovakan plant, who lack the means to comply. The inspectors cannot reach the real sources of the problem: the construction contractor, the research and design institutes, the supply organizations, and the higher levels of the ministries. That is not to say that enforcement has no potential role to play; we shall come back to it later on. But in the Soviet system enforcement is simply not the key to implementation. It cannot even begin to work until it is supported by materials, expertise, and incentives, and these must come from higher up, beginning with the planning process itself.

*Planning and implementation*

Prior to 1974, environmental programs had no formal place in the national plan, and consequently they received no central allocations of funds or supplies. But in the last three years the situation has changed dramatically. In 1974 a Division for the Protection of Nature was created in the State Planning Committee (Gosplan). Annual and five-year economic plans now include a section on environmental quality,[31] which assigns waste-treatment and water-recycling targets to ministries and municipalities, along with the necessary material resources.[32]

The immediate consequence of these changes is that, in principle, responsibility for waste-treatment construction no longer falls on the local enterprise directors but on their ministries, which are now officially accountable for the fulfillment of water-quality plans. Second, the supply of equipment and materials for waste treatment becomes the responsibility of central supply organizations. Finally, there is now a recognized place in which the environmental program can be negotiated as part of the official agenda. But how do things work out in practice?

The negotiating process, as described in interviews with Soviet water-quality officials, works as follows: Draft proposals for water-quality projects originate at the local level and reach Gosplan via two competing channels. The first starts from the basin inspectorates and rises through the hierarchy of the Ministry of Reclamation and Water Management (Minvodkhoz). Minvodkhoz amalgamates the local proposals into a draft water-quality plan that it sends to Gosplan's environmental division. The second channel of proposals runs up the hierarchy of the industrial ministries, or "branches," and leads to the Gosplan departments corresponding to each major type of industry.

Thus at the draft stage of both five-year and annual plans, Gosplan must reconcile two sets of competing proposals. According to water-quality officials, Minvodkhoz's version (as one might expect) calls for considerably more investment than the industries' proposals do – 25 to 30 percent more in the case of five-year plans, 10 to 15 percent more in the case of draft annual plans.

How are these competing versions hammered together? The Division of Environmental Protection does not have actual authority to allocate resources, as the branch divisions do. The latter are given an overall "mark" by Gosplan and must adjust the draft plans submitted by the ministries to fit the assigned mark. They have the power to decide for themselves what part of their investment resources to assign to environmental protection. The Division of Environmental Protection, in other words, is confined to the role of lobbyist for the environment in Gosplan, with a much weaker position in the planning process than the industrial divisions have.[33]

The same conclusion is suggested by the role that Minvodkhoz plays in this bargaining. Minvodkhoz is the lead agency for water use and quality, but it is not yet very effective as an institutional defender of clean water. First, Minvodkhoz, despite its budget of 7 billion rubles a year, is still nowhere near so large or so powerful as the giants it must contend with – especially the Ministries of the Chemical Industry, Oil Refining Industry, and Ferrous Metallurgy.

Second, Minvodkhoz cannot commit its full attention and political resources to water quality. Its main job is reclamation, and the reclamation wing of the ministry dwarfs the water-quality–and–use wing, both in personnel and in resources.[34] By several measures, such as the relative space devoted to the two programs in the ministry's journal and in the minister's speeches or the relative number of R&D institutes working in the two fields, reclamation clearly looms far larger in Minvodkhoz's concerns than water quality. Consequently, Minvodkhoz is not likely to fight hard for its draft water-quality plans when they are whittled down by the industrial-branch divisions in Gosplan.

A further reason for the weak position of water-quality forces in the planning process is that their recommendations are still largely ad hoc. There is no nationwide plan for water use and quality, despite a great deal of talk about a "general scheme" being developed by hydropower planners, and regional or basin plans are still in the development stage. Quality standards are permissive: They must be reached eventually, but the exact timetable is negotiable, and the final standards themselves are still being developed.[35]

What happens next is a familiar chain of events: The subordinate position of the environmental program in the planning system signals to officials at all levels that they may safely divert resources, in case of need, to programs with higher priority. So the program's initial weakness at the top of the system is magnified in the field. Action then falls short in every department: Specialists are not trained, research is not done, construction firms are not reorganized, technology is not developed, facilities are built slowly and inadequately maintained. The final result is that the program does not move. In 1975, for example, only twenty-three out of thirty-eight ministries and agencies fulfilled the plan for "physical and chemical treatment of wastewater," even in the most formal terms.[36] In 1978 a decree of the party Central Committee and the USSR Council of Ministers blasted ministries and party organs alike, not even bothering with the usual ritual praise for good performance that such decrees usually begin with.[37] Obviously, from the Kremlin, the situation must look grim.

As an illustration, consider the problems of constructing waste-treatment facilities. The first obstacle is the structure of the industry: There are still no construction organizations specializing in pollution control, aside from one or two in Moscow. Instead, waste-treatment assignments are handled by general-purpose construction firms (*tresty*), operating on contract.[38]

Second, the system of incentives discourages work on pollution control. Waste-treatment assignments are generally only a very small part of the total work load of construction firms and therefore a small part also of their target and bonuses. They consider waste treatment complicated, labor intensive, and exacting, and they often turn down contracts for waste treatment or put them in last place in their work schedules.[39]

The construction firms, moreover, are just one link in a chain of designers, suppliers, and so on; none of these, according to the press, works particularly well. Everyone blames everyone else: The construction trusts claim that they are fulfilling their plans but that they are given few assignments by their ministries and inadequate supplies by supply organizations and ministries of machine building.[40] Supply offices complain that they cannot provide sets of equipment to construction firms before the systems have been designed, which the design institutes are slow to do. The USSR Ministries of Chemical and Petroleum Machine Building get the blame for not starting series production of key equipment.[41]

Clearly, part of the problem is the suddenness with which the water-quality program was accelerated in 1973. Construction firms were caught unprepared. One of the firms named in the Volga-Ural decree, a petrochemical construction firm in the Ural basin town of Gur'ev, saw its waste-treatment plan jump suddenly from 25 million rubles in 1974 to 55 million in 1975.[42] A Soviet reporter described the firm's plight:

> To use this money is beyond the firm's capability, of course. It lacks the workers, the equipment, and the construction base. The province has only a very small casting yard for reinforced concrete items, and not a single quarry; gravel is hauled in from Aktyubinsk, hundreds of kilometers away. Bricks are shipped in from almost as far as Karaganda. Gur'ev urgently needs help.

The situation was much the same throughout the Ural basin. In Magnitogorsk, investment ran at only one-fourth the rate called for in the 1972 party-state decree.[43] The basin's problems are gradually easing, but a later article remains highly critical and calls the quality of the water there unsatisfactory.[44]

Political priority, of course, influences the rate at which such lags are overcome. Since the beginning of the water-quality program there has been progress in the most important regions and industries and much less in the others. For example, one may read of a biological-treatment facility for a copper-chemical combine in eastern Kazakhstan that has been under construction for ten years,[45] but such stories are now rare in the Volga basin and in Moscow. In Moscow a two-year project may take eight, but in Tadzhikistan the same project may take forever.[46] Similarly, different priorities among ministries show up in differences in construction performance. Light industry and the food industry, having little clout generally, contract with local construction firms instead of national ones.[47] This fact helps to explain the particularly poor record of these two industries.

The basin inspectorates and the other enforcement agencies can do little about these problems. They have no power to fine the construction firms or to give them orders, nor do they have any leverage over the ministries' R&D and design institutes. Minvodkhoz's power of intervention is limited, because it does not contribute funds, supplies, or expertise of its own.

If a new enterprise is completed but the waste-treatment facilities for it are not, the inspectors have, in principle, the power to prevent the enterprise from being commissioned; that is, they can prevent it from being turned over by the construction ministry to the industrial ministry that will operate it. In practice, according to Minvodkhoz officials, the basin inspectors will not resort to such a drastic measure but will insist, instead, on a strict interim schedule for the operation of the enterprise, specifying a firm completion date for the waste-treatment facility and permissible interim levels of discharge of untreated effluent. A reading of the Soviet press, however, suggests that such temporary variances are widespread and tend to become permanent. The participation of basin inspectorate officials on the commissioning committees and their theoretical veto power are apparently not enough to withstand the pressure of enterprise directors who are anxious to get their facilities commissioned and operating and of local party officials who have every incentive to support them.

Is the new environmental program a meaningful reform? That depends on what it is intended to achieve. The program appears, in fact, to have two distinct aims. Each entails a different mix and type of costs and benefits. Each requires a different technology, administrative machinery, and level of commitment. Consequently, they differ also in their significance as departures from the traditional Soviet approach to development and in their chances for success.

The first is aimed at dealing with immediate threats: communicable waterborne diseases (such as the cholera outbreak of the early 1970s), kills of commercially valuable fish, and the like. These can be dealt with relatively quickly and simply through primary and secondary waste treatment at specific point sources, using standard techniques. This first level of aims is the easiest to implement because it relies on well-established, uniform technologies, does not affect industrial production, and demands little from the polluters themselves. Much of the current Soviet effort is of this kind. The press is filled with reports of rapidly growing waste-treatment capacity, especially municipal systems.[48] This side of the program, then, is essentially a long-overdue public-health measure, and there is no reason to believe that it will not succeed.

The second aim is to protect resources for future economic uses, what Americans in the first half of the century called conservation.[49] Conservation is more difficult to achieve than sanitation; because at the level of development the Soviets have now reached it definitely requires jostling industry. Heavy metals, chemicals, and petroleum wastes must be taken out of water or prevented from entering it. Where water is scarce (as it is in the southern half of the USSR), it cannot be used as process water or as coolant with traditional Soviet liberality. Therefore some industries must make process changes, others must be relocated or prevented from moving in. Conservation, in sum, means no longer giving industrial enterprises their accustomed complete latitude in using natural resources.

There is no reason in principle why the traditional political machinery cannot achieve such changes. Conservation involves a redirection of effort but no fundamental change of objectives, since its aim, after all, is to facilitate further economic expansion. Industrial process changes can be considered a type of technological innovation requiring research and development, and this in itself is no radical idea for Soviet industry. To strengthen the claims of new users of scarce water and land, the central leadership simply strengthens the agencies concerned while whittling down those of the previously mighty. The new agencies – reclamation, for example – resemble the old; therefore they require no great adjustments of mind or procedure. In dealing with them, the party apparatus continues to play its accustomed roles of broker, troubleshooter, and expediter, and therefore its power is not threatened. Conservation, then, though it stretches the traditional political system, does not require changing it.

The difficulty is that implementing conservation requires a capacity for subtlety and dosage on a massive scale that the established system of planning and administration has not heretofore shown. No two industrial plants have quite the same processes or the same wastes. Each solution must be essentially tailor-made to local conditions. Justifying it requires a broader frame of reference and a more subtle balancing of objectives than the planning mechanism typically allows, a larger conceptual arsenal (including a system of prices for water) than Soviet economists yet use, better measuring instruments than conservation officials have, and better connections between research and production than Soviet industry can usually muster. Industrial executives and party officials alike tend to concentrate on the near term and the narrow target, because it has so far proved impossible to devise effective signals and levers that will cause them to behave differently. But conservation, on the contrary, requires a delicate balancing act among competing objectives at an infinity of local points.

When looked at in this light, the problem of enforcement stands out as crucial. Only enforcement at the local level by local bodies can guarantee the attention to detail, the case-by-case balancing, that each individual solution requires. One need not look far for reforms that would make the enforcement system more effective. Increased powers over research, design, and construction organizations would give the enforcers leverage over the entire sequence of steps leading to effective waste treatment and process changes at the plant level. Increased clout would make it possible to attract better-qualified personnel into enforcement, especially technical specialists acquainted with the industries each inspectorate must deal with. The practice of according variances and "interim schedules" for compliance with environmental targets should be strictly limited. Enforcement would then have real teeth.

But to name these steps is to name the problem. Such powers would enable local inspectorates to coerce officials at higher levels and across organizational boundaries. Even if those powers were exercised strictly in accordance with the plan (as they would have to be), they would reverse the usual direction of authority and threaten the prerogatives of the local party apparatus, limiting its freedom of action. Such moves would represent more than a refocusing of priorities and resources; they would affect the very structure of the political system. Nothing in the fifteen-year record of the

Brezhnev administration suggests the slightest willingness to try anything so bold.

In conclusion, the new environmental program is an example of the mixed record of the regime's attempts to deal with what one might call third-generation problems. Where the problem has been to ward off an immediate danger, the system has responded well. The elite has shown considerable capacity for new thinking at the top, as the very existence of the environmental program attests. But where the problem is to implement an infinity of intersectoral, hard-to-measure, partial shifts at the local level, performance has been poor. As a result, the "intensive," resource-saving approach, upon which the southern development programs are based, is hindered by the resistance of established users to change. We turn now to the chief water consumers in the southern strategy, the irrigators.

# 9

# SLOW GAINS AT A HIGH PRICE: THE FRUSTRATIONS OF RECLAMATION*

Geography favors Soviet agriculture much less than it does Western Europe or the United States. Rainfall is inadequate and undependable over two-thirds of the Soviet agricultural area.[1] Hence one of the principal aims of the Brezhnev agricultural program is not only to increase crop yields but also to stabilize them against drought.[2] To an extraordinary degree, the new agricultural policy emphasizes reclamation and especially irrigation. For more than a decade, in fact, reclamation has been the fastest-growing category of capital investment in the Soviet economy. Allocations of capital in irrigation, drainage, and other forms of land improvement have doubled in each of the last three five-year plans. More than 32 billion rubles were invested for these purposes during the decade 1965–75, and the pace has grown steadily each year.[3] By the Tenth Five-Year Plan (1976–80), scheduled capital investment for reclamation and land improvement had reached 40 billion rubles,[4] compared with 0.58 billion rubles in 1960.[5] Soviet investment in irrigation is now the largest in the world. Whereas traditionally it had been focused on Central Asian cotton, it has now shifted decisively to the production of grain in the Ukraine and the southern regions of Russia.[6] This means the massive development of a delicate agricultural technology in an area where it had been little used before.

More stable harvests in the Soviet Union would have important consequences for the West. In recent years, droughts in Russia and Kazakhstan have been one of the major uncertainties in Western grain markets, as sudden and massive purchases by the Soviet Union have played havoc with world prices. If the Soviets enjoyed sufficiently consistent surpluses to build up a large grain reserve, they would depend less on food purchases abroad. Soviet foreign currency reserve could be used instead to import advanced technology or to reduce their external debt. Clearly, then, a great deal is riding on the success of the southern strategy.

But the program has had serious problems. First, the costs of reclamation are climbing at an alarming rate, and yields are rising much more slowly

* The original version of this chapter appeared under the title "Transforming Soviet Agriculture" in *Public Policy*, Summer 1977. Copyright 1977 by the President and Fellows of Harvard College. Reprinted by permission of John Wiley & Sons, Inc.

than the leadership would like. Second, the entire irrigation program is threatened because the southern half of the country is running short of water. Both these problems are due in part to natural causes, but they are aggravated by the behavior of the major agencies involved. If the ministries in charge of the land improvement program cannot operate more efficiently than they do now, the leadership may be obliged to make much larger investments than it had anticipated – or to cut down the scale of the program. Major decisions lie ahead.

### Slowly rising yields and fast-climbing costs

Increases in yields are trailing far behind increases in investment.[7] In a speech before the July 1978 plenum of the CPSU Central Committee, Brezhnev observed, "not uncommonly, yields on irrigated land hardly differ from the yields obtained from dryland agriculture."[8] To some extent, this lag is a reflection of a natural fact: The impact of new reclamation construction on crop yields is always both indirect and delayed. It is indirect because many factors other than water affect plant growth, and much depends on the way, and the time, the water is applied. It is delayed because twenty years may be required for a project to reach maturity.

In the meantime, the Ministry of Reclamation and Water Management (Minvodkhoz) points with pride to the canals dug, the masses of earth displaced, and the millions of hectares of projects completed. By these standards the achievements of the reclamation program have been very impressive indeed. Nine million hectares of irrigation and drainage projects were built and turned over to collective and state farms during the Ninth Five-Year Plan (1971–5), far exceeding the plan's original targets.[9] The surface area of irrigated and drained land under cultivation has doubled since 1965.[10] Reclamation soon began making an important contribution to the economy: In 1975, 28 percent of Soviet agricultural output came from lands classified as "improved,"[11] and the average yield for irrigated grain increased from 1.48 tons per hectare in 1964 to 2.77 tons per hectare in 1973.[12] These are not small achievements.

Nevertheless, Soviet newspapers and journals resound with complaints that overall yields are increasing too slowly, and the party Central Committee, in a series of special resolutions, has shown considerable impatience. Of course, we can discount some of that criticism as a reflection of the excessive expectations of politicians. Yet closer examination shows that both the leaders' dissatisfaction over yields and the ministry's glowing construction reports are symptoms of serious underlying problems. The ministry has concentrated on "extensive" tasks, particularly the construction of new networks, while neglecting the more difficult and unprofitable "intensive" jobs, such as improving the efficiency of older projects and helping to put new projects into operation. The latter problem is aggravated by inadequate coordination with the Ministry of Agriculture. Because of these two problems, the reclamation program has strayed off course.

*Reasons for the ministry's bias toward construction*
The Ministry of Reclamation and Water Management concentrated first of all on tooling up. Starting a decade ago as a collection of ill-equipped, low-priority, technically unsophisticated republic-level ministries, Minvodkhoz has turned itself into an industrialized and mechanized giant that now employs considerably more than a million people. Its stock of construction machinery has more than doubled since 1966, and to supply itself with materials and spare parts, the ministry has built a large industry of its own.[13] Observers of the Soviet Union will recognize here a classic pattern: A high-priority program builds an independent, vertically integrated structure to supply as many of its needs as possible, so as not to rely on outside suppliers. But the result has been a definite bias toward construction.

The ministry's bias also arises from another classic Soviet problem, that of designing production targets and incentives that will encourage managers to concentrate on long-term rather than more immediate goals. Two problems in particular plague the ministry: too many new starts and poor quality control. The first is a classic Soviet difficulty. The Soviet landscape is dotted with unfinished construction of all kinds, and the reclamation program is no exception. One of the culprits is the incentive system. When the heads of construction units negotiate monthly output targets, they find it to their advantage to bargain for labor-intensive assignments, thus securing a high monthly wage fund and a large quota of workers. Then, when they execute the plans, they concentrate instead on the *least* labor-intensive tasks, which enables them to meet their principal output targets. Through these two strategies in tandem, they maximize their bonuses.[14] But because the least labor-intensive tasks typically come at the beginning of project construction rather than at the end, it is more advantageous to start a new project than to complete an old one.

In reclamation as elsewhere in the Soviet economy, the incentive system rewards gross output – so many miles of canals, so many tons of earth moved – rather than the number of completed projects turned over to state and collective farms, let alone their contribution to improved yields. Minvodkhoz is now striving to remedy the situation with a new incentive system that pays bonuses for completed projects only.[15] But this reform will be successful only if it does not aggravate the second major problem – poor quality control.

The quality-control problem stems in part from the builders' inexperience and inferior professional qualifications, weaknesses inevitable in an organization that has grown so fast. But it is also a by-product of the ministry's established procedures. Construction firms reportedly do not have an effective system for checking the quality of work, and supervision by the designers is weak.[16] Yet without adequate quality control from above and from outside, an incentive system based on completed projects rather than gross output tempts construction firms to skip part of the work specified in the designs, so as to label the projects "complete."[17] But as far as the farmers are concerned, they are nothing of the sort, and so in reality the result is more unfinished construction.

Finally, for a time the Ministry of Reclamation's official policy favored the creation of new projects over the reconstruction of older ones. According to one source, only 16 percent of the capital allocated to reclamation construction during the Eighth Five-Year Plan (1966–70) was used to rebuild older projects.[18] This is hardly surprising. To the Ministry of Reclamation, reconstruction appears difficult and unprofitable. It requires specialized labor, a large number of small-scale operations, detailed knowledge of local conditions and careful adaptation to them, and close coordination with agricultural authorities and local farms, as well as imaginative research and design – factors that do not mesh well with the ministry's emphasis on mechanization and automation.

Yet there is abundant evidence that painstaking reconstruction is badly needed. Older Soviet networks (most of which are located in Central Asia) are highly inefficient. Most canals and ditches are open and unlined; and water losses resulting from seepage and evaporation typically amount to 40 or 50 percent of the total amount drawn from the water source. Most of the older projects are poorly suited to mechanization and modern irrigation. In Central Asia, in particular, irrigated fields are as a rule not leveled, and they tend to be small and bordered by trees and other vegetation. This prevents farmers from using modern machinery, such as sprinklers mounted on wheels, designed for movement over large, level surfaces. Irrigation water is widely overused. The result is disappointing crop yields[19] and widespread poisoning of the soil by salt.[20]

*Poor cooperation between the Ministries of Reclamation and Agriculture*
A second major reason why yields are rising slowly is that the Ministry of Reclamation and the Ministry of Agriculture work badly together in the field. Since 1965 they have disagreed on their respective duties. In general, Reclamation handles basic engineering development: canals, laterals, control structures, and preparation of the fields (clearing, grading, and the like). The Ministry of Agriculture, for its part, is responsible for developing farming operations: settling or resettling the land, training personnel (an especially important task in view of the recent expansion of irrigation to areas where it had not been part of the local tradition), putting up residential and service buildings, obtaining seed and fertilizer, and so forth. Once the network is operating, the Ministry of Reclamation supervises the allocation of water, performs capital repairs, and cleans and maintains local networks on contract; the farms supply ditch riders and other manpower for small jobs.

In actual practice, however, the division of tasks can never be so neat, and close cooperation between reclamation and agricultural officials is essential. Yet reclamation construction organizations in the field tend to take the position that their duties end with the completion of construction, and farm officials act as though irrigation development were none of their concern. The party leadership and the top executives of the two ministries see this failure to cooperate as an extremely serious problem. In 1973, in response to a strongly worded resolution of the party Central Committee, the USSR

Ministries of Reclamation and Agriculture issued a self-critical statement in which they acknowledged that

> in many republics yields in the fields are rising too slowly. Responsibility for this lies with the *irrigators* (who in a number of cases have not fulfilled their design and construction work on time or with sufficient quality), and also with the *agricultural personnel* (who are not giving enough attention to reclaimed land, to the introduction of leading methods of agronomy and crop rotation, or to the application of mineral fertilizers in the necessary quantities).[21]

Yet the problem has not been solved, for three years later another Central Committee resolution repeated several of the same points,[22] as did Brezhnev in a speech in 1978.[23]

This problem of coordination can be seen in every aspect of irrigation development, from the planning and financing of new projects and the supply of materials in the field to operations and maintenance. In general, funding for agricultural development lags behind funding for construction, even though a new project costs nearly as much to develop as to build. One source estimates that for each hectare of irrigated grain, proper development requires from 50 to 70 percent as much capital investment as irrigation construction, and the proportion reaches 100 percent for other types of irrigated crops.[24] In the case of new irrigation networks in previously unsettled areas, the cost of agricultural development significantly *exceeds* that of the basic construction.[25] As of the late 1960s, however, capital funds allocated for this purpose by the Ministry of Agriculture averaged no more than 27 percent of the capital outlay of the Ministry of Reclamation.[26]

The farms themselves, once new projects have been turned over to them, are expected to bring them into operation with their own revenues or central funds allocated by the Ministry of Agriculture. When such funds are not forthcoming, the land is damaged. For example, along the newly constructed Kara-Kum Canal in Turkmenia, an irrigation network has been built to bring water to 350,000 hectares of arid land, but funds for farming development have been allocated to cover only about a third of that area.[27] The local farms, left to their own resources without proper drainage or fertilizers, are exhausting the soil and causing a rapid buildup of salt.[28]

The traditional division of duties between the two ministries affects the allocation of supplies as well as funds, even for high-priority projects. For example, the deputy head of the construction administration for the middle Volga, one of the prime target areas, stated to an interviewer:

> We are fully aware of our responsibility, not only for construction, but also for the agricultural development of new irrigation projects. But here's an example: we turn over irrigated pastureland to the farms unfenced and unsown. Why? Because we don't have any grass seed or wire for fencing. The agricultural organizations and the farms have a far simpler time acquiring all that than we do.[29]

These problems of capital and equipment point once again to the misplaced priorities of the ministries involved.

*Weak organization of operation and maintenance at the local level*

Another symptom of the ministry's priorities is weakness in the local organizations that handle operation and maintenance. The district irrigation system administrations (*raionnye upravleniia orositel'nykh sistem – UOS*) are responsible for maintaining and repairing canals, lateral feeders, and pumping equipment; for allocating water among regions and farms; and for desalinating irrigated land where necessary. Their bonuses are tied to the performance of the irrigated farms in their district, but they do not have the money and resources to execute their tasks. A typical UOS is a small outfit with a large territory to cover. In 1970 the average UOS served about thirty-three collective and state farms with a staff of 150 people. Few of these had much formal training: In that same year, about 15 percent of the personnel in the entire Operations and Maintenance branch of the ministry had higher or secondary education, and presumably few of these were located at the district level. One-third of the personnel of the branch were classified as "engineering-technical workers" (*inzhenerno-tekhnicheskie rabotniki*), but most of these slots (especially at the district level) were occupied by *praktiki*, that is, people whose technical knowledge was acquired on the job rather than through formal training.[30]

Because they are small, the district UOSs must rely on other organizations for manpower and other services. Labor and transportation for maintenance come from the farms, particularly in Central Asia, where district UOSs are especially short of communications facilities and transportation of their own.[31] For major jobs, such as capital repair and desilting for the major canals, the UOSs sign contracts with the nearest reclamation construction firms, which have the necessary machinery.[32] The UOSs receive funds from the state budget for these contracts. The construction firms for their part have an annual plan for such contract work, which is negotiated between the firms and the UOSs and cleared up the ministry's chain of command. The same device is used for the other duties of many of the local UOSs: The reconstruction of existing networks and the improvement of the water supply, the grading of irrigated fields, and the agricultural development of new irrigation networks appear to be handled on contract.[33] Annual plans for such contract work are reported "fulfilled" and "overfulfilled," but until recently the volume was very low, compared to construction.

A real problem appears to be the maintenance of the intrafarm network. Small canals and ditches are vulnerable to silt. In most places, especially in Central Asia, they are still maintained by manual labor.[34] The farms are expected to care for their networks either through their own means or through contracts with reclamation construction firms. In either case, the farms bear the costs. In principle, should a farm fail to maintain its network in working condition, the district UOS has the right to intervene, pay for the work itself, and demand reimbursement from the farm. This would appear to be a great potential source of power, but it is hedged about with many constraints and is apparently seldom invoked: The local UOS must obtain clearance from the District Executive Committee of the local Soviet (*raiispolkom*) before it can move; and besides, it usually does not have the resources to do the job or the money to contract it out, because its annual funding is drawn from the state budget according to a fixed schedule.[35] To give the district UOS a greater incentive to assume responsibility for the upkeep of the intrafarm networks, the ministry in 1970 began linking their bonuses to the output of the local farms, but this has apparently not improved the ability of the UOSs to deal with the problems.[36]

The UOS are also responsible for allocating water among the farms, but the district level is apparently not able to exploit this source of power either. Local requests are balanced at the province level against anticipated stream-flow, canal capacity, and demands from other users.[37] Thus the chief deci-sion-making level in these matters appears to be the province.[38] The district UOSs have little authority over the drawing up of the plans and next to none over their implementation. The Division of Water Use in the district UOS makes daily corrections in the plans,[39] depending on the actual availability of water, but it cannot prevent each farm from distributing its own water as it sees fit, nor can the UOS interfere in the agricultural activities of the farms.[40] Thus, despite the labor the local UOS invests in the allocation process and the stake (both legal and financial) it has in the efficient use of the water, the UOS must apparently stand by helplessly if excess water is allowed to run into a field because, say, the part-time ditch riders have been called off to another job or have left the intake valve open when they go home at night.[41] The farms do not pay for the water, and neither do the UOSs. And although it is occasionally reported that the UOSs fail to stick to the allocation plan,[42] I have never seen any suggestion that the UOSs actually interrupt – or even threaten to interrupt – the supply of irrigation water as a means of forcing the farms not to waste water or to perform their other duties.

In sum, the district organizations for operations and maintenance have no means and no leverage, neither over the farms nor over construction firms in their own ministry. They are, in effect, the ministry's basement. Nothing shows more clearly the bias of the Ministry of Reclamation toward con-struction during the reclamation program's first decade.

*Manpower problems*

The operation of irrigation networks is further hindered by a shortage of trained manpower and the fact that the Ministry of Reclamation has been able to outbid the Ministry of Agriculture by offering incentives that the latter cannot. For example, irrigation construction workers on the Kuibyshev project in the Volga basin are given housing in nearby cities, to which their families are assigned and where they spend weekends. The workers are veterans of the Irtysh-Karaganda project in Central Asia and are permanent employees of construction firms, which move from project to project as a unit.[43] The same arrangements have been used for Central Asian construc-tion crews working in the non-black-earth zone.[44]

The Ministry of Reclamation can call upon party and state authorities in each republic for additional manpower. In 1972, republics were assigned recruitment quotas of additional workers to be assigned to the Ministry of

Reclamation by a special All-Union party-state decree.[45] Consequently, manpower has not been lacking for construction. But for subsequent development of new projects, or their operation, the shortage of qualified personnel on the farms is serious. Specialized irrigation workers on the farms, such as ditch riders, operators for sprinklers and pumping stations, and agronomists specializing in irrigation, are all in short supply. Like drivers, mechanics, and other agricultural workers with technical skills, they can take their talents to the cities, and so they leave in large numbers. The problem is acute even in the highest-priority areas, such as the Volga basin. A party secretary in charge of irrigation development there had this to say:

> We are timely in organizing the training of operators for sprinklers and pumping stations, and ditch riders, in agricultural professional-technical schools; we draw students from the high schools into irrigation work. But for a specialist to stay and work on the farm, you've got to create the right living conditions, supply him with living quarters, cultural and everyday services. But *Glavsredvolgovodstroi*,[46] which is giving most of its attention to irrigation construction, doesn't have the engineering or the materials to build living quarters or services. And that kind of construction is very labor-intensive, it demands skilled hands.[47]

The same secretary went on to give as an example of labor shortages the Dimitrov collective farm in the Red Partisan region of his province: Some 1,750 acres were under the ditch, he said, but on the entire collective farm there were only twenty-two "mechanizers" (i.e., usually driver-mechanics – not necessarily people with skills in irrigation). "On other farms," the secretary said, "the situation is no better."[48]

In the long run, prevailing patterns of migration may ease irrigation's manpower problems, eventually making it a better bet than the northern strategy of developing the non-black-earth zone. Many southern regions, especially Central Asia and the Caucasus, have growing labor surpluses, resulting both from in-migration and high birthrates. Within the Russian Federation, people are moving south, instead of east as they once did. In contrast, the northern and eastern regions of the Soviet Union suffer from out-migration, and so the population there is heavily weighted toward unskilled farmers and pensioners. Consequently, the current expansion of irrigation into southern areas where there has been little before (like the southern Ukraine, the Volga basin, and the northern Caucasus) – in addition to the continued growth of irrigation in traditional centers such as the Transcaucasus and Central Asia – will eventually satisfy several aims simultaneously: not only to increase and stabilize agricultural output, but also to head off the potential problems engendered in Central Asia by a surplus of youthful rural labor and by the relative lag in per capita income of many southern regions.

But in the meantime irrigation planners must constantly take the manpower problem into account. Even within an area of overall labor surplus it may not be possible to coax workers away from settled areas to develop nearly virgin territory unless careful coordination is maintained between

Reclamation and Agriculture, so as to build housing and basic amenities at the same time as the network. This has been achieved in certain important projects, such as the Golodnaia and Karshinskaia steppes and the zone around the Karakum Canal.[49] Even in the most favorable cases, however, resettlement can be expensive and involves delays. For example, despite the inducement of good housing and high salaries, it reportedly took some time before Uzbek farmers consented to settle in sufficient numbers in the Golodnaia Steppe. Recent population trends may be one of the main reasons why so much of the new irrigation effort has been concentrated in the European USSR. For example, it was originally planned to irrigate more than 2.5 million hectares in the Kulunda Steppe between the Ob' and the Irtysh rivers in West Siberia, but the project would have required 140,000 additional agricultural workers, who were not available and probably could not have been attracted to the area. So priority was shifted to the Volga basin instead.[50] Such problems have prompted some experts to oppose any further expansion of construction in new areas and to recommend reconstruction and improvement of existing networks instead.[51]

In the last five years, under steady prodding from the party leadership, the Ministry of Reclamation has taken several steps to deal with its problems. To prevent waste, many new canals are lined with concrete, and water is applied in the fields with mobile sprinklers. These now service 35 percent of the irrigated area of the USSR, compared with 4 percent in 1965.[52] Some of the emphasis of the program has been shifted toward consolidation and project development. Under the last five-year plan (1976–80), funding for reclamation continued to grow as fast as before, but the rate of expansion of new project area was cut.[53] Resources are being channeled preferentially into "integrated" projects – that is, into state farms in which agricultural development is executed in tandem with network construction under a single plan and a single management. In 1976, the first year of the Tenth Five-Year Plan, funding for such projects increased by 23 percent, as against 14 percent for the Ministry of Reclamation as a whole.[54] Agricultural development too is getting more money than in the past. The Volga basin projects, in particular, were scheduled to receive five times more resources for agricultural development during the Tenth Plan than they did during the preceding plan.[55]

In recent years the Ministry of Reclamation has tended to take over a growing share of responsibility for maintenance and operation, even inside the farms.[56] The volume of contract work to be performed on the farms by reclamation crews has been growing rapidly, from 11.2 billion rubles in the Eighth Plan (1966–7) to 21.9 billion rubles in the Ninth Plan (1971–5). But a new problem has cropped up: Many construction organizations are not meeting their plan targets on such contract work, whereas for new network construction, the plan is overfulfilled by a wide margin.[57] Clearly, the incentive structure still favors the latter. As Brezhnev observed at the July 1978 plenum of the Central Committee of the CPSU, agricultural development of new projects continues to lag far behind construction; and many a news item in the Soviet press continues to call attention to problems of maintenance and operation.[58]

In sum, the irrigation program in its first two decades has been wasteful, often ineffective, and in some places even harmful. But does that really matter? What difference does it make for the southern strategy if irrigation is slower to show results than impatient politicians would like? The answer is that water and capital are now so short that Minvodkhoz's misuse of both is driving party leaders into a dilemma.

### Policy consequences

Consider first the implications of scarce water. Delays in bringing new irrigated lands into cultivation mean that over the next few years the actual consumption of water for irrigation will lag behind the levels planned for it. This will give a breathing space to competing water users in the area, which (on past form) they will use to further their own plans, committing the scarce water of the region as though irrigation were not to be a factor. "Business as usual," their behavior seems to say, "until irrigation actually needs the water, and then we'll see." Thus, each year's delay by the Ministry of Reclamation in taking up its planned share of water leads to a distorted mix of outputs, longer on industry, hydropower, inland navigation, and shorter on irrigated agriculture than Moscow intends. But more than that, when the new irrigation systems reach full operation, they will require *more* water than planned because they will use it inefficiently. Further conflict and delay will follow, as irrigators struggle with other water users. The Kremlin will then have the unpleasant task of deciding which of the competitors to curtail, or whether to cut the Gordian knot by committing additional billions to bring in more water from the north. Regardless of the course adopted, we may be sure that the eventual costs of the southern strategy will be far higher, and the benefits longer in coming, than the Kremlin could have imagined in 1966.

Of course, the irrigation program may be curtailed. Capital is now so short in the Soviet Union that that is becoming a distinct possibility. Having enjoyed for so long a virtual blank check, the reclamation program cannot be expected to continue much longer at its present level of funding unless it proves itself. Therefore, the real danger raised by the problems we have discussed in this chapter is that the post-Brezhnev leadership may soon tire of throwing ever more water and capital into the southern strategy. If such is the case, then it will fall short of its only justifying aim, to provide a solid buffer against drought.

Why has the leadership been unable to deal with the Ministry of Reclamation's bias toward new construction and its tendency to neglect other tasks? Such a bias is not an exclusively Soviet phenomenon. The early years of the federal reclamation program in the United States, for example, were marked by the same problem (which nearly caused mass bankruptcy among farmers in the American West).[59] Irrigated agriculture, after all, begins with engineering; and it is therefore a natural tendency for reclamation in the early years to be dominated by engineers. The crucial question is whether this tendency can be overcome. In the United States, it took an outright purge (which was never completely successful) of the powerful chief engineer's office in the Bureau of Reclamation to weaken the engineers' hold over the agency.[60] What will happen in the Soviet Union? The death in early 1979 of the longtime head of Minvodkhoz, E. E. Alekseevskii, may create the occasion for a sweep of personnel. His replacement, N. F. Vasil'ev, comes not from the ministry but from the post of first deputy prime minister of the Russian Federation. Recent Soviet practice has been to appoint the heads of technical ministries from within,[61] and the fact that Vasil'ev is an exception may be a sign that personnel changes are in store for Minvodkhoz. Yet as of this writing there have been no major changes in the ministry's top command since Vasil'ev's appointment.[62]

But as this chapter has sought to show, the sources of the ministry's bias run deeper than any simple matter of dominance by engineers or an entrenched leadership, and it will take more than a shake-up of the ministry's top hierarchy to overcome the problem. The underlying causes have to do partly with the overall style of the Brezhnev agricultural policy, which favors large, centralized programs run by large, centralized ministries. The ministry's bias also stems from the constraints and temptations of the traditional system of management. Construction poses fewer problems of coordination and management than agricultural development or operation and maintenance do, because it is more amenable to large-scale, centralized operation. Under the conditions of a vertically integrated command economy, large-scale, centralized construction is easier to insulate from undependable suppliers, uncooperative partners, and so forth than the ministry's local operations are. It is more easily mechanized, and it can attract manpower. Its performance is easier to evaluate, and its rewards are more direct. We have seen enough of the details of the ministry's operations to conclude that the bias toward construction, and the tendency to neglect development and operations, will be very hard to correct by traditional administrative means.

Finally, a major underlying cause of the program's problems is the technology of irrigation itself. It is not as simple an art as it seems. To work properly, irrigation must be carefully adapted to local conditions, to a great variety of soil types, patterns of rainfall, crop mixes, and locally available manpower. When water runs short, only the people on the spot have the experience and the information to make fast and efficient redistribution among different farms and crops. In other parts of the world, this fact has enabled irrigation communities to maintain an often surprising degree of local autonomy in the face of the pressure and demands of central authorities.[63] This phenomenon has not been apparent in Soviet irrigation because Moscow has long put political control above efficiency of output. But because of its stake in the success of irrigation and because of the latter's demanding technology, the leadership may be persuaded to delegate more authority to local farms and regions, to give them both the latitude and the motivation to use scarce water efficiently. How probable or feasible that is we shall take up again at greater length in the concluding chapter.

In the meantime, what common lessons can be drawn from the three aspects of the Brezhnev program we have just analyzed? That is the subject of the next chapter.

# 10

## CARRYING OUT A THIRD-GENERATION PROGRAM WITH SECOND-GENERATION METHODS

It is apparent from the preceding three chapters that carrying out the Brezhnev programs in the southern USSR has been anything but easy. Moscow's efforts have been plagued by conflict and dissipation of effort, which the central authorities have been unable so far to remedy. The southern strategy is already costing far more, and returning far less, than Khrushchev's hopeful successors could have believed possible in 1965. But in this respect it is faring no worse than the agricultural program in most of the rest of the country.[1] What is the explanation? Why has implementation proved so difficult?

Three main problems, as we have seen in the previous chapters, account for much of the difficulty in implementing the southern programs. The first is evasion. Local managers bend new priorities and rules by taking advantage of weak enforcement, uncertainty, and the leaders' competing objectives. We have seen many examples: Industrial plants spill accumulated wastes when they think they can get away with it; waste-treatment facilities often lag behind primary construction and are not maintained even when they are in operation; power-station operators use uncertainties in streamflow to manipulate reservoir levels to their own advantage; reclamation construction crews take advantage of the fact that most project completions are scheduled for the winter quarter to cut corners, because the project cannot be properly inspected in deep snow;[2] irrigators exceed their quotas even if it damages the soil or causes the farms downstream to run dry. The injured howl; the press denounces the selfish; a few individuals – remarkably few – are punished, but over the last decade the situation does not seem to have changed much.

Over the longer term, the main problem is the agencies' passive obstructiveness. In their planning they have consistently failed to adapt willingly to impending changes in investment and resource use, behaving as though they could not see them coming or as if they believed they would never arrive. In the south of the European USSR, the Ministry of Power has been slow to develop alternate sources of peaking power; the Ministry of the River Fleet lagged in reacting to anticipated reductions in the channel depth of major inland waterways; the Ministry of Agriculture has not made any special effort, even under steady prodding, to bring new irrigation projects into production. Industrial ministries continue to expand into water-short areas, including the critically overused Don basin, and their efforts to make water-saving or waste-reducing process changes are still hardly more than symbolic. Construction firms have delayed in organizing departments to deal specifically with waste treatment. Even then, when the deadlines come and the ministries are caught short, they demand variances and delays; and they get them – at least much of what they ask for – because they too perform indispensable economic functions.

The third problem is misdirected effort. More work has gone into construction than into operation and maintenance; more into starting new projects than into completing them; more toward the development of large-scale, uniform techniques than into adaptation to local conditions; and more into speed and pro forma plan fulfillment than into attention to ultimate results. The agencies have tended to measure their progress by what they put into their programs, not what they are getting out. Consequently, there has been little success in improving quality and correcting shoddy performance in operation and maintenance.

Beneath these problems of evasion, passive obstructiveness, and misdirection lie deeper causes: Local officials have the wrong stake in what they do; no one in particular bears the costs of low-quality or misdirected performance, and no one really knows what those costs are, for there exist few detailed loss functions relating causes to effects.[3] Centralization along vertical lines produces indifference to horizontal integration, and the pressure of taut plans and demanding targets leaves people little opportunity to think more broadly even if they had any incentive to do so.

If these problems have a familiar ring, that is because they are very familiar indeed. To carry out the agricultural program, the Soviet leaders have chosen a strategy of centralized capital investment along traditional lines, and they are executing it by traditional means. It is not surprising, therefore, that they are running into the traditional problems that such an approach has always given them in the past. The Kremlin's response to this has likewise been traditional. To deal with the agencies' evasions, obstructiveness, and misdirected effort, it has used three familiar devices:

1. *Redirection of effort at the margin.* Faced with unanticipated drifts and obstacles, the leadership has attempted to correct them by marginal adjustments in policy. To correct an excessive bias toward "end-of-the pipe" waste treatment, for example, it encourages industries to cut both wastes and water consumption by changing production processes. The Ministry of Reclamation is exhorted to shift toward consolidation instead of expansion and toward reconstruction rather than new construction (which may entail a partial shift of attention back toward Central Asia, where most of the older networks are located). Focusing on "complex" projects is likewise a way of redirecting resources toward a small number of carefully supervised, high-priority projects, another traditional strategy.

This approach relies mainly on administrative fiat and publicity. In the last ten years the Kremlin has drummed out a steady beat of decrees and regulations, usually as joint *postanovleniia* of the Central Committee and the USSR Council of Ministers. Such decrees include unpublished appendixes consisting of long lists of detailed assignments to specific enterprises and locations, with target dates for execution. Although one often reads of cases in which these assignments are not met, they are far from vague exhortation. Through such decrees, formal authority over water use and water quality has gradually been made stricter, clearer, and more detailed.

2. *Manipulation of the incentive system.* Fines, bonuses, and performance indicators have been adjusted here and there. Polluters know they are slightly more likely to be fined or prosecuted than ten years ago. Reclamation construction crews can collect their bonuses – in principle – only if their work is certified complete, and local irrigation districts now find their bonuses tied to the performance of the farms they service. In some areas, like Kirgizia and the Don basin, charges are being levied for water use. Higher compensation is demanded when industry or hydropower take over agricultural land. Charges on capital have been raised in project planning. On the whole, however, there have been few new uses of economic levers. For example, despite the fact that charges have been levied for water use in Kirgizia and the Don basin, a decade's discussion of effluent charges and pricing systems for water elsewhere in the country has produced no change in official policy, and water remains underpriced or free.

3. *Direct local application of political authority.* Through the pages of the Soviet press we catch frequent glimpses of the local party apparatus at work, ramrodding through a high-priority irrigation system or the construction of rural roads in Saratov province,[4] overseeing pollution control in Iaroslavl' province[5] and allocating scarce irrigation water in Stavropol' province,[6] arbitrating among clashing bureaucracies over the Cheboksar project on the Volga, or knocking heads at a high-level meeting of the *collegia* of the Ministries of Reclamation and Agriculture.[7] This is undoubtedly the most important of the four mechanisms, as the party plays its traditional roles of broker, expediter, overseer, and coordinator.

These responses employ familiar organizational and administrative levers, applied from Moscow by central political authority and mediated by the local party apparatus. They have worked well enough in the past. Will they not do so now, again, enabling the southern programs to muddle through as the rest of the Soviet economy does, eventually producing – if the leadership perseveres long enough and pays the price – more or less the results the Kremlin desires?

The answer is that the southern programs pose a more delicate and demanding challenge, and impose more serious constraints, than most Soviet development has faced in the past, and in these respects they foreshadow the Soviet economy of a very near tomorrow.

## The future: constraints and objectives

*The leadership is severely constrained by its own objectives.* In any optimization problem there are as many constraints as there are objectives. The present generation of Soviet leaders is experiencing the force of this principle more than their predecessors ever did, for unlike the Kremlin in

Stalin's day, which kept its objectives few and simple, today's leaders are pursuing a mix of numerous aims. Consequently, they are correspondingly more constrained. Much of the delicacy of reallocating effort and resources in the southern USSR comes from the fact that none of the major aims being pursued there can be sacrificed more than marginally, whether we are talking about peaking power, industrial water supply, waterway channel depths, irrigation water, or spawning grounds and commercial fishing. The semblance of interest-group power, incidentally, comes from these constraints. It is not the clout of power-grid operators as an interest group, for example, that prevents the party leadership from turning over hydropower stations to the Ministry of Reclamation, or that of the Ministry of the Chemical Industry that keeps the water-quality basin inspectors on a tight leash, but the multiple and competing objectives of the leaders themselves, in which electricity and chemicals loom large. The Kremlin is constrained to a large extent by its own choices, which confront the leaders with painful trade-offs at every margin, not just in agriculture but in the other major sectors of the economy as well. To name only a few: Stressing technological innovation exacts a cost in lost current production; raising birthrates in Slavic areas means losing women from a tight labor force; arresting the deterioration of air and water quality constrains industrial expansion, particularly in the Moscow region; buying grain on foreign markets consumes foreign exchange that might be used instead for the purchase of technology; increasing capital investment means holding back consumer welfare in the near term, with attendant effects on worker morale and productivity – the list goes on, underscoring the one central fact about the Soviet economy in its third generation: The trade-offs themselves are not new (they are inherent in the scarcity of resources anywhere), but they are more tightly binding, because the leadership is pursuing a broader and more interdependent set of objectives, whereas at the same time there are fewer uncommitted resources left to throw into battle. Any marginal change of course in the country's economic policy must be carved out of the growth plans of some other crucial objective. More important, the danger that any such changes may cause a chain of unforeseen consequences for other vital objectives naturally makes the Kremlin cautious about pushing hard. The example of Khrushchev's impulsiveness and its disastrous results has not been forgotten.

Further, the leaders' objectives are constraining not merely because there are more of them and fewer uncommitted resources than a generation ago. The objectives themselves are more demanding, for two reasons in particular: *Every local situation must be treated differently* and *the costs of uncertainty make planning difficult.*

The traditional Soviet system has done well at producing either a small number of large, integrated, custom-designed projects (such as hydropower plants, strategic rockets, BAM, the Kama River truck complex) or a *large* number of smaller, relatively uniform systems (mass housing, fighter planes, consumer durables). Its great weakness lies in its lesser ability to produce quickly large numbers of custom-made systems, each one adapted to a highly individual setting (computer software systems, small and medium research instruments, novel architectural design, automation of local workplaces and auxiliary tasks, and imaginative use of new construction materials). The general reasons for this are well known: Vertical segregation prevents customers from obtaining components and materials quickly from several ministries simultaneously.[8] The customer, unless he has high priority, has little leverage in what is still in most areas a seller's market. And the customer's own plan encourages him to reach for ready-made solutions and uniform designs.

In the programs underlying the southern strategy, these defects are serious. Each irrigation area, for example, has its own complex mosaic of soil structures; regimes of moisture, streamflow, and temperature; crops; industrial wastes; available manpower and machinery. Therefore, construction, operation, and maintenance for reclamation and conservation must be carefully tailored to each. The price for applying uniform approaches is not merely inefficiency; it sometimes results in severe losses, even eventual abandonment of the land.[9] The same is true of waste-treatment technology, for the composition of pollutants in any given stretch of stream depends not only on the production processes of the industries located there but also on the highly variable chemical changes that occur once effluents mix together and react to local conditions of temperature, sunlight, and so on. Each plant's waste-reduction scheme must be its own. But there has been a tendency instead for the Soviet environmental program to skimp on research and focus on building general-purpose municipal facilities instead, and for local industries simply to dispose of their wastes through them, with bad results for the systems' operation.

As the Soviet economy matures, it faces more and more situations of this kind, branches of activity in which a thing must be done well if it is to be done at all, and that means there must be closer attention to quality and detail. The common feature of these modern tasks is not necessarily that they are technologically advanced (although an increasing number are) but that they are varied and exacting. An irrigation project that is lost to salt from inadequate drainage or that delivers water without regard to the requirements of individual soils and crops is as worthless as an industrial plant that allows dust to come in contact with integrated microcircuitry, imperfections in high-performance alloys, bubbles in optical glass, or leaky welds in pipelines or nuclear-power-plant cooling systems. In agriculture, as in industry, the trend is toward closer tolerances, purer and newer and custom-made materials, technologies that draw on several branches of industry simultaneously, stringent quality requirements, and individually tailored designs.

The special problem of dealing with water as a natural resource is that it flows in random, unpredictable amounts. In the most general sense, all the programs used as examples in this book have the purpose of fighting this problem: diversions, reclamation networks, effluent storage tanks, and all the rest. But as resources approach full use, as competing purposes become more tightly bound to one another, uncertainty, however much it may be reduced through buffers of all kinds, has greater consequence. Can the central authorities successfully control the costs of uncertainty and their distribution? In the southern programs the answer so far appears to be no. As we have seen, no mechanism of sufficient subtlety exists at the local level to prevent hydropower operators from passing on the costs of unforeseen variations in streamflow to other users, to enable local irrigation districts to respond efficiently to local shortages or to control cheating among farms,[10] or to allow basin inspectors to cope with local crises in pollution control.

Like the last two trends we have just discussed, reducing and allocating the costs of uncertainty is a growing problem not just for the southern agricultural programs but for the entire Soviet economy. The country's greater involvement in international trade exposes it more than ever before[11] to uncertainties in price and supply (to say nothing of political uncertainties) for such commodities as grain, oil, high-technology manufactured goods, bauxite and other minerals, and so on. The Soviets' greater dependence on internally generated research and development means they owe progressively more of their economic growth to science, a notoriously unpredictable enterprise, rather than other countries' proven technologies. Most of all, the country's growing shortage of labor confronts the leadership with the uncertainties resulting from millions of individual decisions on migration and family size.

Of course, uncertainty is nothing new in Soviet managerial experience, especially the uncertainties produced by the command economy itself. But the Soviet manager's standard response to it – to ward off uncertainty by creating a buffer zone around himself, thus making himself as independent as possible[12] – has itself become a costly liability. Managers who react to the uncertainties of technological innovation by refusing to innovate are passing along the costs of obsolescence to their ministry or to the economy as a whole. Enterprise heads who deal with uncertainty of supply and manpower by hoarding materials and labor are likewise making the rest of the economy pay for their extra security. Hydropower operators who respond to uncertainties in streamflow by arbitrarily cutting off other users are transferring the costs to the entire basin. The techniques used are evasion, false reporting, and passive resistance, and there is nothing in the traditional arsenal of Soviet administrative instruments that has succeeded so far in correcting the problem, except high-priority attention, which by definition cannot be applied to more than a handful of places.

In sum, the stringency of the southern programs' requirements, together with the delicacy of balancing them against one another and against other established programs, magnifies the effects of the traditional behavior of individuals and institutions in a command economy; but it also constrains the ability of the leaders to deal with those effects through the traditional instruments of power. Whatever the existing machinery can do, it is doing, but it is apparently unable to prevent local officials from evading, obstructing, or displacing the leaders' aims. The practical consequence is that implementation is not moving fast enough to save the leadership from being cornered into the unpleasant choice of cutting its losses by cutting back the irrigation program or accepting the much greater expense of bringing in additional water from the north. The latter would mean, in effect, retreating to an "extensive" strategy in place of the present "intensive" one, definitely a failure by comparison to the leaders' present aims.

Part of the explanation for this state of affairs is undoubtedly to be found in the dual character of the Brezhnev programs: On the one hand, they call for rapid and massive infrastructural investment; on the other, they call for efficiency and fine tuning. The first has naturally tended to dominate the second, because once the basic idea of investing in the countryside was accepted, it could be treated as just another industrialization program, a familiar business to Soviet officials at all levels. But the second aim is unfamiliar, its complexities unanticipated and therefore underestimated. In that sense, the real reform in implementation will begin when the present massive infusion of capital begins to decline, and not before.

But the more fundamental problem is that the Kremlin's traditional instruments are unable to produce fine tuning on a large scale, and developing new ones poses the problem of maintaining control. Do we find that the leaders use thumbs? Consider now the implications of trying to use fingers: Suppose that the central leadership attempts to overcome the obstacles to the southern programs by developing regional authorities, thus placing decision-making power in the hands of people close enough to the ground to be familiar with local conditions and enabling them to span the several interests that are currently in conflict. Examples of such organizations would be irrigation districts that would have authority over both the networks and the farms; reservoir authorities in charge of both water supply for irrigation and supply of peaking power; and water-quality agencies with real enforcement powers over industrial ministries and extensive freedom to contract with (and, in case of nonperformance, to recover damages from) ministerial research institutes and construction firms for waste-treatment design and construction. What would happen, in short, if the central authorities attempted to carry out the southern programs by building local organizations with a horizontal span instead of a vertical one?

Any such arrangement would require an overhaul of the incentive system to enable the leadership to retain overall control through indirect leverage rather than through direct administrative dictation. Price levers are the most obvious means. For example, Soviet specialists have long discussed ways of putting a price on the various uses of water, including effluent charges and charges for delivery of industrial process water and irrigation water. There is no consensus on the precise principles to be used, but there is already general agreement among the experts that some pricing system is the only way to attach commensurable values to the many competing uses for water in each locality, thus creating the basis for a smooth balancing at the margin between competing uses.

For economic measures to work, however, they must take precedence over administrative orders. In the Soviet Union today, money quantities are simply not the determining influence over behavior, because their effects are muted, distorted, or drowned out altogether by administrative overrides and countermands, such as last-minute changes in plan targets, supply orders, or simply a phone call from the party *raikom* (district committee). Economic contracts lose much of their force because, in the event of nonfulfillment, the injured party cannot sue for significant compensation or damages. Despite the recent spread of jurisconsults attached to each enterprise, whose job is to monitor compliance with contract agreements, everyone in the enterprise knows that the really important indicator is the system of plan targets contained in the enterprise planning documents – an administrative quantity, not an economic one.[13] Profits too are a secondary consideration, despite the publicity given to them in the last ten years, because the target that really matters is the volume of "realized output," which is but one small step up from the traditional war-horse of Soviet indicators, the *val*, or gross output. The same would inevitably be true of a pricing system for water: If a fine, an effluent charge, or punitive prices for above-plan water use began to bite seriously into an agency's capacity to meet its assigned targets, one can be sure that its parent ministry would pay the price, or appeal to political authority, but would not change spontaneously its pattern of output or investment. The Kremlin would find itself bombarded with pleas for variances, even as it is now.

We are now getting to the heart of the problem of reform. Measures like deconcentration and the use of economic mechanisms require the leadership (and for that matter the administrative class as a whole) to accept explicitly more uncertainty, more local latitude, more local control of information, more individual leeway – in short, to accept explicit constraints on their own power and freedom of intervention. This they are manifestly not ready to do. To leaders who have come up through the old school, the proposition that less power is more must sound absurd. And they are not wrong, at least for the present, for nothing would lead sooner to disaster than to turn over the economy to that withered and deformed hidden hand that is the Soviet system of prices and incentives as it is today, a system so distorted by artifice and inconsistency that it is incapable of clearing markets or encouraging efficient behavior. That point aside, it is difficult to see how any doctrine of restrained central power could be reconciled with official Soviet ideology, Russian political tradition and culture, or the understandable concern of the party apparatus to preserve the source of its power.

Throughout this book we have seen a certain self-restraint on the part of the leaders, as though, despite their frustration over the constraints that surround them, they do not quite know what else to try. Frequently, they react with no more than a scolding in *Pravda* to instances of malperformance that in earlier times would soon have sent the offenders to lesser jobs in colder places, convulsed the organization charts of the agencies involved, and launched the media into all-too-familiar campaigns of sloganeering and exhortation. By and large, the leaders have not done these things, and the ironic result is that, by half-acquiescing in the constraints bearing on their traditional powers without at the same time confronting the problem of developing new ones, the leaders have had to endure even higher levels of uncertainty, more local latitude (but of a highly unproductive, even anarchic, sort), and greater constraints on their ability to get their way, than they might have under a deconcentrated system. They watch as capital and resources are diverted in directions they did not intend; they are gradually cornered into accepting a stepped-up timetable for a project (the interbasin diversions) that they initially envisioned as lying well over the horizon; and they find themselves forced to choose between cutting their losses in agriculture (thus settling for modest results in a program of great importance to them) and venturing even greater sums of money (but without any real assurance of success).[14] Far from being exceptional, moreover, such frustrations are increasingly typical of the Soviet system in its third generation, not just in agriculture but in other areas of the economy as well. What kind of power is that? What accounts for the curious powerlessness of a leadership that, in principle, has absolute power?

This book argues that the explanation lies, first, in the multiple constraints bearing upon the leaders, arising partly from their own objectives and partly from the increasing delicacy and complexity of the policies they are pursuing, as well as the growing scarcity of the resources available to them and the intractability of the human material. The leaders' traditional instruments of power are well suited to mobilizing masses of people and resources for large undertakings, suppressing or inhibiting opposition to them, and intervening to make mid-course corrections in the cases that have sufficiently high priority to warrant the leaders' scarce attention. But the demanding technologies, scarce resources, and unpredictable and only partially governable human behaviors of a post-mobilizational, late-industrial society transform the leaders' absolute power into blunt tools, which the leaders themselves are reluctant to use. The essential problem of third-generation reform, to repeat, is ultimately that of developing new instruments of power – fingers instead of thumbs – that will give the leaders a capacity not for closer control but for finer tuning. Yet at the same time the thumbs, however much their use may be suspended here and there, remain the main instrument of power in the political system. This state of affairs cannot change quickly or broadly or too explicitly without disrupting long-established careers, institutions, procedures, habits, and beliefs – in short, shaking the political system itself. The result is a partial political paralysis that the Brezhnev leadership has never succeeded in resolving.

It is worth stressing, however, that this partial paralysis does not mean that power is slowly passing from the hands of those who have traditionally held it – the Politburo and the party apparatus – into other hands. The power of the party leaders to make the key decisions is not being questioned, challenged, or taken over by any organization or group. But the ultimate success or failure of new programs depends less on the big decisions than on the myriad small ones (or even nondecisions) by which policies are designed, carried out, adjusted, and refined. That is why the greatest enemy of the party leadership, and the main threat to their effective power, is not opposition but diversion, obstruction, and erosion.

At times, if the central leaders happen to be divided, such obstruction can be so nearly open that it verges on defiance: The USSR Academy of Sciences, at the height of the Lysenkoite repression of Mendelian genetics, bootlegged molecular biology and genetics research through its chemistry and physics divisions, bypassing the Lysenkoite strongholds in the biology division.[15] Soviet jurists ground down and finally defeated Khrushchev's "anti-parasite" laws,[16] and the military resisted his attempts to reduce the size of the armed forces. But these instances are exceptional compared to the leaders' greater problem: the quiet but universal gnawing of bureaucratic termites, who quietly undermine the policy that looks sound in *Pravda* editorials. Thus Gosplan and the other state committees routinely reallocate resources to cover shortages and emergencies as they arise, and the leaders discover at the end of each plan period that their priorities have drifted, sometimes by a great deal. The Academy of Sciences manages in a variety of ingenious ways to deflect the leaders' efforts to make it assume a greater role in technological innovation at the expense of pure research. The Ministry of Instrument Making resists expanding the manufacture of new types of research instrumentation.[17] The Ministries of Agriculture and Reclamation have the dysfunctions we have already seen. Soviet development of atomic power has been hampered by the failure of the relevant ministries to work together.[18] Industrial ministries resist new products and processes developed in other ministries. In short, getting the ministries and state agencies to march together in time to the beat of the official music turns out to be the leaders' most frustrating task. And what state organizations can do, ordinary people can do even better. Their decisions to reproduce or not, to migrate or not, to learn Russian themselves or have it taught to their children, to buy or not, and what, and when, frustrate the leaders' plans even more than the behavior of bureaucrats.

The sum of all these small decisions deflects the central authorities from their course, forcing them either to alter their priorities or to expend additional resources and effort to get their way. The unresponsiveness of the instruments industry, for example, has left the leadership no choice but to commit foreign exchange to purchase Western equipment, especially in biology and medicine. Similarly, lagging technological development in the oil industry and local misallocations of effort in geological exploration are forcing the Soviet Union to turn to the West for advanced drilling equipment, and the reluctance of workers to settle in Siberia makes it necessary to fly in drilling crews for temporary duty, an expensive and inefficient stopgap. The project to divert northern rivers is due to a combination of agency resistances and Central Asian demography. In their cumulative impact on the leaders' priorities and performance, such microdecisions add up to major constraints on the leaders' power.

What are the implications of these constraints for our understanding of power in the Soviet political system? They do not mean that the Soviet Union is evolving toward pluralism, although it is not hard to understand why Western specialists on Soviet politics are at loggerheads on this question. If we gauge power according to the final outputs of the political system, we shall be tempted to say that what the central leadership is losing, the technical specialists, institutional or interest groups, or even the masses must be gaining. On the other hand, if we restrict the definition of power, as many Western political scientists do, to the ability to win in observable conflicts or issues, then we shall conclude instead that institutional subverters and obstructors, however much they deflect the Kremlin's aims, do not have power, but at most a sort of negative capacity for drag,[19] which can be overcome, at any one place and time, if the political authorities choose to make an issue and are willing to devote the necessary attention and effort to getting their way. Much of the disagreement among Western scholars over whether interest groups exist in Soviet politics, and over whether it is proper to call the Soviet system pluralistic, thus revolves around implicit differences in the definition of power.[20]

Perhaps we should start instead from the question of where *resources* for power in Soviet politics come from. Part of the answer, at least, is clear: The resources that give organizations their latitude (and thus their ability to frustrate the leadership) do not derive from them but from the sum of the leaders' own objectives and values. No competing resources exist in the Soviet Union that can serve as a basis for autonomous, organized political power. "Industrial authority, scientific knowledge, military expertise, national popularity, personal wealth, ethnic-group support," wrote Huntington and Brzezinski in a phrase that has yet to be improved upon, "are neither autonomous nor deployable on the plains of politics."[21] Instead, they are, so to speak, on loan from the center. The latitude they allow to those below fluctuates, as we have seen in this book, with the leaders' own objectives and the extent of unity or disunity within the top leadership. The spectacular glory, collapse, and partial renaissance of hydropower is a vivid illustration. It follows that the relative tolerance of a united leadership for institutional obstruction and diversion below, which has been one of the most remarkable features of the Brezhnev period, is due not to any power in the hands of interest groups but to the leaders' expedient or baffled self-restraint (we cannot yet know which – perhaps both) in the face of the complex and frustrating situations before them. The ability of the oil industry to ignore the environmental program, that of the Ministry of Power to deny water to competing users, that of hydropower to lord it over reclamation (or the opposite a decade later), of Gosplan to short-change agriculture as soon as the leadership appears to waver – all these seeming instances of political clout in the hands of interest groups are ultimately contingent upon the rise and fall of priorities in the Kremlin, and most of what looks like interest-group politics is in reality no more than the playing out of the leaders' own objectives.

To be sure, the leaders do not live in a vacuum. Their objectives, their perceptions, and their calculations are the product of constant interaction with their surroundings, through which the leaders absorb new facts, new ideas, and even new values. Consequently, one can make too much of the distinction between "state" and "society" in the Soviet system or between "the central leaders" and "the rest." Nevertheless, in the third generation of Soviet power as in the first two, there is no evidence that the bureaucratic resources delegated by the suzerains of the command state are appropriable by the vassals (and still less by their clerics), and therefore, unlike land or capital, delegated bureaucratic resources do not engender the basis for power independent of the center. In this sense it is still possible, more than twenty-five years after Stalin's death, to construct a plausible case for calling the Soviet system totalitarian.[22]

But that does not necessarily mean that the leaders are able to get their way quickly or cheaply. To shift policies in any large industrial economy is like changing the course of an ocean liner under full steam. In addition, there are in the Soviet system obstacles to the ready flow of information and new ideas, of people, and even (because of things like unfinished construction and "hidden reserves") of material resources. These reinforce the ability of organizations to obstruct and deflect the leaders' aims. But that is not the same thing as power, as we can see from the following illustrations:

Rearguard resistance.
Political resources can be taken away from a program that has lost priority, but they cannot be taken away *quickly*. And in the meantime, while a previously high-priority program is being scaled down, a declining agency can use the resources remaining to it to fight a rearguard action. Such "slowly decaying" resources take several forms: (a) survival of attitudes corresponding to the earlier set of priorities; (b) survival of "former" people in established bureaucratic positions (e.g., the continuing influence of Lysenkoites in the bureaucracy of the Academy of Sciences);[23] (c) monopoly of key personnel and skills by the previously dominant agency; difficulty of reassigning them quickly to new agencies and tasks; control over key positions in the field (e.g., continued control by hydropower operators over allocation and timing or water resources, despite the official shift of power to reclamation and agriculture).

Carry-over from related high-priority tasks.
A program in decline may belong to an institution whose other missions remain vital and close to the leadership's own values and highest priorities. Thus Khrushchev had great difficulty in cutting down the traditional land forces in the military, because the armed forces as a whole remained vital to the leadership, and therefore the leadership had to proceed cautiously against the opposition of old tank commanders and artillerists. The Ministry of Power managed to retain a commanding voice in water-resource management through the operation of hydropower facilities because energy as a whole remains a high-priority concern. On a lesser level, the hydropower design agency, Gidroproekt, remained influential partly because it was given new high-priority tasks, like the design of nuclear-power plants on the Kama River project, and partly because hydropower remained important east of the Urals.

Congruence of values.
Some approximation to autonomy is gained by groups whose functions and outlooks are so close to those of the political leadership that no disagree-

ment exists between them on basic values. Within such overall basic agreement, however, serious smaller disagreements can occur. A prominent recent example is the ability of the USSR Academy of Sciences to resist pressure to expel Andrei Sakharov (or, for that matter, Trofim Lysenko), and to delay for several years the admission of party administrators like S. P. Trapeznikov to full membership.But as the Sakharov episode also shows, the leadership does not lack the power to get its way if it wishes badly enough to override self-imposed inhibitions and competing objectives (such as the desire to conciliate Western public opinion).

In sum, an institution that *once* had high priority manages to retain some of its influence for a time. And the power of an institution whose *basic* mission has high priority spills over to those parts of its job that have less, because of its fundamental indispensability to the leadership. So even though the power resources of institutions are essentially *derived* from the priorities of the leadership, their flow is neither even nor instantaneous.

So far in discussing resources for power we have dealt only with the relations between the central leadership and the state institutions. Properly speaking, what the former delegates to the latter (money, materials, manpower, and authority) should more appropriately be called instruments of power rather than resources, because the ultimate resources for power are nowhere but in the minds of ordinary people, that is, in the faith, greed, or fear that cause them to move in response to the will of others. The leader with power is the one who finds the right levers to engage these individual motives for his purpose through appropriate instruments. The dilemma of *both* central leaders and state institutions in the Soviet Union today is that the levers traditionally available to them, which were successful enough in the first two generations of Soviet industrialization, are now insufficient. The responses they bring from local officials and people in the field are slow and grudging, and attended by such severe side effects that the original aims of leaders and institutions alike are diluted or diverted. This is perhaps the ultimate reason why Soviet government institutions do not develop power vis-à-vis the party leadership and apparatus: Hamstrung themselves by their inability to command effective performance from their own personnel, they require the party's intervention and helping hand. How then can they offer the central leadership the initiative and effective performance that might give them a basis for bargaining for autonomy? The only exception here may be the military.

Controlling diversion, obstruction, and erosion is of course not a new problem in Soviet administration; in fact, it is one of the oldest. Much of the importance and power of the party apparatus stems from its functions as a corrector of the "unplanned and irrational" behavior of local officials and people. Over the years, a characteristic Soviet administrative style has developed in response to the leaders' mistrust of the latitude of organizations. One of its rules is to delegate as little as possible. Compared with their Western counterparts, Soviet leaders and apparatus officials attend personally to a great mass of detail, handling decisions that in Western organizations would be disposed of lower down. Another device is to multiply watchdogs, inspections, "raids," formal reports at district party headquarters, and so forth. Still another traditional device is to surround agencies and officials with targets, plans, and performance indicators of all kinds, to bind their behavior to the desired pattern. These classic devices of Soviet administration have well-known consequences, familiar to Westerners and Soviets alike. Ordinary decision making is made slow and rigid, dependent upon the energy and health of the top-ranking officials; watchdogs are eventually co-opted into "family circles" of common interest by the local officials they supervise; party officials are overwhelmed with detail and end up spending much of their time putting out fires; and performance indicators do their job so well that they bind the lion but encourage the fox. These side effects were harmful enough in the days of coal-and-steel industrialization; but in the age of microelectronics and high-technology agriculture, they are disastrous.

The solutions to these problems do not lie in simple-sounding expedients like deconcentration or market socialism. The cardinal issue in Soviet reform is how to reconcile the third-generation requirements we have seen illustrated in this book with the leaders' imperative requirement for control. Is such an apparent squaring of the circle possible for a political system that inherits from its first two generations a lingering distrust in the truth-revealing virtues of public conflict, apprehension over the likely behavior of the autonomous individual, acute discomfort over uncertainty, and a total rejection of the hidden hand?

The answer depends above all on how dire the need for change will appear to Brezhnev's heirs, and this question brings us back to agriculture, to the future of reform, and to the questions raised at the beginning of the book.

# 11
# CONCLUSIONS: LESSONS
# OF THE BREZHNEV
# POLICIES AND THE
# FUTURE OF REFORM

Prior to the 1970s there was not a decade in the turbulent history of the Soviet Union that did not put the political system to the test. By comparison, the last ten years were a period of calm; consequently, we must bear in mind that the policies we have examined in this book were formed and carried out in an unusually benign atmosphere. But beginning in the 1980s the Soviet political system faces two further tests, one political and one economic. The first is a sweeping change in political leadership. Within the next few years power will pass to a new generation of rulers, not only in the Politburo, but also in the top several hundred positions of the party and government. Incredible as it may seem, this will be the first true succession in the Soviet elite since the Great Purge of 1938–9.[1] One may say without much exaggeration that nearly two-thirds of a century after the 1917 Revolution, the Soviet political system is just beginning its third generation. The second test is economic. The country will face shortages of several key resources, particularly energy, manpower, and capital, each of which has the potential to create a crisis as serious as the one in agriculture in the 1960s.[2] Together these two impending challenges may create a climate with more possibilities for changing the traditional structure and rules of Soviet politics than at any time since the 1920s.[3]

As they react to this grim and complex picture, Brezhnev's would-be successors are bound to be influenced by their perception of the success or failure of his agricultural and natural-resource programs, not only because these have grown into one of the largest segments of the Kremlin's budget, but also because they are the only instance in their recent experience of a high-priority, country-wide innovation in policy. Accordingly, in this concluding chapter we evaluate the lessons of the Brezhnev policies and attempt to draw from them the implications for the future of policy reform in the next two decades.

## A preliminary balance sheet

How does the record of the last fifteen years of agricultural and related reforms appear from Moscow? The results can be measured by three different standards. The most basic one is whether, thanks to the Brezhnev program, the Soviet leaders have successfully countered the clear and immediate threats that created an agricultural crisis in the first place. In particular: After fifteen years of the Brezhnev policy is the country now safe from the humiliation of periodic crop failure, with all its consequences?

The answer so far is no. Year-to-year variations in farm output remain as dizzying as a generation ago, mainly because of weather; the difference in grain output between 1975 and 1976, for example, was 84 million tons. Soviet farmers are once again resorting to some of the risky practices of the Khrushchev years, planting in marginal lands and reducing clean fallow in arid areas.[4] Soviet grain reserves provide a buffer, but only a partial one.[5] In bad years, such as 1972, 1975, and 1979, Soviet agriculture has seemed more vulnerable and more dependent upon the outside world than ever. Though in the last fifteen years Soviet farm output (as measured by a three-year moving average) has increased by half,[6] the leadership expected to do better than that and on the basis of that expectation pursued a rapid expansion of animal husbandry. Demand for fodder has far outrun supply,[7] and neither the tripling of agricultural capital stock that has taken place in the last fifteen years nor the greatly expanded output of fertilizer and farm machinery has closed the gap.

However, the gap exists not simply because agricultural output failed to increase as fast as was expected but also because the leadership evidently made a deliberate choice, once the gap appeared, not to allow it to interfere wth their plans for livestock expansion but to rely instead on imports to cover the shortfall as much as possible.[8] This represented a very substantial change in traditional Soviet behavior. In the 1950s and 1960s the Soviet leaders' first goal was autarky, as it had been more or less continuously since the end of the First Five-Year Plan. When the harvest was bad, they slaughtered livestock to economize on feed, but until 1963 they had never imported more than 1 million tons of grain in any year. In 1975, in contrast, the Soviets imported 26 million tons of foreign grain from the United States and limited the slaughter of livestock as much as possible.[9] For the next four years the Soviet Union imported considerably more than 10 million tons of grain each year, spending billions in foreign exchange to maintain livestock, apparently reconciled to the idea of depending on foreign suppliers in one of the world's most unstable markets.

This apparently deliberate policy means that massive imports by themselves should not be interpreted as a failure of Brezhnev's policy, but simply that foreign suppliers were being used to provide a buffer that an overextended Soviet agriculture as yet could not. This was a very different situation from the pathetic agricultural failures of the 1950s and 1960s. Soviet leaders may worry about the opportunity costs of so much imported grain and about the future availability of oil to pay for it,[10] but they are no longer on the brink of disaster as they once were. In this sense, then, the Brezhnev program by the end of the 1970s had succeeded in moving the country well away from the nadir of 1963.

Then came the American grain embargo of 1980. At this writing the embargo has failed to cause the Soviets major or lasting hardship. From July 1979 to June 1980 they managed to import, by one path or another, 31.5

million tons of grain, compared to their original target of 34 million tons. Though they had to pay as much as 25 percent more than the American selling price, the extra hard currency was easily available at a time of record gold and oil prices.[11]

More interesting, however, are the possible effects of the embargo on the attitudes of the Soviet leadership. These men, who were reared on Stalinist autarky and for whom it was a large step to allow themselves to depend on world markets for a major and vital commodity, have been given a stunning reminder of the risks. What lesson will they draw from it? They may well conclude that it was unwise, in retrospect, to have allowed themselves to slip into a situation in which the centerpiece of their agricultural policy became a *pièce en prise*, hostage to the goodwill of the American adversary. If they do, then it will not be hard to explain to the Soviet people who is responsible for the lack of meat on their plates. The net effect of the embargo may simply be to hand the Soviet leadership a ready way to liquidate a gap that, in view of the foreign exchange it ate up, may have been dimly viewed within a part of the Soviet elite to begin with.[12] On the other hand, the failure of the attempted embargo may encourage the Soviet leaders to persevere in the present course, as they may reason that they have too much invested in the livestock program to turn back.

A second and stiffer standard by which to evaluate the Brezhnev program is whether Soviet agriculture can soon reach a sustained takeoff. What such a takeoff means in economic or agronomic terms may be difficult to define, but in political terms it is quite clear: The infrastructural transformation currently under way must reach a point soon at which the heaviest part of the job is done and the need for further massive investment declines, before the political coalition behind the Brezhnev program weakens and agriculture's bloated share of the capital investment budget comes under attack. How soon? The grace period may be no longer than Brezhnev's dwindling lifetime, for capital is now so short that agriculture is certain to be cut as soon as he is gone, or maybe even before.

Read in terms of this looming deadline, the latest statistics must make discouraging reading in the Kremlin. The major indexes of productivity and return on capital say that, far from producing a takeoff, agricultural investment is yielding rapidly diminishing marginal returns.[13] Of course, to a degree, that is just what one would expect. The Brezhnev program involved nothing less than a wholesale transformation of the countryside, and it will not produce a fast return. Whole industries have been launched, millions of people trained or retrained, and so forth. Until the enormous input has been assimilated, returns are bound to be very low, but in time they are also bound to improve.

Presumably this is also the argument of the program's supporters, but it is bound to weaken politically as time goes on, for two reasons. First, the requirements for investment in agricultural infrastructure seem to have no end, and filling one need only exposes another. For example, the latest of many Soviet concerns is rural roads. Only 40 percent of all collective and state farms have any hard-surface roads at all, and only 17 percent have ten kilometers or more. What exists is poorly built and maintained. Now that Soviet farms are increasingly mechanized and interdependent, their inaccessibility in bad weather (which traditionally includes much of the late winter and spring, the infamous *rasputitsia*) has become intolerable. Yet the job of building an all-weather network of rural roads has hardly begun, and it promises to cost further billions.[14] Other tasks that are still at their beginning include construction of service buildings and rural housing, supply of spare parts and maintenance services for agricultural machinery, transportation, storage, processing and preservation facilities for produce – the list goes on and on, seemingly endless.

Second, looming in the 1980s are serious shortages of manpower, water, fuel, and foreign exchange. We shall consider their larger implications in a moment, but as far as agriculture is concerned they raise the very unpleasant prospect that to make good on what has already been invested, the leaders may be required to invest even more. Consider manpower first: Despite major efforts to raise farm incomes and increase the amenities of rural life, Moscow has failed to dissuade the young and the skilled from leaving the farm. From 1971 to 1974, 2.6 million tractor drivers and combine and machine operators were trained in what must rank as one of the world's most ambitious rural education programs. Yet during that period the net number of rural workers in those categories rose by little more than a quarter million;[15] in fact, for the entire period from 1965 to 1979 it has increased by only 1.3 million (from 3.1 million to 4.4 million).[16] Some vital agricultural regions are especially affected, such as the non-black-earth zone, the Volga basin, and Kazakhstan. But people with employable skills will undoubtedly continue to leave these areas, for the major Russian cities do not reproduce their own numbers, warmer climates and better living conditions beckon, and Soviet industry adds to urban demand for labor by hoarding reserve workers just as it does raw materials. The one great exception to the overall shortage, Central Asia, does not help the rest of the country because most Central Asians do not wish to move.[17] The result is a seller's market for labor in which agriculture is in most places the loser.

To stem the flight from the farms, the government is working in four directions at once, by raising incentives to stay, mechanizing farm operations, favoring private farming, and even, in some places, moving in contract workers from other regions. The overall statistics are impressive: The real income of kolkhoz farm workers more than doubled between 1965 and 1979; the power available per agricultural worker passed from 7.7 horsepower to 22; and rural electricity consumption quadrupled.[18] Some recent straws in the wind indicate the lengths to which the government may be prepared to go, either toward liberalization or coercion: Since 1978, both in speeches and in his official autobiography, Brezhnev has advocated a greater role for private plots, the acre-size allotments that peasant families are allowed to cultivate for their own profit and which still provide an important share of Soviet fare.[19] Another straw is that in certain provinces of the non-black-earth zone, Central Asian reclamation workers are so numerous that the road signs are written in both Russian and Uzbek.[20] But these are partial measures, which do not offset the fact that many farm operations are still performed by hand, that most Central Asians are reluctant to leave their home villages, and that private plots account for a steadily declining share of total agricultural output.[21] Only more investment, more time, and the availability of more amenities in the countryside will make a dent in the rural manpower problem. The situation will get worse before it gets better.

The second problem is fuel and its connection with foreign exchange. If current forecasts that Soviet oil production will peak in the early 1980s are accurate,[22] Soviet agriculture will be affected in two ways. First, because mechanization and modernization are transforming it into a major consumer of petroleum and petrochemicals for fertilizer and pesticides, rural electricity, farm machinery, food processing, and so on, agricultural modernization becomes more difficult and expensive if oil runs short. Second, if Soviet oil exports decline, then Brezhnev's successors may not be able to afford the foreign exchange to import from 10 million to 35 million tons of grain each year to support the country's livestock, even if (in the wake of the American embargo) they should be inclined to do so.

The third key shortage of the 1980s is water, which has been the common theme of this book. Without repeating the points already made, suffice it to say here that shortages of water are tied to the other two, and none can be addressed separately from the others. Farms overuse irrigation water, for example, partly because they lack manpower to control the water, maintain the ditches, and repair the pumps and sprinklers. In Central Asia, on the other hand, it is the excess of rural manpower and its reluctance to leave the region that is causing Moscow to consider bringing in water from Siberia. Interbasin diversions would require energy to pump water uphill, and the resulting loss of hydropower to other uses might have to be covered by fossil fuels. One may well speak, then, not of individual shortages but of a massive triple squeeze that must somehow be gotten through before the Brezhnev agricultural program can reach takeoff. The prospect is for even greater investment, not less, and therefore by our second standard also, the Brezhnev program is in trouble.

The last and most demanding standard is whether Soviet agriculture is moving toward eventual self-sufficiency in its day-to-day operations. Will it always be the sick man of the Soviet economy? Will there ever come a day when it will not require the pure oxygen of high-priority political support, the daily intravenous feeding of subsidies, or periodic emergency rescue through massive foreign imports? This was Brezhnev's own ultimate vision, but can it be attained through the agricultural program as it is presently being conducted?

To judge from the experience of other industrial countries, a self-sufficient modern agriculture can be achieved only if the following three elements are present: specialized and vigorous industrial support oriented toward the needs of the farms; a prestigious and high-quality agricultural science closely tied to local operations through extension services and experimental stations; and an agricultural labor force consisting not of peasants but of educated agricultural technicians and entrepreneurs. All three elements must be responsive to local conditions, changes in demand, requirements of different groups, the availability of different inputs – in short, to both local needs and national demand.

Soviet progress in these respects has been uncertain. Much of the industrial support for agriculture comes from ministries whose main jobs are anything but agricultural. Brezhnev has committed the defense-related ministries to support the agricultural program, and they bring to it their high priority and abundant skills and resources.[23] But because their main business lies elsewhere, they cannot be expected to make special efforts in agriculture unless they are continually prodded. This means that if the commitment of the Politburo to agriculture should weaken even slightly, much of this industrial support could vanish, as it did in 1966–7. Yet so long as constant political attention is required to maintain full industrial involvement in agriculture, we can safely say that the third standard is not being met.

The same is true of scientific support. The growth of the agricultural sciences has been among the slowest of all the scientific specialties in the last quarter century, and there is no sign of a change in that respect. The Lenin Academy of Agricultural Sciences (VASKhNIL) does not compare in prestige or in quality with the USSR Academy of Sciences, and within the Academy of Sciences itself most agricultural research is performed by the republican academies, which have much lower prestige and funding than their Union-level counterpart. Despite the revival of genetics in the Soviet Union since 1964, plant breeding and seed selection are weak areas, especially when judged by their actual contributions to farming.[24] For example, according to the CIA, Soviet wheat growers largely use only one spring variety and two winter varieties for strong wheat, and for durum wheat they rely almost totally on one older variety. These were developed before the Brezhnev program began and are considered inadequate for mechanized, irrigated farming.[25] Similarly, Soviet chemical engineering for the production of modern fertilizers has not improved enough in the last two decades to give the Soviets an independent and modern industry, and for the production of compound and nitrogenous fertilizers, the Soviets have chosen to rely instead on foreign suppliers of production equipment.[26]

Some of the main problems in securing industrial and scientific support for agriculture are similar to those encountered elsewhere in the economy. Only very gradually is Soviet industry beginning to think of its products as packages that must include maintenance and spare parts, training for users, and arrangements for responding to the users' needs and to their suggestions for further innovations.[27] Similarly, the classic weakness of Soviet research and development lies not so much in the quality of its science as in its separation from the users' needs and its relative neglect of field experimentation and diffusion of successful innovations. These well-known Soviet problems have especially serious consequences in agriculture. For example, though Soviet agricultural geneticists have a network of some fifteen hundred stations through which they test some twelve thousand new plant varieties annually, only a few of the stations actually have their own land

and equipment. Nearly all of them rely on contracts with local farms, but because the farms have pressing production targets of their own, experimental plots have the last claim. Meanwhile, in Moscow, seed selection is in the hands of a minor and relatively powerless State Commission in the Ministry of Agriculture.[28] In other words, agricultural technology suffers from the same problem of *vnedrenie* (i.e., introduction of new developments into production) as the rest of Soviet technology.

As for the growth of a modern agricultural labor force, important changes are taking place, but slowly. Alongside the traditional work force is appearing a rural but nonfarm working class, employed in service functions related to agriculture. In agriculture management, educational levels are rising. Between 1965 and 1978 the proportion of agricultural personnel with higher or specialized secondary education increased from 20 to 61 per 1,000.[29] These people include farm managers, agronomists, and assorted specialists, who altogether make up about 7 percent of total farm personnel.[30] Eventually these trends will transform local agricultural management, but how soon?

The kinds of changes involved here require more than high-priority investment; they require time, the redirection of incentives, and the disappearance of a tenacious bias in favor of cities and heavy industry. And because problems of industrial support, technological innovation, and skilled manpower affect not merely agriculture but the entire economy, one should not expect them to disappear in agriculture ahead of other sectors. Success by the third standard may be a generation away.

To sum up: After fifteen years of sustained, high-priority effort and the investment of more than 600 billion rubles[31] in agriculture and related programs, the Brezhnev policies have produced some progress toward meeting the first, and politically most urgent, standard; they may meet the second if given sufficient further investment and time; but they are not yet even close to meeting the third. Put another way, the Brezhnev reform has succeeded in improving and stabilizing Soviet diets and diminishing the danger of massive crop failure and has begun to reverse the consequences of long neglect of the countryside. But even if the present effort continues for another decade at its present level (which is unlikely), it will not free the country from periodic reliance on foreign imports, heavy infrastructural investment, and constant intervention and subsidy. This is both a great failure, and yet, all the same, no small achievement. It is a failure in terms of the goals the Brezhnev coalition set for itself and the resources it expended to pursue them (and therefore we may expect the future of the agricultural program to be one of the major issues of the coming succession). The figure that best captures this partial success is that in 1978 one Soviet farm worker still fed only 9.7 people compared to 7.3 people in 1965.[32] But at the same time we should not overlook the fact that, faced with a crisis that would soon have threatened its legitimacy and stability, the Kremlin reacted decisively and with considerable effect. We should not underestimate the vitality and power of a political system that can act to ensure its survival by diverting hundreds of billions into a previously neglected – in fact, despised – sector of the economy. Those who ask themselves whether the Soviet regime will survive beyond 1984 should look elsewhere than to agriculture as the source of the regime's fatal weakness, for with their gigantic investment, the Soviet leaders have bought themselves at least a measure of security. But they aimed higher, and when we appraise their efforts in that light we can only wonder at the relative modesty of the results gained at such cost.

The causes are obviously complex. Two generations of deliberate neglect of agriculture (and many generations of rural backwardness before that) did not leave merely a physical legacy of damaged soils and primitive infrastructure but also a social and cultural legacy of contempt for the countryside and a system of administration and political power biased toward industry and cities. No crash program could erase that in a mere fifteen years. But this book argues that the basic weakness of the Brezhnev program is more fundamental: In its genesis, development, and implementation, it is not a third-generation reform at all but the last of the great industrializing campaigns. It is therefore limited to what such campaigns can achieve; and it is attended by the same problems that have always bedeviled such campaigns in the past: excess, overoptimism, subversion, and waste.

Does that mean that the present political system is incapable of producing reforms appropriate to the requirements of a third-generation economy? To judge that question, we must look beyond the performance record of the Brezhnev policies to the political lessons they contain.

## Political lessons of the Brezhnev programs

The first and most important lesson of the Brezhnev conservation and agricultural programs is that even a leadership as conservative and as fearful of change as the Brezhnev coalition was able to perform successfully a major shift in its priorities, reorient investment funds and resources against the bias of tradition and established lines of priority and prestige, rethink long-established assumptions and approaches, develop new programs and new agencies, and pursue this new course systematically, consistently, and energetically.

What is most striking about the rise of the new agricultural policy, however, is how long it took to establish it securely, especially if one bears in mind that it entailed no change in the Kremlin's most basic objectives (economic development and so on) nor any alteration of the system's basic structures or rules. Therefore, while giving appropriate credit to the evident energy of the Soviet political system, we may wonder whether the changes it produces in the future will always be so slow and so conservative.

Not necessarily. True, this book has stressed the theme of an increasingly constrained leadership, but we should remember that those constraints are largely economic, technological, and social, rather than directly political. Compared with their predecessors of the 1960s, the leaders of the 1980s may actually be *less* constrained in waging the intra-elite politics that lead to new coalitions and new policies. In the 1960s there were several unique circumstances at work that combined to make the process slower: First the post-Khrushchev succession was not a true replacement of the ins by the outs. Second, the political elite's strong reaction against Khrushchev's freewheeling ways produced unprecedented constraints on his successors' ability to use the traditional instruments of power and contributed to the selection of a leader who, whether by necessity or by temperament (or both), ruled by slow concertation. Third, in the 1960s there was still widespread optimism in Moscow about the effectiveness of traditional economic methods and remedies, and this in turn undoubtedly produced a strong bias in favor of the kind of industrializing agricultural policy that Brezhnev advocated. None of those circumstances will necessarily hold in the 1980s. In short, when the next succession comes, the new occupants of the Kremlin may find themselves freer to seize and wield the instruments of intra-elite power, to develop new policies, and to do it more quickly.

Indeed, behind the scenes, the basis for consensus on new and bolder policies may already be taking shape, just as it did in agriculture in the five years or so before Khrushchev's fall. As we look back a decade or two from now, we may see that a similarly slow process of change in elite attitudes was taking place in the apparently inconclusive discussions of the 1970s about different management arrangements, price and incentive systems, energy policy, and so on. Through such debates (or, rather, the discussions behind the scenes of which they are the imperfect shadow), Soviet minds are perhaps even now being prepared for changes that we cannot yet see, even though they may require a change of leadership to emerge.[33]

The second important lesson of the Brezhnev programs is that the Soviet political leadership was able to draw upon new thinking in several fields long frozen, to expand its horizons and incorporate new ideas into policy, while channeling innovations in conservative and safe directions and keeping control of issues with radical potential. The leaders' treatment of agricultural specialists during this period was very different from the contempt, exploitation, and harassment to which agronomists, geneticists, soil scientists, and others had been subjected in the past; and specialists in those fields responded energetically to the new opportunities, creating or re-creating with astonishing speed established professions where there had been only barren ruins or undeveloped sites a few short years before.

In an earlier chapter I argued that despite this change of atmosphere and the strong response it evoked, the essential features of the traditional relationship between Soviet political leaders and their sources of ideas and advice appear unchanged. One is almost equally tempted to argue the exact opposite, because the relaxation of negative controls and the resulting vigor of public debate have been so striking in so many "technical" fields. To be sure, negative controls unrestrained by countervailing power may be reimposed at any time (as the case of IKSI eloquently demonstrates). But is it not clearly in the interest of the leaders *not* to reimpose them? And does not power, even absolute power, rest ultimately on the values, habits, and expectations of leaders and led alike, so that power long unused decays? Would not an attempt to reimpose ideological controls on, say, cybernetics seem illegitimate and absurd, not least to the leaders themselves? One is tempted to say that compared to a generation ago something in the Soviet political culture has changed and the relationship of knowledge to power along with it.

Nevertheless, as far as the participation and influence of technical specialists in actual policy making are concerned, I do not think one can go quite so far. The position of Soviet specialists, in the end, remains entirely dependent upon the goodwill and needs of political authorities; their participation is governed by the authorities' pleasure; the advice given is largely secret; the portion of it that is subject to public debate is for the most part a weak echo of what is really being discussed behind the scenes; and there is no appeal – none, that is, that the leaders are obliged to take account of. The Soviet expert, at least in the areas of policy as we have discussed here, is clearly on tap, not on top, however much he may be useful or necessary.

What are the consequences for policy making? The cases we have discussed suggest that barriers (both vertical and horizontal) to the flow of information may have aggravated the tendency of the leadership to proceed too fast and too far in their new policies, because of a lack of open, expert, countervailing criticism. In the future, as technical issues grow ever more complex and interconnected, the usefulness to the leaders of having them thrashed out publicly will increase, for only a wide airing will preserve the leaders from the biased information "interested" ministries may provide or from the one-sided advocacy of specialist-entrepreneurs and regional "patriots." In policy formation, as in implementation, an increase in effective power may require continued relaxation of traditional powers.

The third lesson suggested by the Brezhnev programs is that the apparent influence of institutional groups derives not from resources and instruments of power of their own but from constraints that the political leadership tacitly accepts, largely because they arise from the leaders' own objectives, the complexity and interrelatedness of tasks in a modern economy, and the growing scarcity of resources, including manpower. Therefore, if throughout this book we see evidence of argument and conflict on nearly every page, it is not the precursor of political pluralism but the playing out of delegated powers of state agencies, which, as we have seen, can be granted or withdrawn on short notice. The playing out is neither fast nor smooth; state agencies can use their delegated powers (for a time) to obstruct and divert, but not to oppose official policy openly or impose an alternative (though they may propose one). The most carefully drafted initiatives from specialists or agencies below, painstakingly threaded through the bureaucracy to gain the approvals of all the agencies concerned and earnestly argued for years through the consultants of the Central Committee or the *referentura* of the Council of Ministers, may be reversed at a moment's notice by the leadership's sudden decision, without possibility of public appeal or countervailing action. Thus, to take a recent example, the gradual development of a balanced energy policy in response to concern about declining oil reserves, which one can trace through Soviet journals in the 1970s, was abruptly pushed aside at the November 1977 plenum of the Central Committee in favor of a massive return to a strategy based on western Siberian oil, even in the face of mounting evidence from the experts that such a policy was extremely risky.

This means that the Soviet leaders retain awesome power, but, this book argues, it is power of the wrong kind. The genie produced by the command economy is ham-handed, capable of flooding the countryside with half-finished irrigation projects and agroindustrial livestock combines, but not of producing stable harvests or substantial increases in meat output. *Krokodil* captures the absurdity neatly with a standard cartoon that comes straight from Gogol: A tractor roars across the fields of Russia, drawn by a flying troika of plowhorses.

It follows that the Soviet leaders will not soon be able to afford another such "reform," and consequently it will not do as a model for meeting third-generation economic problems across the board, not even as a stopgap, because it is simply too expensive and too slow. Brezhnev's successors will not be able to deal simultaneously with energy, transportation, industrial modernization, housing, and so on by the same methods that were used in the Brezhnev agricultural program. In energy policy, for example, the balance to be struck is between conservation and further development of new sources. Naturally, the Soviet economy will need plenty of both; but the point is that if the Soviet energy policy of the 1980s ends up being channeled in the same lopsidedly "extensive" directions as the Brezhnev agricultural policies of the 1960s and 1970s, that is, toward production rather than conservation, one may safely predict that the country will be in trouble. The Soviet Union is already the least efficient producer and user of energy of any modern industrial power (despite some zones, it should be said, of outstanding efficiency); and its energy intensiveness, instead of declining as in most advanced economies, is rising.[34] A policy that stresses development of new sources of energy without dealing with the organizational structures and economic incentives that produce overconsumption will not solve the Soviet Union's energy problems. And although a second-generation approach, though inadequate, still has some relevance when applied to a problem like energy or Central Asian development or transportation, it has almost none when applied to some of the other problems rising up in the 1980s, such as geographically unbalanced birthrates, labor shortages and low labor productivity, slow or inappropriate technological innovation, low-quality output, hidden inflation, or the spread of the underground "second economy." In short, second-generation reform, as we have seen it in the pages of this book, is not enough to enable the Soviet political system to deal with the problems of a third-generation economy.

How the Soviet leaders react to this problem depends mainly, of course, on how severe the 1980s turn out to be. If the decade proves to be relatively benign, the Kremlin may be able to pursue further the partial evolution it has already undergone in the last fifteen years. One might reasonably expect further experimentation with new schemes to promote technological innovation (such as profit-making associations geared toward export markets), greater reliance on material incentives and even local enterprise (such as a further elaboration of the present trend toward specialized "brigades" in the factory and on the farm), a gradual acceptance of the need for the "hidden hand" of meaningful prices but also (as Joseph Berliner puts it) for the "hidden foot" of possible unemployment – one can go on. The Brezhnev period has not been a treadmill of meaningless reform;[35] there has been slow, but definite, learning. But what is needed is the right mixture of stress and leisure for the political elite to accustom itself to the meaning of governing by fingers instead of thumbs and to reconcile itself to the political price that will have to be paid by abandoning some degree of formal control. The danger is that they will not have that leisure.[36] If oil output falls to 9 million barrels a day or less by 1990, if during the decade of the 1980s the weather is bad, if perceived international pressures (or opportunities) incline the leaders toward even higher levels of military spending, if migration patterns and labor turnover worsen – all of which are quite conceivable – then there will be neither time nor patience for slow experimentation. Soviet leaders will be forced to use what power they have, which may mean Draconian measures to enforce labor discipline, curtail the second economy, limit fuel use, cut back consumption, reallocate manpower, and so on. Such stopgap devices could get the country through the rapids of the 1980s and into the calmer waters of the 1990s. For example, by accepting a partial cutback in the objectives for meat production, the Soviet Union could use some of the foreign exchange now being spent for foreign grain to buy foreign energy technology instead.

The government can also free investment resources by cutting back the entire agricultural sector, which many Soviets now openly view as the most bloated sector in the Soviet investment budget. This can be done by cutting back selectively on the least successful programs, such as the non-black-earth zone, and postponing programs that are not immediately needed, such as the major interbasin diversions. A second measure immediately available to free capital and lessen energy consumption is to concentrate resources on the large number of unfinished investment projects now dotting the countryside.[37] In sum, if the 1980s prove to be harsh, the Soviet leadership has a range of stopgap measures available, which in order to see them through the decade need not do more than help out in the short run and at the margin. As for the prospect of calmer waters by the 1990s, it would not take much optimism to reason as follows: The labor shortage will be relieved slightly in the 1990s; the energy problem will abate, for it is due in the first place to the decline of European sources and the premature peaking of west Siberian oil; but natural gas will take up the slack, followed in the longer term by other sources of energy from the resources of Siberia. As for agriculture, the front-end investment already made is bound to yield results, especially in fodder production. Consequently, the 1980s will not necessarily be a decade of crisis and Draconian reaction in the Soviet Union. On the contrary, the combination of political succession and policy pressures may be just the combination required to shake the political elite out of its immobilism.

But in what direction will it choose to move? We began this book by asking whether the Soviet political elite is capable of responding to the social and economic problems gathering before it in the third generation of

Soviet rule, to promote greater balance, quality, longer horizons, and efficiency. After observing the response of the Brezhnev leadership to the agricultural problem in its many ramifications, we cannot doubt the energy of this political system. But whether it has the ability to develop the instruments of power appropriate to modern reform cannot yet be judged. As this book has tried to show, the success of the next generation of Soviet leaders in matching the evolution of their increasingly modern society and economy with modern political instruments will depend less on their ability to launch new programs and reorganizations, incentive systems and indexes, than on their capacity to rethink the inherited relations between knowledge and power, between control and autonomy, and between a safe conservatism and progress.

# NOTES

## 1 Challenge of the third generation of Soviet power

1 By referring to the upcoming generation of leaders as the "third generation," I am adopting here the usage of Seweryn Bialer in *Stalin's Successors* (Cambridge: Cambridge University Press, 1980), who points out that, because of extremely slow personnel turnover under Brezhnev, the political generation now leaving the scene can still be considered "Stalinist."

2 For general treatments of the economic challenge facing the Soviet leadership in the last two decades of the century, see U.S., Congress, Joint Economic Committee, *The Soviet Economy in a Time of Change*, 2 vols. (Washington, D.C.: U.S. Government Printing Office, 1979), hereafter cited as *Time of Change*; and Alec Nove, *The Soviet Economic System* (London: Allen and Unwin, 1977). Finally, see the annual series published by the Central Intelligence Agency's National Foreign Assessment Center, *The Soviet Economy and Outlook*.

3 Charles E. Lindblom, *Politics and Markets* (New York: Basic Books, 1977), pp. 65–75.

4 On the essential functions performed by the regional party apparatus, see Jerry F. Hough, *The Soviet Prefects: The Local Party Organs in Industrial Decision–Making* (Cambridge, Mass.: Harvard University Press, 1969), esp. pp. 289–305.

5 For a Soviet discussion of the "unorganized and irrational" character of recent migration patterns, see A. V. Topilin, *Territorial'noe pereraspredelenie trudovykh resursov v SSSR* (Moscow: Ekonomika, 1975).

6 For a discussion of this and related issues, see N. C. Davis and S. E. Goodman, "The Soviet Bloc's Unified System of Computers," *ACM Computing Surveys* 10, No. 2 (June 1978): 93–122.

7 See, e.g., B. E. Paton, "Nerazryvnoe edinstvo nauki i proizvodstva," *Ekonomika i Organizatsiia Promyshlennogo Proizvodstva* 5 (1973): 4; and V. Trefilov, "Konveier vnedreniia," *Izvestiia*, 19 February 1977.

8 On the evolution of Brezhnev's thinking, see George Breslauer, *Dilemmas of Leadership in the Soviet Union Since Stalin: 1953–1976* (Berkeley: University of California Press, forthcoming). On the evolution of debate among leaders on the importance of technological innovation and its

relation to dependence on Western technology, see the essay by Bruce Parrott, "Soviet Technological Progress and Western Technological Transfer to the USSR: An Analysis of Soviet Attitudes" (Washington, D.C.: Department of State, Office of External Research, Bureau of Intelligence and Research, July 1978).

9  L. I. Brezhnev, Report of the CPSU Central Committee, Twenty–fifth Congress of the CPSU (Moscow: Novosti, 1976), pp. 52, 58.

10  See, e.g., Gertrude E. Schroeder, "The Soviet Economy on a Treadmill of 'Reforms,' " in *Time of Change*, 1: 312–40.

11  Paul Cocks has written several excellent descriptions of Soviet experiments in management and organization. See, e.g., "The Policy Process and Bureaucratic Politics," in Paul Cocks, Robert V. Daniels, and Nancy Whittier Heer, eds., *The Dynamics of Soviet Politics* (Cambridge, Mass.: Harvard University Press, 1976), pp. 156–78.

12  See, e.g., the chapter by Julian Cooper in the forthcoming second volume of R. Amann, J. M. Cooper, and R. W. Davies, eds., *The Technological Level of Soviet Industry* (New Haven, Conn.: Yale University Press), of which the first volume appeared in 1977. Further discussion may be found in Paul Cocks, "Organizing for Innovation in the 1970's," an occasional paper of the Kennan Institute for Advanced Russian Studies, Smithsonian Institution, Washington, D. C., No. 54 (November 1978).

13  See Nove, *op. cit.*, pp. 172–99. See also Morris Bornstein, "Soviet Price Policy in the 1970's," in U.S., Congress, Joint Economic Committee, *The Soviet Economy in a New Perspective* (Washington, D.C.: U.S. Government Printing Office, 1976), pp. 17–66. See also Morris Bornstein, "The Administration of Soviet Prices," *Soviet Studies* 30, No. 4 (October 1978): 466–90.

14  See, e.g., the recent decree of the CPSU Central Committee and the USSR Council of Ministers, "Ob uluchshenii planirovaniia i usileniia vozdeistvia khoziaistvennogo mekhanizma na povyshenie effektivnosti proizvodstva i kachestva raboty," *Pravda*, 29 July 1979.

15  In addition to the works already cited, see Louvan E. Nolting, *The Reforms of Scientific Research, Development, and Innovation in the USSR*, U.S., Department of Commerce, Foreign Economic Report No. 11, September 1976.

16  Abram Bergson, "Toward a New Growth Model," *Problems of Communism* 22, No. 2 (March–April 1973): 1–8: For background, see Alexander Erlich, "Development Strategy and Planning: The Soviet Experience," in National Bureau of Economic Research, *National Economic Planning: A Conference of the Universities – National Bureau Committee for Economic Research* (New York: Columbia University Press, 1967), pp. 247–9.

17  Peter Wiles, *Distribution of Income: East and West* (Amsterdam: North–Holland, 1974). See also Breslauer, op. cit.

18  See, e.g., N. Shmelev, *Ekonomicheskie sviazi vostok–zapad: problemy i vozmozhnosti* (Moscow: Mysl', 1976).

19  Theodore Shabad, "Raw material problems of Soviet aluminum industry," *Resources Policy* (U.K.), December 1976. See also Marshall I.

Goldman, "Will the Soviet Union Be an Autarky in 1984?" *International Security* 3, No. 4 (Spring 1979): 18–36; and Marie Lavigne, *Les Relations économiques Est-Ouest* (Paris: Presses Universitaires de France, 1979).

20 The reader is referred to an excellent research paper by Geoffrey Levitt of the Harvard Law School, "The Legalization Movement in the Soviet Enterprise" (seminar paper, Harvard University, Department of Government, Spring 1978).

21 For economics 1950–72, see D. M. Gvishiani, S. R. Mikulinskii, and S. A. Kugel', *The Scientific Intelligentsia in the USSR*, English trans. (Moscow: Progress Publishers, 1976), p. 130.

22 See Gertrude E. Schroeder, *Organization and Management in the Soviet Economy: the Ceaseless Search for Panaceas*, ER77-10769 (Washington, D.C.: Central Intelligence Agency, National Foreign Assessment Center, December 1977).

23 See Schroeder, "Treadmill of 'Reforms.' "

24 For an interesting recent example, see "Poshla ASU s molotka," *Pravda*, 13 March 1978. For background, see V. Glushkov, "Zaboty na polputi," *Literaturnaia Gazeta*, No. 29 (January 1975): 10; and in the same issue, V. Rapoport, "Stadiia vtorichnogo skepsisa." A good general account of the computerized management program can be found in N. V. Makhrov, A. A. Modin, and E. G. Iakovenko, *Parametry razrabotki sovremennykh avtomatizirovannykh sistem upravleniia predpriiatiiami* (Moscow: Nauka, 1974).

25 See, e.g., the criticism of industrial research contained in the series of articles published in *Literaturnaia Gazeta* under the general heading "Akademiia – dlia neakademicheskikh nauk," 14 March, 21 April, 28 July, 18 August, and 6 October 1976.

26 Louvan E. Nolting, *The Structure and Functions of the USSR State Committee for Science and Technology*, U.S., Department of Commerce, Foreign Economic Report No. 16, 1979.

27 For the best general analysis of the reasons for resistance to technological innovation in Soviet industry, see Joseph S. Berliner, *The Innovation Decision in Soviet Industry* (Cambridge, Mass.: M.I.T. Press, 1976).

28 For an interesting series of case studies, see the Soviet discussion of problems in diffusion of the technology of explosion welding. Zamira Ibragimova, "Tiazhkii put' vnedreniia," *Ekonomika i Organizatsiia Promyshlennogo Proizvodstva*, No. 5 (1973): 37–50; "Vzryv-masterovoi," *Pravda*, 10 May 1978; "Vzryv–metallurg," *Izvestiia*, 15 February 1977.

29 Igor Birman, "From the Achieved Level," *Soviet Studies* 30, No. 2 (April 1978): 153–73.

30 Albina Tretyakova and Igor Birman, "Input-Output Analysis in the USSR," *Soviet Studies* 28, No. 2 (April 1976): 157–86.

31 For some of the recent writings along these lines, see William Taubman, "The Change to Change in Communist Systems: Modernization, Post-modernization, and Soviet Politics," in Henry W. Morton and Rudolf L.

Tokes, eds., *Soviet Politics and Society in the 1970s* (New York: Free Press, 1974), pp. 369–94. See also Zbigniew Brzezinski, ed., *Dilemmas of Change in Soviet Politics* (New York: Columbia University Press, 1969) and Jerry F. Hough, *The Soviet Union and Social Science Theory* (Cambridge, Mass.: Harvard University Press, 1977), Chap. 1. A prominent theme in this literature is the tension between the technical requirements of administering an industrial society and the political requirements of maintaining the leaders in power. One of the best and most careful examples of such analysis, written shortly after Stalin's death, is Barrington Moore's *Terror and Progress USSR* (Cambridge, Mass.: Harvard University Press, 1954), which the author described as "an attempt to weigh, with an eye to the future, the sources of stability and the potentialities for change in the Bolshevik regime."

32  The energy sector does not yet qualify, for the Soviet leadership is only now beginning the job of creating a mechanism for unified decision making and developing policies to lessen their dependence on oil and to conserve energy. The energy sector may be the greatest area of reform of the 1980s and 1990s, but it was not under Brezhnev. See Grey Hodnett, "The Energy Problem and Soviet Foreign Relations in the 1980's" (Paper prepared for the Council of Foreign Relations' Study Group on Domestic Sources of Soviet Foreign Policy, January 1980).

33  I. Ivannikov, "Kapital'nym vlozheniiam v sel'skoe khoziaistvo-effektivnoe napravlenie," *Planovoe Khoziaistvo* 10 (1978): 62–8. This figure includes major categories of off-farm investment, what the Soviets term the *agroindustrial complex*.

34  Brezhnev himself is a partial exception. He was trained initially as a reclamation engineer and was heavily involved in agriculture as first secretary of the party in the Moldavian Republic and then in the Kazakh Republic.

35  Leslie Dienes and Theodore Shabad, *The Soviet Energy System* (Washington, D.C.: Winston, 1979), pp. 185–7.

36  I. A. Gerardi, "Osobennosti prirodnykh i meliorativnykh uslovii zony nedostatochnogo uvlazhneniia i problemy pereraspredeleniia stoka rechnykh basseinov po territorii SSSR," mimeographed (Moscow: Soiuzvodproekt, 1969), p. 14.

37  Of the net increase in Soviet irrigated area in the last ten years, 75% is located in the European zone. E. E. Alekseevskii, "Melioratsiia zemel'– osnova polucheniia vysokikh i ustoichivvkh urozhaev," *Vestnik sel'skokhoziaistvennoi nauki* 5 (1976): 4. During the Tenth five-year plan (1976–80), 600,000 new hectares of irrigated land were scheduled for the Volga basin alone – an increase of 25% over the previous Five-Year plan. A. Vorotnikov, O. Dronov, and G. Ivanov, "Preobrazhenie Povolzh'ia," *Pravda*, 19 and 20 February 1977, p. 2.

38  See, e.g., E. K. Alatortsev, "Rezervy ispol'zovaniia meliorirovannykh zemel'," *Vestnik sel'skokhoziaistvennoi nauki* 5 (1976): 24. Apparently some debate is going on over what should be the upper limit to irrigation in the European USSR. Some geographers caution against expanding

much beyond 10 million hectares. See I. P. Gerasimov et al., "Large–Scale Research and Engineering Programs for the Transformation of Nature in the Soviet Union and the Role of Geographers in their Implementation," *Soviet Geography* 17, No. 4 (April 1976): 235–45 (reprinted from *Materialy VI S"ezda Geograficheskogo Obshchestva SSSR* [Moscow, 1975], pp. 3–18).

39  Michael D. Zahn, "Soviet Livestock Feed in Perspective," in *Time of Change*, 2: 165–88.
40  This array of projects is discussed in Chapter 5.
41  L. K. Davydov and N. G. Konkina, *Obshchaia Gidrologiia* (Leningrad: Gidrometeoizdat, 1958), p. 309.
42  S. L. Vendrov and I. S. Glukh, "O nekotorykh problemakh preobrazovaniia rechnoi seti russkoi ravniny," in *Voprosy preobrazovaniia prirody russkoi ravniny* (Moscow: Institute of Geography, USSR Academy of Sciences, 1973), pp. 171–73.
43  "Napoiat Aral sibirskie reki," *Pravda Vostoka*, 17 August 1978.
44  These novels from the late 1920s and early 1930s, by the Russian satirists Il'ia Il'f and Evgenii Petrov, capture as no other literature ever has the art of getting by in Soviet society. Most educated Russians are familiar with every episode in the two novels, and many can quote long passages.

## 2  Building authority around a new agricultural policy

1  For background on Soviet agricultural policy, see Roy D. Laird, Joseph Hajda, and Betty A. Laird, eds., *The Future of Agriculture in the Soviet Union and Eastern Europe: The 1976–1980 Five-Year Plan* (Boulder, Colo.: Westview Press, 1977). For descriptions of Soviet agricultural policy before 1965, see Lazar Volin, *A Century of Russian Agriculture* (Cambridge, Mass.: Harvard University Press, 1970), and Alec Nove, *An Economic History of the USSR* (Baltimore, Md.: Penguin Books, 1969). The political background of recent changes in agricultural policy is discussed in Werner G. Hahn, *The Politics of Soviet Agriculture, 1960–1970* (Baltimore, Md.: Johns Hopkins University Press, 1972); and Michel Tatu, *Le Pouvoir en URSS* (Paris: Grasset, 1967). See also Martin McCauley, *Khrushchev and the Development of Soviet Agriculture: The Virgin Land Programme 1953–1964* (London: Macmillan, 1976). For assessments of agricultural performance during the five-year plan 1971–5, see David W. Carey, "Soviet Agriculture: Recent Performance and Future Plans," in U.S., Congress, Joint Economic Committee, *The Soviet Economy in a New Perspective* (Washington, D.C.: U.S. Government Printing Office, 1976), pp. 575–600, and W. Klatt, "Reflections on the 1975 Soviet Harvest," *Soviet Studies* 28, No. 1 (October 1975): 485–98. I have benefited particularly from the opportunity to read the manuscript of George Breslauer's *Dilemmas of Leadership in the Soviet Union Since Stalin, 1953–76* (Berkeley: University of California Press, forthcoming).

2 See *Plenum Tsentral'nogo Komiteta KPSS, 24–26 marta, 1965, steno-graficheskii otchet* [Plenum of the Central Committee of the CPSU, 24–26 March, 1965, stenographic report] (Moscow: Politizdat, 1965).

3 See Hahn, op. cit. pp. 117–67.

4 For example, central capital allocations for reclamation doubled between 1960 and 1965. See *Sel'skoe khoziaistvo SSSR* (Moscow: Statistika, 1971), p. 361.

   Similarly, the main outlines of the grain-oriented, Europe-centered irrigation policy, which is now dominant, were laid down in a memorandum by Khrushchev to the CPSU Politburo in 1963. See "On Development of Irrigated Agriculture in Order to Assure the Grain Harvest," in N. S. Khrushchev, *Stroitel'stvo kommunizma v SSSR i razvitie sel'skogo khoziaistvo*, 8 vols. (Moscow: Politizdat, 1964), 8: 91–102. That program, in turn, was a revival of the approaches that Khrushchev had proposed in the Ukraine in the 1940s. The Kakhovka irrigation project in the Ukraine, ultimately completed in the 1960s, had been promoted by Khrushchev after the drought of 1946. At the time, it was rejected in favor of a plan to build a canal in the southern Ukraine. See Sidney Ploss, *Conflict and Decision-Making in Soviet Russia: A Case Study of Agricultural Policy, 1953–63* (Princeton, N.J.: Princeton University Press, 1965), pp. 36–7.

   For the story of the expansion of chemical fertilizer production under Krushchev, see Hahn, op. cit., pp. 114–16.

5 The November 1964 plenum of the CPSU Central Committee removed the incapacitated F. R. Kozlov from the Party Presidium (as the Politburo was then known) and added P. N. Demichev as a candidate member.

6 See Hahn, op. cit., and Tatu, op. cit.

7 For a major, detailed study of Khrushchev, see the forthcoming work by Breslauer, op. cit.

8 On this point, see Tatu, *Le Pouvoir en URSS*, p. 269; and Jerry Hough, *The Soviet Prefects: The Local Party Organs in Industrial Decision-Making* (Cambridge, Mass.: Harvard University Press, 1969), pp. 201–3.

   Khrushchev's use of the party apparatus to implement his agricultural policies reached such lengths that Tatu speculates that the first secretary's Politburo colleagues may have acquiesced quite willingly in the 1962 division of the party because they hoped in this way that at least half the apparatus could be turned to industry, with the latter half possibly becoming the preponderant one. If this was their hope, it was apparently a vain one. According to Hahn, 80% of the pre-bifurcation first secretaries of the *oblast* party committees (*obkoms*) were moved into agriculture, and 31 of the 39 *obkom* first secretaries named to the CPSU Central Committee in 1963—4 were from the agricultural side (op. cit., p. 97).

   Since 1964, the emphasis has shifted back to appointment of persons with industrial backgrounds as *obkom* first secretaries. See T. H. Rigby, "The Soviet Regional Leadership: The Brezhnev Generation," *Slavic Review* 37, No. 1 (March 1978): 1–24.

9 Fedor T. Morgun, *Khleb i liudi* (Moscow: Politizdat, 1975).

10 L. I. Brezhnev, "Tselina," *Novyi Mir*, No. 10 (1978): 3–55.

11 Ibid., pp. 12, 13, 35, 49–55.

12 Ibid., p. 52.

13 Ibid., pp. 14, 15, 43.

14 In his speech before the USSR Supreme Soviet on 9 August 1953, Malenkov called for a policy of intensification but did not mention the additional investment that such a program would require. Malenkov's address to the same body the following year called for higher labor productivity in agriculture but again failed to mention any increase in investment (required to make higher productivity possible) (McCauley, op. cit. pp. 46, 65).

15 Nikita S. Khrukshchev, *Khrushchev Remembers. The Last Testament*, trans. and ed. Strobe Talbott (Boston: Little, Brown 1974), p. 122.

16 Brezhnev, op. cit., p. 23.

17 Morgun, op. cit., p. 170.

18 McCauley, op. cit., pp. 209–13.

19 Brezhnev, op. cit., p. 42.

20 Ploss, op. cit.; Carl A. Linden, *Khrushchev and the Soviet Leadership, 1957–64* (Baltimore, Md.: Johns Hopkins University Press, 1966).

21 Ploss, op. cit., pp. 61, 111, 112.

22 See V. Khlebnikov, "O dal'neishem ukreplenii ekonomiki kolkhozov," *Voprosy ekonomiki* 7 (1976): 49–57. The figure 12% comes from examination of the graph: Khlebnikov's figures may be a good guide to the general trends of investment in the Khrushchev years, but the overall levels he gives appear to be seriously inflated. At least this is one interpretation of the figures given in later editions of *Narodnoe Khoziaistvo*. These later figures suggest that the share of agriculture during those years was actually about 3 percentage points lower, on the average, than Khelbnikov says. If one combines Khlebnikov's trend line, therefore, with the average figures reported in *Narodnoe Khoziaistvo*, one arrives at a low of 12% in 1960.

23 Breslauer, op. cit., Chap. 3, quoting Khrushchev's speech reproduced in *Stroitel'stvo kommunizma*, 4: 109.

24 Roman Kolkowicz, "The Military," in H. Gordon Skilling and Franklyn Griffiths, eds., *Interest Groups in Soviet Politics* (Princeton, N.J.: Princeton University Press, 1971), pp. 160–4.

25 Khrushchev, *Stroitel'stvo kommunizma*, 4: 181, quoted in Hahn, op. cit., p. 86.

26 January 1961 plenum, stenographic record, p. 527. Quoted in Hahn, op. cit., p. 87. Breslauer, op. cit., comments on the January 1961 plenum in Chapter 4.

27 Breslauer, op. cit. Chap. 4, quoting Khrushchev, *Stroitel'stvo kommunizma*, 4: 286–90.

28 Tatu, op. cit., pp. 228–31 and 388.

29 *Narodnoe Khoziaistvo SSSR*, relevant years.

30  Hahn, op. cit. pp. 87, 89, 90, 115. Tatu, op. cit., pp. 138, 229. Ploss, op. cit., pp. 219, 241.
31  In addition to the references already mentioned, see Khrushchev, *Stroitel'stvo kommunizma*, 8: 175. See also Tatu, op. cit., pp. 466–7.
32  *Plenum Tsentral'nogo Komiteta KPSS marta 1965 g., stenograficheskii otchet* (Moscow: Izdatel'stvo politicheskoi literatury, 1965), pp. 6–9.
33  *Plenum Tsentral'nogo Komiteta KPSS fevralia 1964 g., stenograficheskii otchet* (Moscow: Izdatel'stvo politicheskoi literatury, 1964), p. 401.
34  Ibid., p. 399.
35  Ibid., p. 413.
36  Ibid., p. 409.
37  Ibid.
38  Ibid., p. 431.
39  Ibid., p. 456.
40  Ibid., pp. 409–10.
41  Ibid., p. 418.
42  Robert F. Miller, *One Hundred Thousand Tractors* (Cambridge, Mass.: Harvard University Press, 1971), Chaps. 14 and 15.
43  Hahn, op. cit., p. 3.
44  See Breslauer, op. cit., Chap. 3.
45  Rigby, op. cit.
46  This is also the conclusion of George Breslauer.
47  Maryruth Coleman, "The Agricultural Planning Debate, 1965–68: Plan and Market in the Management of Soviet Agriculture" (seminar paper, Harvard University, Department of Government, 1977; available from Ms. Coleman).
48  Hahn, op. cit., p. 194.
49  Breslauer, op. cit., Chap. 9, quoting Kosygin speeches published in *Pravda*, 9 and 11 June 1966, and *Sovetskaia Belorussia*, 15 February 1968.
50  An excellent analysis of this debate and the positions of the various specialists and politicians involved can be found in Coleman, op. cit.
51  Hahn, op. cit.
52  T. Sokolov, "Nekotorye problemy agropromyshlennogo kompleksa strany," *Planovoe Khoziaistvo*, No. 2 (1974): 8.
53  Rigby, op. cit.
54  For extensive treatment of Voronov see Hahn, op. cit., also Tatu, op. cit., pp. 137–9 and 237–9.
55  Breslauer, op. cit., Chap. 12.
56  Coleman, op. cit., pp. 20 and 21.
57  Paul Cocks, "The Rationalization of Party Control," in Chalmers Johnson, ed., *Change in Communist Systems* (Stanford, Calif.: Stanford University Press, 1970).
58  See the articles by Arcadius Kahan and Roy and Betty Laird in Laird, Hajda, and Laird, op. cit., pp. 9–48.
59  Sidney Ploss notes a characteristic episode: "B. G. Gafurov, the Party secretary of Tadzhikistan, tried to prove that it was possible to narrow the rows in sowing cotton. But U. Yusupov, former premier of Uzbeki-

stan, took a skeptical view. According to Khrushchev, 'This, comrades, was not just an argument between Ivan Ivanovich and Ivan Nikiforovich. It was a dispute on a question of principle" (op. cit., p. 98).

60  The impact of this on genetics is well known. For a review of the effects on plant physiology and agricultural practices, see David Joravsky, *The Lysenko Affair* (Cambridge, Mass.: Harvard University Press, 1970).

61  D. M. Gvishiani, S. R. Mikulinskii, S. A. Kugel', eds., *The Scientific Intelligentsia in the USSR (Structure and Dynamics of Personnel)* (Moscow: Progress Publishers, 1976), pp. 141–5.

62  Hahn, op. cit., pp. 7, 43, 63, and elsewhere.

63  Tatu, op. cit., p. 408.

64  N. P. Dubinin, *Vechnoe Dvizhenie* (Moscow: Politizdat, 1973), pp. 357, 358, 388.

65  Ibid., pp. 358 and 393.

66  Morgun, op. cit., pp. 168, 254, 265–6, 320–3.

67  Hahn, op. cit., pp. 26–7.

68  Ibid., pp. 103, 113.

69  Khrushchev, *Stroitel'stvo kommunizma*, 6: 145, cited in McCauley, op. cit., p. 165.

70  A. I. Baraev authored *Osnovnye polozheniia po bor'be s vodnoi i vetrovoi eroziei pochv* (Moscow, 1962) and another volume on the same subject the following year.

71  Hahn, op. cit., p. 104.

72  P. M. Zemskii, *Razvitie i razmeshchenie zemledeliia po prirodno-khoziaistvennym raionam SSSR* (Moscow, 1959), discussed in McCauley, op. cit., Chap. 8.

73  *Plenum TsK KPSS*, March 1965, pp. 25–6.

74  But some of the old style still remains. A *Pravda* article describes Poltava First Secretary Morgun striding into the fields to lecture the local farm administration about the virtues of the Baraev method (24 February 1979).

75  In his recent memoirs dealing with the early years of the Virgin Lands campaign, Brezhnev pays tribute to Baraev and Mal'tsev, implying that only orders from above prevented their ideas from being implemented (op. cit.). Morgun, more convincingly, admits in his memoirs that he was initially unimpressed by Baraev's recommendations for shallow plowing and only gradually became a convert (op. cit., p. 265).

76  I. A. Gerardi, "Osobennosti prirodnykh i meliorativnykh uslovii zony nedostatochnogo uvlazhneniia i problemy pereraspredeleniia stoka rechnykh basseinov po territorii SSSR," (Moscow: Soiuzvodproekt, mimeographed, 1969), pp. 6–7. Gerardi gives full listings of the organizations involved and summarizes their findings in detail.

77  In the 1960s plowland was being taken over at a rate of more than 500,000 hectares per year. A. A. Stepankov, "Ekonomicheskaia otsenka zemli i ushcherba ot zatoplenii vodokhranilischchami GES," in Vsesoiuznyi Zaochnyi Politekhnicheskii Institute, *Sbornik Trudov*, No. 64, series Ekonomika energetiki (Moscow, 1972), p. 3. See also A. B.

Avakian, "Nekotorye problemy sozdaniia vodokhranilishch v SSSR," *Izvestiia Akademii Nauk SSSR*, seriia geograficheskaia 4 (1972): 60.

78 Gerardi, op. cit., pp. 21–5.

79 Ibid., p. 38.

80 G. L. Magakian, "Irrigatsiia v SSSR: sovremennoe sostoianie i perspektivy razvitiia," in *Vodnye resursy i ikh kompleksnoe ispol'zovanie*, Vol. 73 *Voprosy Geografii* (1968): 38–43. See also M. S. Filimonov and G. G. Shiler in *Ratsional'noe ispol'zovanie obvodnitel'no-orositel'nykh sistem* (Moscow: Kolos, 1970), pp. 72–87.

81 Gerardi, op. cit., pp. 9, 10, 17, 29.

82 G. V. Kopanev, "Vodnoe khoziaistvo i kompleksnoe ispol'zovanie vodnykh resursov," in *Razvitie i razmeshchenie proisvoditel'nykh sil SSSR: Sredneaziatskii ekonomicheskii raion* (Moscow: USSR Academy of Sciences and USSR Gosplan Council on the Use of Productive Resources, 1972), pp. 178–80.

83 This issue is discussed at length in Chapter 5.

84 This argument is central to Breslauer's book, and this chapter owes a great deal to his reflection on the subject.

3 *Environmental issues rise to official legitimacy*

1 P. S. Neporozhnii, ed., *Gidroenergetika i kompleksnoe ispol'zovanie vodnykh resursov SSSR* (Moscow: Energiia, 1970), p. 101. For a more detailed discussion of the priority of industrial uses over drinking water, even as late as the 1960s, see *Kompleksnoe ispol'zovanie vodnykh resursov SSSR* (USSR Gosplan Soviet po izucheniiu proizvoditel'nykh sil, Otdel kompleksnogo ispol'zovaniia vodnykh resursov, Moscow, 1965). See also Marshall Goldman, *The Spoils of Progress: Environmental Pollution in the Soviet Union* (Cambridge, Mass.: M.I.T. Press, 1972), pp. 104–8.

2 See Geoffrey Hosking, "The Russian Peasant Rediscovered: Village Prose of the 1960s," *Slavic Review* 32, No. 4 (December 1973): 705–24; and Gleb Zakulin, "The Contemporary Countryside in Soviet Literature: A Search for New Values," in James R. Millar, ed., *The Soviet Rural Community* (Urbana: University of Illinois Press, 1971), pp. 376–404.

3 S. Enders Wimbush, "Great Russians and the Soviet State" (Paper presented at the 1977 Meeting of the American Political Science Association, Washington, D.C., October 1977).

4 Boris Komarov, *Unichtozhenie prirody* (Frankfurt: Possev, 1978), p. 11.

5 N. Chistiakov and E. Kuznetsov, "Neobkhodimye utochneniia," *Literaturnaia Gazeta*, 10 April 1965.

6 Ibid.

7 Goldman, op. cit., p. 183.

8 V. Chivilikhin, "Svetloe oko Sibiri," *Oktiabr'* 4 (1963).

9 Sholokhov's words are quoted in Komarov, op. cit., p. 8.

10 Goldman, op. cit., p. 189.

11 Chistiakov and Kuznetsov, op. cit.

12 Chistiakov and Kuznetsov, ibid.
13 Volkov, "Tuman nad Baikalom," *Literaturnaia Gazeta*, 6 February 1965.
14 A. Trofimuk, "Tsena vedomstvennogo upriamstva," *Literaturnaia Gazeta*, 13 April 1965; Oleg Volkov, "Tuman ne rasseialsia," *Literaturnaia Gazeta*, 13 April 1965, and "Tuman nad Baikalom."
15 Chistiakov and Kuznetsov, op. cit.; "Tol'ko dokumenty–eshche raz o Baikale," *Komsomol'skaia Pravda*, 9 June 1966, p. 4.
16 The State Committee was then headed by K. N. Rudnev, whose entire previous career had been spent in military procurement and technology. Since 1947 the State Committee under its various names and forms had always been headed by figures drawn from defense-related industries. See Organization for Economic Cooperation and Development, *Science Policy in the USSR* (Paris, 1969), p. 55.
17 B. P. Konstaninov et al., "Baikal zhdet," *Komsomol'skaia Pravda*, 11 May, 1962, p. 2.
18 "Tol'ko dokumenty," op. cit.
19 Konstaninov et al., op. cit.
20 Komarov, op. cit., p.14 and passim.
21 N. M. Zhavoronkov, "Obsuzhdenie dokladov," *Vestnik Akademii Nauk SSSR*, No. 7 (1967): 52–4.
22 Ibid., p. 53.
23 G. Gorin, letter to the editor, *Literaturnaia Gazeta*, 20 December 1967, trans. in *Current Digest of the Soviet Press* 19, No. 51 (1968): 12.
24 Trofimuk, op. cit.
25 Academician Zhavoronkov was the host at a dinner for a visiting American delegation in Moscow in September 1976 at which the author was present.
26 Volkov, "Tuman ne rasseialsia."
27 Trofimuk, op. cit.
28 A. Merkulov, "Alarm from Baikal," *Pravda*, 28 February 1965, trans. in *Current Digest of the Soviet Press* 17, No. 9 (1965): p. 25.
29 S. Mokshin and N. Chernavin, "Gnev Baikala," *Sovetskaia Rossiia*, 28 May 1966, p. 3.
30 Trofimuk, op. cit.
31 Volkov, "Tuman ne rasseialsia."
32 Konstantinov et al., op. cit.
33 Volkov, "Tuman ne rasseialsia."
34 Komarov, op. cit., p. 17.
35 *Komsomol'skaia Pravda*, 11 May 1966, quoted in Goldman, op. cit., pp. 193–4.
36 Oleg Volkov, "Lessons of Lake Baikal," *Literaturnaia Gazeta*, 11 October 1967, p. 12, trans. in *Current Digest of the Soviet Press* 19, No. 48 (1967): 6.
37 Ibid.
38 A. Gaidai, "The Secrets of Baikal," *Pravda*, 16 February 1969, trans. in *Current Digest of the Soviet Press* 21, No. 7 (1969): 28.

39  Yu. A. Kravchenko, "Baikal ostanetsia zhemchuzhinoi Sibiri," *Komsomol'skaia Pravda*, 11 February 1969, p. 1; "Baikal vziat pod okhranu," *Priroda*, No. 5 (1969): 108–9; "Zabota o Baikale," *Izvestiia*, 8 February 1969, p. 2; K. G. Pysin, letter to the editor, *Komsomol'skaia Pravda*, 11 February 1969, p. 1.

40  *Komsomol'skaia Pravda*, 11 August 1970, quoted in Goldman, op. cit., p. 206–7.

41  Komarov, op. cit., p. 15 and passim.

42  K. Prodai-Voda, "Chistye vody Baikala," *Trud*, 7 September 1976, p. 2; I. Borodavchenko, "Baikal: novaia stranitsa biografii," *Literaturnaia Gazeta*, No. 49 (4 December 1974): 11; A. Golovanov, "Dar Baikala," *Sovetskaia Belorussiia*, 5 January 1975, p. 4; Iurii Khromov, "Zhemchuzhina Sibiri," *Sovetskaia Estoniia*, 10 December 1974, p. 3; V. Khodii, "Baikalu – okhrannaia gramota," *Pravda*, 20 November 1974, p. 6; Iurii Belichenko, "Chtoby sberech' Baikal," *Komsomol'skaia Pravda*, 23 November 1974, p. 2; A. Larionov, "V Listvianke na Baikale," *Sovetskaia Rossiia*, 18 March 1975, p. 4. Also A. Veretennikov, "Preserve the Siberian Pearl" *Ekonomicheskaia Gazeta*, No. 4 (January 1977), trans. in *Current Digest of the Soviet Press* 29, No. 5 (1977): 15; A. Starukhin, "Ozero dlia vsekh," *Pravda*, 15 May 1978; V. Riashin, "Zapret na pol'zu," *Literaturnaia Gazeta*, 21 December 1977, p. 13; O. Volkov, "Nad Baikalom veter peremen," *Pravda*, 3 December 1977.

43  Komarov, op. cit., p. 22.

44  These findings are summarized and discussed in S. L. Vendrov and K. N. D'iakonov, *Vodokhranilishcha i okruzhaiushchaia prirodnaia sreda* (Moscow: Nauka, 1976), and S. L. Vendrov, *Problemy preobrazovaniia rechnykh sistem* (Leningrad, 1970).

45  S. L. Vendrov, et al., "O rabotakh IG AN SSSR v oblasti inzhenerno-geograficheskikh problem proektirovaniia i ekspluatatsii krupynykh ravninnykh vodokhranilishch," *Trudy koordinationnykh soveshchanii po gidrotekhnike*, No. 53 (1969): 41–3.

46  See Chapter 5.

47  Interviews conducted by the author during two six-week stays at the Institutes of Geography and Water Problems in late 1972 and early 1973.

48  P. L. Pirozhnikov, "Rybokhoziaistvennoe ispol'zovanie vodokhranilishch kompleksnogo naznacheniia," *Koordinatsionnye soveshchaniia po gidrotekhnike*, No. 53 (Leningrad: Energiia, 1969), pp. 81–93. See also V. V. Delitsyn, "Razmnozhenie ryb na volgoakhtubinskoi poime v usloviiakh zaregularivannogo rechnogo stoka," in *Volga-1* (Abstracts from a Conference on the Reservoirs of the Volga Basin, sponsored by the Institute of Freshwater Biology of the USSR Academy of Sciences) (Tol'iatti, 1968). These are just two examples from an enormous literature.

49  Vendrov and D'iaKonov, op. cit., p. 46.

50  A. I. Makarov and O. S. Ligun, "Nekotorye rezul'taty analiza svodnykh dannykh o vokokhranilishchakh SSSR," *Koordinatsionnye soveshchaniia po gidrotekhnike*, No. 70 (Leningrad: Energiia, 1972).

51 The project review process for the Krasnoiarsk Dam is described in detail in Iu. A. Kilinskii and V. S. Smetanich, *Kompensatsiia poter' sel'skogo khoziaistva pri sozdanii krupnykh vodokhranilishch: obzor literatury* (Moscow: VNII informatsii i tekhniko-ekonomicheskikh issledovanii po sel'skomu khoziaistvu 1970), pp. 40–1.

52 See Chapter 4 for further discussion of these issues.

53 V. S. Matveev, "Sushchestvuiushchii poriadok soglasovaniia i utverszhdeniia proektov po organizatsii vodokhranilishch: Kriticheskie zamechaniia i predlozheniia po uluchsheniiu sushchestvuiushchego poriadka soglasovaniia i utverzhedeniia proektov," in *Tezisy dokladov seminara-soveshchaniia obobshcheniia opyta proektirovaniia vodokhranilishch* (Moscow: Gidroproekt, 1969), pp. 75–76.

54 A. A. Korobchenkov, "Osnovnye zadachi nauchno-issledovatel'skikh rabot po obobshcheniiu opyta proektirovaniia, stroitel'stva i ekspluatatsii vodokhranilishch," *Trudy koordinationnykh soveshchanii po gidrotekhnike*, No. 53 (1969): 9.

55 The results were presented at periodic interagency conferences (*koordinationnye soveshchaniia*) hosted by the Vedeneev Research Institute for Hydro-Engineering in Leningrad. The proceedings of these conferences were published as *Trudy koordinationnykh soveshchanii po gidrotekhnike*, Nos. 53 (1969), 59 (1970), and 83 (1973).

56 Kilinskii and Smetanich, op. cit.

57 Interview with economist A. B. Gokhshtein, formerly with the Central Scientific Research Institute for Inland Waterways (Moscow).

58 See *Kompleksnoe osvoenie vodnykh resursov obskogo basseina* (Novosibirsk: Nauka, 1970), and A. B. Avakian et al., "Problemy sozdaniia vodokhranilishch v Sibiri," in *Prirodnye usloviia osvoeniia perspektivnykh raionov v Sibiri* (Novosibirsk, 1969).

59 Vendrov, *Problemy* (1970), pp. 115, 185, 188. See also P. S. Neporozhnii, "Gidroenergetika v vodokhoziaistvennom komplekse strany," *Vodnye Resursy*, No. 3 (1972): 11.

60 *Izuchenie i osvoenie rek Dal'nego Vostoka* (Moscow: Nauka, 1969), esp. pp. 25–9.

61 P. S. Neporozhnii, ed., *Gidroenergeticheskie resursy* (Moscow: Nauka, 1967), p. 100.

62 P. M. Dmitrievskii, "Kompleksnyi metod issledovanii i proektirivaniia, ego primenenie pri razrabotke problemy Angary," in *Biulleten' po vodnomu khoziaistvu*, No. 3 (1968): 99–106. See also A. I. Makarov and G. V. Sergachev, "Perspektivy sozdaniia i ispol'zovaniia vodokhranilishch v basseine Eniseia i Angary," *Issledovaniia beregov vodokhranilishch (Tezisy dokladov tret'ego soveshchaniia po izucheniiu beregov sibirskikh vokokhranilishch)* (Irkutsk: Siberian Division of the USSR Academy of Sciences, 1972), p. 15; and N. N. Iakovlev, "Ispol'zovanie unikal'nykh gidroenergoresursov v basseine Eniseia i Angary," *Trudy Gidroproekta* (Leningrad edition), No. 25 (13) (1971): 17–42.

63 See Chapter 4.

64  A. D. Orlov, "Nekotorye itogi vypolneniia proektnykh i stroitel'nykh rabot sozdanii vodokhranilishcha Saratovskoi GES," in *Tezisy dokladov*, op. cit., p. 89.

65  Vendrov, *Problemy*, pp. 41–5 and 136–46.

66  O. A. Dzhougarian, "The Sevan Lake Problem: Economic and Ecological Aspects," in U.S., Department of Commerce, Office of Environmental Affairs, *Proceedings of the First US/USSR Environmental Economics Symposium, Erevan, USSR,* October 1977 (Washington, D.C.: U.S. Government Printing Office, 1978) pp. 116–19.

67  *Sel'skoe Khoziaistvo SSSR* (Moscow: Statistika, 1971) p. 361. E. E. Alekseevskii, "Tretii god piatiletki i zadachi vodokhoziaistvennykh organizatsii," *Gidrotekhnika i Melioratsiia,* No. 1 (1973): 3, and "Melioratsiia v chetvertom gody deviatoi piatiletki," *Gidrotekhnika i Melioratsiia,* No. 1 (1974): 8.

68  M. N. Loiter, "Rezervy povysheniia effektivnosti ispol'zovaniia vodnykh resursov," in *Intensifikatsiia i rezervy ekonomiki* (Moscow: Nauka, 1970), p. 70, and *Sel'skoe khoziaistvo SSSR* (Moscow: Statistika, 1971), p. 361.

69  *Gosudarstvennyi piatiletnii plan razvitiia narodnogo khoziaistva SSSR na 1971–75 gody* (Moscow: Politizdat, 1972), p. 102.

70  Robert W. Campbell, "Issues in Soviet R&D: The Energy Case," in U.S., Congress, Joint Economic Committee, *The Soviet Economy in a New Perspective* (Washington, D.C.: U.S. Government Printing Office, 1976), pp. 97–112.

71  One of the few public utterances about the possible dangers of nuclear power came from Petr L. Kapitsa at a plenary session of the USSR Academy of Sciences. See P. L. Kapitsa, "Energiia i fizika," *Vestnik Akademii Nauk,* 1 (1976): 34–43. Of late, there has been some concern about the use of nuclear power for co-generation near large urban centers. See N. Dollezhal' and Iu. Koriakin, "Iadernaia elektroenergetika: dostizheniia i problemy," *Kommunist,* No. 14 (September 1979): 19–28. For an official rejoinder (which does not mention Dollezhal' directly, however), see F. Ia. Ovchinnikov, "Atomnoi energetike – chetvert' veka," *Teploenergetika,* No. 7 (1979): 4.

72  B. N. Laskorin et al., "Kachestvo i okhrana vody v basseine reki-Volgi," *Vodnye Resursy* 4 (1975): 23–25.

73  Ibid.

74  O. M. Voronova, "Uvelichenie stoimosti ochistki stochnykh vod i tekhniko-ekonomicheskie aspekty etoi problemy," *Vodnye Resursy* 1 (1976): 141.

75  I. I. Borodavchenko, "Problemy ispol'zovaniia i okhrany vodnykh resursov SSSR," *Gidrotekhnika i Melioratsiia,* No. 4 (1976): 9.

76  Interview with the USSR minister of reclamation, E. E. Alekseevskii, "Vodu nado berech'," *Trud,* 24 January 1976.

77  L. I. Brezhnev, "Report of the Central Committee of the CPSU," *XXVvi. s"ezd Kommunisticheskoi Partii Sovetskogo Soiuza (stenograficheskii otchet),* (Moscow: Politizdat, 1976) 1: 67.

78  Statement by K. A. Efimov, chief of Gosplan's Department of Planning of Scientific Research and Development, at a meeting of the US/Soviet Working Group on Management of Technological Innovation, State Committee on Science and Technology, Moscow, February 1979 (author's notes).

79  A translation of the USSR Principles of Water Legislation can be found in Irving K. Fox, ed., *Water Resources Law and Policy in the Soviet Union* (Madison: University of Wisconsin Press, 1971), pp. 221–39.

80  On the Volga-Ural: Decree of the CPSU Central Committee and the USSR Council of Ministers: "O merakh po predotvrascheniiu zagriazneniia basseinov rek Volgi i Urala neochishchennymi stochnymi vodami," *Pravda*, 17 March 1972. On the Baltic Sea, Decree of the USSR Council of Ministers, "O merakh po usileniiu okhrany ot zagriazneniia basseina Baltiiskogo moria," *Izvestiia*, 20 August 1976. On the Black and Azov seas: Decree of the CPSU Central Committee and USSR Council of Ministers, "O merakh po predotvrashcheniiu zagriazneniia basseinov Chernogo i Azovskogo morei," February 1976, described in I. Gasiev, "Voda i zhizn'," *Zaria vostoka*, 21 May 1976, p. 4.

81  Decree of the USSR Council of Ministers and the Central Committee of the Communist Party of the Soviet Union, "Ob usilenii okhrany prirody i uluchshenii ispol'zovaniia prirodnykh resursov," Decree No. 898, 29 December 1972.

82  P. Poletaev, "Plan i okhrana prirody," *Planovoe Khoziaistvo* 4 (1976): 28–35.

83  For Western discussions of the beginnings of the Soviet water-quality program, see Goldman, op. cit. See also Donald R. Kelley, "Environmental Policy-Making in the USSR: The Role of Industrial and Environmental Interest Groups," *Soviet Studies* 27, No. 4 (October 1976): 570–89, and "Environmental Problems as a New Policy Issue," in Karl Ryavec, ed., *Soviet Society and the Communist Party* (Amherst: University of Massachusetts Press, 1978), pp. 88–107; Fred Singleton, ed., *Environmental Misuse in the Soviet Union* (New York: Praeger, 1976); David E. Powell, "The Social Costs of Modernization: Ecological Problems in the USSR," *World Politics* 23, No. 4 (July 1971): 618–34; and John W. Kramer, "The Politics of Conservation and Pollution in the USSR" (Ph. D. diss., University of Virginia, Charlottesville, 1973).

84  Secondary treatment is already the general rule there, and Moscow sanitary engineers are now moving on to tertiary treatment by means of filtration through sand and gravel. Moscow is also the first city in the country to have begun to build treatment facilities for polluted runoff from city streets.

 Moscow clearly represents a special case: Although it appears that more pollution control is being done there than elsewhere in the country, more also needs to be done, because of the very great concentration of industry and population and the limited natural streamflow from outside the area. For example, the flow of the Moscow River inside the city limits is composed of: treated sewage water, 47 m$^3$/sec; industrial effluent, 8 m³/sec; surface runoff, 10 m³/sec; as well as the augmented inflow of the river itself, which is 40 m³/sec. The city's streamflow consists of such a large proportion of treated sewage water that even secondary biological treatment is not enough; much of the city's sewage is industrial in origin and contains toxic and poorly degradable substances; consequently, the efficiency of biological waste treatment is considerably lowered.

In view of these special circumstances, it is not surprising that, even though 400 million rubles was spent on waste treatment in Moscow from 1965 to 1975 and nearly 1,000 enterprises were equipped with waste-treatment facilities, the same complaints can be heard as in the rest of the country about poor design, delays in construction, and negligent operation. A recent article concludes that the quality of the Moscow River has increased only "somewhat" in the last ten years. See A. N. Lavrenov, S. V. Il'inskii, and E. E. Scherbakov, "Vodoemam byt' chistymi," *Gorodskoe khoziaistvo Moskvy* 4 (1976): 31–2.

For a background description of environmental policy in Moscow, see David E. Powell, "Politics and the Urban Environment: The City of Moscow," *Journal of Comparative Political Studies* 10 (October 1977): 433–54. See also M. G. Riabyshev, "Okhrana vodnykh resursov Moskvy," *Vodnye Resursy* 5 (1975): 15–32. Finally, an account of the early history of sanitation engineering in Moscow can be found in A. Rubinov, "Saving the River," *Literaturnaia Gazeta*, 4 October 1978, p. 11, trans. in *Current Digest of the Soviet Press* 30, No. 46 (13 December 1978): 5.

85  Poletaev, op. cit.
86  This figure is derived from a comparison of nationwide net addition to capacity for the period 1971–3 with the corresponding figure for the Volga River alone during the period 1972–4. The former figure comes from Iu. P. Belichenko and Iu. B. Egorov, "Ob opyte raboty organov vodnogo nadzora," *Problemy okhrany vod*, No. 5 (1974): 13. The latter figure comes from K. I. Akulov, "Public Health Aspects of the Protection of Water Resources in the Light of the Decree of the CC CPSU and the USSR Council of Ministers, 'Regarding Measures to Prevent the Pollution of the Volga and Ural Rivers by Untreated Wastewater,'" *Gigiena i Sanitariia* 2 (1976): 1–7.
87  V. Golovin, "Khraniteli chistoi vody," *Kazakhstanskaia Pravda*, 21 January 1975, p. 4.
88  I. Gasiev, "Voda i zhizn'," *Zaria Vostoka*, 21 May 1976.
89  T. Mukhamedov, "Khranite vodu v chistote," *Kommunist Tadzhikistana*, 12 May 1976, p. 3.

4   *Displacing Stalinist dogma on the price of capital*

1  For a few examples from a large literature, see Richard W. Judy, "The Economists," in H. Gordon Skilling and Franklyn Griffiths, eds., *Interest Groups in Soviet Politics* (Princeton, N.J.: Princeton University Press, 1971), pp. 209–52; Herbert S. Levine, "Economics," in George Fischer,

ed., *Science and Ideology in Soviet Society* (New York: Atherton Press, 1967), pp. 107–38.

2 Moshe Levin, *Political Undercurrents in Soviet Economic Debates: from Bukharin to the Modern Reformers*, (Princeton, N.J.: Princeton University Press, 1974); Michael Ellman, *Planning Problems in the USSR: the Contribution of Mathematical Economics to Their Solution, 1960–1971* (Cambridge: Cambridge University Press, 1973); Albina Tretyakova and Igor Birman, "Input-Output Analysis in the USSR," *Soviet Studies* 27, No. 2 (April 1976): 157–86; Alfred Zauberman, *The Mathematical Revolution in Soviet Planning* (London: Oxford University Press, 1975); Aron Katsenelinboigen, "Conflicting Trends in Soviet Economics in the Post-Stalin Era," *Russian Review* 35, No. 4 (October 1976): 373–99; same, "Soviet Science and the Economists/Planners," in John R. Thomas and Ursula M. Kruse-Vaucienne, eds., *Soviet Science and Technology: Domestic and Foreign Perspectives* (Washington, D.C.: George Washington University Press, 1977), pp. 230–43.

3 From 1950 to 1974, the number of scientific personnel working in economic sciences grew by an average of 12.7%, far above the national average for all scientific and technical specialties of 8.5%. In second place came engineering sciences, with 11.4%. See S. A. Kugel' and P. B. Shelishch, "The Scientific Intelligentsia of the USSR: Factors and Trends in its Development," *Sotsiologicheskie issledovaniia* 1 (1979): 33–42, trans. in *Current Digest of the Soviet Press* 31, No. 9 (28 March 1979): 15. It is true that most of these newly minted economists are not scholars but rather low-level clerks who perform simple calculations in planning offices. But the figure is still revealing as a surrogate of the profession's rising status and practical importance.

4 See Chapter 3 of the author's doctoral dissertation "Organizational Adaptation to Stress: A Study of Water Resource Development in the US and the USSR," Harvard University, 1974. For further information see D. M. Iurinov, "Institut 'Gidroproekt' imeni S. Ia. Zhuka i gidroenergetika strany za 50 let," *Trudy Gidroproekta* 16 (1969): 22. See also Boris Komarov, *Unichtozhenie prirody* (Frankfurt: Possev, 1978), pp. 86–91.

5 N. V. Razin, "Vklad institut 'Gidroproekt' v delo razvitiia gidroenergetiki i kompleksnogo ispol'zovaniia vodnkykh resursov SSSR," *Trudy Gidroproekta* 16 (1969): 34.

6 The early issues and events surrounding the problem of capital intensity from the 1920s to the early 1950s have been thoroughly analyzed by Gregory Grossman in "Capital-Intensity: A Problem in Soviet Planning" (Ph.D. diss., Harvard University, 1952). I have borrowed freely from his account to bring the reader quickly to the recent period of change.

7 For a discussion of Soviet price formation and its implications, see Alec Nove, *The Soviet Economy*, 3rd ed. (London: Allen and Unwin, 1978).

8 Grossman, op. cit., p. 157.

9 Ibid., pp. 158–60.

10 Ibid., p. 16.

11  A. A. Beschinskii, "Energetika i razvitie teorii effektivnosti kapital'nykh vlozhenii," in Akademiia Nauk SSSR, Institut ekonomiki, *Metody i praktika opredeleniia effektivnosti kapital'nykh vlozhenii i novoi tekhniki,* No. 21 (Moscow: Nauka, 1972): 8–9. GOELRO, a state commission of the 1920s which formulated a pioneering long-range plan for the electrification of Russia, used an interest rate of 6%.

12  E. A. Elokhin and B. L. Erlikhman, "Narodnokhoziaistvennoe znachenie proektiruemogo gidroenergostroitel'stva," *Trudy Gidroproekta* 16 (1969): 217–18. The "pay-out period" (*srok okupaemosti*) is defined as the reciprocal of the "norm of capital effectiveness," the saving in current costs (between two alternative projects) per unit of additional capital investment:

$$E = \frac{I_2 - I_1}{K_1 - K_2}$$

where $I_1$ and $I_2$ are the current costs of alternatives 1 and 2, respectively, and $K_1$ and $K_2$ are the corresponding capital investments. Gregory Grossman calls this ratio the "cost-saving ratio." It is equivalent to an interest rate if a minimum cost-saving ratio is set for all such pair-wise comparisons. See Grossman, op. cit., pp. 29–36.

13  Grossman, op. cit., pp. 237–9. Curiously though, thermal-power designers, according to Grossman, used no capital-intensity criterion whatsoever. In fact, policy on this question varied widely from *glavk* to *glavk* within the Ministry of Power Station Construction, to which both hydro and thermal power belonged. At times there were as many as four different values of the capital-intensity norm in use simultaneously.

14  Gregory Grossman qualifies this observation with the following comment: "True, it was the engineers who reinvented the capital-intensity criterion and applied it (mostly clandestinely). But they never did arrive at the theory of the 'norm' of either the CRE, or the recoupment period, or the time factor. An economist, Khachaturov, gave their work an economic cast and content, though he, too, being an orthodox Marxist, did not and could not provide the theory of the norm. This was done by two 'underground' economists, Novozhilov and Kantorovich. While also a Marxist, Novozhilov was familiar with neoclassical economics, so his theorizing may have had an inspiration from the West, although I would not deny it a great deal of originality. Kantorovich, on the other hand, started with his plywood machines and apparently invented the whole theory from scratch via the mathematics of 'efficient use of resources.' " (Personal communication to the author, May 1979.)

15  Gregory Grossman, "Scarce Capital and Soviet Doctrine," *Quarterly Journal of Economics* 67, No. 3 (August 1953): 311–43.

16  These developments are described in Razin, op. cit., p. 34. On the story of the Volga-Baltic Canal, see Tsentral'nyi Institut Normativnykh Issledovanii i Nauchnotekhnicheskoi Informatsii "Orgtransstroi" Ministerstva Transportnogo Stroitel'stva SSSR, *Tekhnicheskii otchet o*

*stroitel'stve Volgo-baltiiskogo vodnogo puti im. Lenina*, Vol. II: *Organizatsiia stroitel'stva i proizvodstva rabot* (Moscow, 1968), pp. 10–11.

17 Beschinskii, op. cit., p. 9.

18 *Tipovaia metodika opredeleniia ekonomicheskoi effektivnosti vlozhenii i novoi tekhniki v narodnom khoziaistve SSSR* (Moscow: USSR Academy of Sciences, 1960).

19 I. I. Fain, "Sovremennoe sostoianie metodiki tekhniko-ekonomicheskikh raschetov v energetike," in *Tezisy dokladov seminara-soveshchaniia obobshcheniia opyta proektirovaniia vodokhranilishch* (Moscow: Gidroproekt, 1969), pp. 5–8.

20 Elokhin and Erlikhman, op. cit., p. 221.

21 Fain, op. cit.

22 Gosudarstvennyi komitet pri Sovete Ministrov SSSR po nauke i tekhnike, "Metodika tekhniko-ekonomicheskikh raschetov v energetike" (Moscow, 1966). This document was not directly available to me, but it is discussed in E. A. Elokhin, "O normativnoi effektivnosti kapital'nykh vlozhenii i norme ucheta faktora vremeni," in *Trudy Gidroproekta* 17 (1969): 10–30.

23 Elokhin and Erlikhman, op. cit.

24 Elokhin, op. cit., p. 17.

25 B. L. Baburin, "Napravleniia metodicheskikh issledovanii effektivnosti gidroenergostroitel'stva," *Trudy Gidroproekta* 29 (1973): 5.

26 Ibid., p. 6.

27 I. I. Fain, "Otsenka rentabel'nosti kapitalovlozhenii pri stroitel'stve gidroelektrostantsii," *Trudy Gidroproekta* 29 (1973): 22.

28 Baburin, op. cit., p. 5.

29 USSR Gosplan, USSR Gosstroi, and USSR Academy of Sciences, *Tipovaia metodika opredeleniia ekonomicheskoi effektivnosti kapital'nykh vlozhenii* (Moscow: Ekonomika, 1969).

30 Gosplan SSSR and Akademiia Nauk SSSR, "Metodika opredeleniia ekonomicheskoi effektivnosti vnedreniia novoi tekhniki, mekhanizatsii i avtomatizatsii proizvodstvennykh protsessov v promyshlennost'," described in *Gidroenergeticheskie resursy* (Moscow: Energiia, 1967), p. 231.

31 Ibid.

32 E. G. Skvortsova, "Sushchestvuiushchie metody tekhniko-ekonomicheskikh raschetov v vodnom khoziaistve," in *Tezisy dokladov k nauchno-tekhnicheskomu soveshcheaniiu, "Tekhniko-ekonomicheskie voprosy proektirovaniia kompleksnykh vodno-khoziaistvennykh ob"ektov i vodno-khoziaistvennykh sistem"* (Leningrad: Leningrad Polytechnical Institute, 1969), p. 6.

33 Grossman, "Scarce Capital," p. 313. There is another necessary condition for norm equality through the economy; namely, that *interbranch* transfers of capital be responsive to differences in marginal returns. If this condition does not hold, there is no clinching efficiency argument for norm equalization through the economy. Rather, the norm in each branch should take into account internal demand for capital and in-

ternal supply (autonomously determined). I am grateful to Professor Grossman for calling this point to my attention.

34 T. S. Khachaturov, *Ekonomicheskaia effektivnost' kapital'nykh vlozhenii* (Moscow: Ekonomika, 1964), pp. 83–7.

35 M. N. Loiter, *Prirodnye resursy i effektivnost' kapital'nykh vlozhenii* (Moscow: Nauka, 1974), p. 117.

36 Beschinskii, op. cit., p. 17.

37 V. P. Zakharov and V. A. Kiktenko, "Normativ effektivnosti kapital'nykh vlozhenii i kriterii optimizatsii vodnokhoziaistvennykh sistem," in *Tezisy dokladov,* op. cit., p. 6.

38 M. N. Marmer and N. M. Chernyi, "K metodike raschetov ekonomicheskoi effektivnosti kapitalovlozhenii,' *Trudy Gidroproekta* 29 (1973): 19.

39 See M. Troitskii, "Na novom etape," *Novyi Mir,* No. 1 (1975): 169–79.

40 Beschinskii, op. cit., p. 14.

41 The time factor ($E_p$ – *Koeffitsient privedeniia zatrat,* or *faktor vremeni*) as defined in the most recent methodology (1969) is used simultaneously with the capital-effectiveness coefficient ($E_n$) as follows:

$$\sum_{t=1}^{T} (E_n K_t + \Delta I_t)(1 + E_p)^{\tau - t} = \min$$

where: $E_n$ = capital-effectiveness norm (*normativnyi koeffitsient effektivnosti kapital'nykh vlozhenii*); $E_p$ = time factor (*koeffitsient privedeniia zatrat*); $K_t$ = capital outlay in year $t$; $I_t$ = costs of operation, maintenance, capital repair, and replacement (*tekushchie izderzhki*); $\tau$ = basis year to which all quantities are discounted; $T$ = construction and gestation period (period of temporary operation, during which capital outlays and current costs are variable); and $\Delta I_t$ = increase in current costs in year $t$-$1$ over year $t$ (includes operation, maintenance, capital repair, and replacement). *Tipovaia metodika* (1969), op. cit.

42 Beschinskii, op. cit. p. 14.

43 Loiter, op. cit. pp. 118–19.

44 Elokhin, op. cit. pp. 10–15.

45 Ibid., p. 15.

46 For a fuller discussion of these issues, see *Gidroenergeticheskie resursy* (Moscow: Nauka, 1967), pp. 238–9; for background, see R. W. Campbell, "Accounting for Depreciation in the Soviet Economy," *Quarterly Journal of Economics* 70 (November 1956): 481–506, and Otto Eckstein, *Water Resource Development: The Economics of Project Evaluation* (Cambridge, Mass.: Harvard University Press, 1958), pp. 91–4.

47 Beschinskii, op. cit. p. 16.

48 Ibid.

49 See Levine, op. cit.

50 M. N. Loiter, "Rezervy povysheniia effektivnosti ispol'zovaniia vodnykh resursov," in *Intensifikatsiia i rezervy ekonomiki* (Moscow: Nauka, 1970), p. 78.

51 G. E. Moskalev, "Kanal Volga-Ural i ego rol' v razvitii khoziaistva Severnogo Prikaspiia," in Geograficheskoe obshchestvo SSSR, zapadno-kazakhstanskii otdel, *Voprosy geografii severnogo Prikaspiia* No. 1 (Leningrad, 1971): 82.

52 In 1970, 93% of the useful capacity of the 205 largest reservoirs in the country was accounted for by those reservoirs having hydropower as their leading component. A. I. Makarov and O. S. Ligun, "Nekotorye rezultaty analiza svodnykh dannykh o vodokhranilishchakh SSSR," *Koordinatsionnye soveshchaniia po gidrotekhnike*, No. 70 (Leningrad: Energiia, 1972): 148.

53 Elokhin and Erlikhman, op. cit., p. 220.

54 L. G. Goruleva et al., "Nekotorye voprosy raspredeleniia zatrat," *Trudy Gidroproekta* 29 (1973): 196.

55 In all three cases the cause of the failure was a significant increase in the project costs assigned to hydropower, as a result of controversy over compensation for losses of agricultural output because of inundation by the reservoirs. The increase came after construction had already begun. The test was applied essentially ex post facto. See Razin, op. cit., p. 29.

56 P. S. Neporozhnii, ed., *Gidroenergetika i kompleksnoe ispol'zovanie vodnykh resursov SSSR* (Moscow: Energiia, 1970), pp. 97–8.

57 A. A. Makeev, "Voprosy ekonomicheskogo obosnovniia vodokho-ziaistvennogo kompleksa," *Trudy Gidroproekta* 29 (1973): 25.

58 See, e.g., Marmer and Chernyi, op. cit., p. 18; T. S. Khachaturov and M. N. Loiter, "Effektivnost' kapital'nykh vlozhenii i ekonomicheskaia otsenka vodnykh resursov," *Vodnye Resursy*, No. 1 (1973): 7, and V. P. Zakharov, "Voprosy ekonomicheskoi effektivnosti kapital'nykh vlozhenii v vod-noe khoziaistvo," *Problemy gidroenergetiki i vodnogo khoziaistva* (Kazakhskii NII Energetiki), No. 7 (1970): 5–6.

59 Marmer and Chernyi, op. cit., pp. 22–3; Khachaturov and Loiter, op. cit., p. 7.

60 B. G. Kovalenko, "Nekotorye voprosy optimizatsii ispol'zovaniia vodozemel'nykh resursov basseinov gornykh rek (primentiel'no k bas-seinam Srednei Azii)," *Voprosy vodnogo khoziaistva* (Kirgizskii NII vodnogo khoziaistva), No. 10 (1967): 10.

5   *Technology assessment Soviet style*

1 U.S., Congress, Senate, Committee on Public Works, Special Subcom-mittee on Western Water Development, *Western Water Development: A Summary of Water Resources Projects, Plans, and Studies Relating to the Western and Midwestern United States* (Washington, D.C.: U.S. Government Printing Office, 1966). Soviet specialists have followed with interest the fate of the North American Water and Power Alliance (NAWAPA) project and the rise of environmental regulation in the United States. The fact that environmental opposition has brought a halt to projects like NAWAPA has not been lost on Soviet geographers. For an example of a Soviet description of the American situation, see the

account of a symposium held at the International Institute for Applied Systems Analysis, "Mezhregional'nye perebroski rechnogo stoka," *Vodnye Resursy*, No. 3 (1979): 199–203.

2 See Chapter 9 and Philip P. Micklin, "Irrigation Development in the USSR during the Tenth Five Year Plan (1976–1980)," *Soviet Geography: Review and Translation* 19 No. 1 (1978): 1–24.

3 See Chapter 8.

4 See, e.g., Brezhnev's long review of the agricultural situation at the July 1978 plenum of the Central Committee of the CPSU, "O dal'neishem razvitii sel'skogo khoziaistva SSSR," *Pravda*, 4 July 1978; this concern was even more evident at the November 1979 plenum (see Chapter 11).

5 S. Enders Wimbush and Dmitry Ponomareff, *Alternatives for Mobilizing Soviet Central Asian Labor: Outmigration and Regional Development*, R-2476-AF (Santa Monica, Calif.: Rand Corporation, 1979).

6 The geographical and ecological aspects of the Soviet diversion idea have been followed and analyzed for many years by Philip P. Micklin, notably in the following articles: "Soviet Plans to Reverse the Flow of Rivers: the Kama-Vychegda-Pechora Project," *Canadian Geographer* 18, No. 3 (1969): 199–215; "NAWAPA and Two Siberian Water-Diversion Proposals: A Geographical Comparison and Appraisal," *Soviet Geography: Review and Translation* 18, No. 2 (February 1977). "Environmental Factors in Soviet Interbasin Water Transfer Policy," *Environmental Management* 2, No. 6 (1979): 567–80; and "Disciplinary Plans for USSR Rivers," *Geographical Magazine* 51 (July 1979): 701–6.

7 A. N. Kosygin, "Kurs na effektivnost' – vazhneishee zveno ekonomicheskoi politiki Partii," *Planovoe Khoziaistvo* 7 (1979): 13.

8 CPSU Central Committee and USSR Council of Ministers, "O provedenii nauchno-issledovatel'skikh i proektnykh rabot po problemam perebroski chasti stoka severnykh i sibirskikh rek v iuzhnye raiony strany" (Decree No. 1084, 21 December 1978), *Sobranie postanovlenii pravitel'stva SSSR*, No. 4 (1979): 90–5; hereafter cited as 'O provedenii."

9 For a capsule history of the Pechora project up to 1968, see G. L. Sarukhanov, "Perebroska stoka severnykh rek," in *Trudy Gidroproekta* 16 (1969): 446–8. See also V. P. Repkin, "Letopis' gidrotekhnicheskogo stroitel'stva za 50 let," *Trudy Gidroproekta* 16 (1969): 547, and "Nam eto teper' po plechu," *Ekonomicheskaia Gazeta*, 21 February 1961, p. 3.

10 The chain of hydropower projects in the Kama-Volga basin and their environmental consequences are described in Philip P. Micklin, "International Environmental Implications of Soviet Development of the Volga River," *Human Ecology* 5, No. 2 (1977): 113–33.

11 The political troubles of hydropower during the 1950s and 1960s are described in the last two chapters of this book.

12 For reviews of the anticipated environmental impact of the early version of the Pechora project, see G. I. Varlamov, "Podschet zatrat neftegazovoi promyshlennosti pri sozdanii vodokhranilisch KVP vodokhoziaistvennogo kompleksa," and A. F. Anufriev, "Osobennosti energeticheskogo osvoeniia rek Komi ASSR," pp. 52–55, *Problemy ekonomiki Komi*

ASSR, Trudy Komi filiala AN SSSR, No. 20 (Syktyvkar, 1970). See also L. A. Brattsev, V. A. Vitiazeva, and V. P. Podoplepov, *O vlianii pere-broski stoka severnykh rek v bassein Kaspiia na narodnoe khoziaistvo Komi ASSR* (Leningrad: Akademiia Nauk SSSR, Komi filial, 1967); and L. A. Brattsev and V. A. Vitiazeva, "Novye idei v proektnykh resheniiakh po probleme perebroski stoka severnykh rek," *Izvestiia Komi filiala geograficheskogo obshchestva SSSR*, Pt. 2, No. 2 (12) (1970): 3–5.

13 This description of the institutional background is based on interviews conducted by the author at the Institutes of Geography and Water Problems, USSR Academy of Sciences, in Moscow in 1972 and 1973.

14 I. A. Gerardi, "O povyshenii vodoobesbechennosti reki-Volgi i perebroske chasti stoka severnykh rek na iug," *Gidrotekhnika i Melioratsiia*, No. 11 (1973): 112–17.

15 Ibid., and M. I. L'vovich, "Geograficheskie aspekty territorial'nogo pereraspredeleniia vodnykh resursov," *Izvestiia Akademii Nauk SSSR (ser. geograficheskaia)*, No. 2 (1977): 22–37; and S. L. Vendrov and I. S. Glukh, "O nekotorykh problemakh preobrazovaniia rechnoi seti rus-skoi ravniny," in *Voprosy preobrazovaniia prirody russkoi ravniny* (Moscow: Institute of Geography, USSR Academy of Sciences, 1973), pp. 174–7.

16 "Puti perebroski vod," *Vodnyi Transport*, 2 July 1977, p.4. Gidroproekt is still calling for both versions to be executed simultaneously.

17 G. Voropaev, "Chtoby dat' vodu iugu," *Izvestiia*, 13 August 1978.

18 "O provedenii," op. cit.

19 Brattsev, Vitiazeva, and Podoplepov, op. cit.

20 Varlamov, op. cit.

21 Anufriev, op. cit., pp. 52–5.

22 Brattsev and Vitiazeva, op. cit., pp. 3–5.

23 V. P. Podoplepov and L. A. Brattsev, "Shestoe uslovie," *Literaturnaia Gazeta*, No. 46 (17 November 1976): 10.

24 Ibid.

25 See I. A. Gerardi, "Vtoraia Amu-Dar'ia dlia Srednei Azii," *Pravda Vostoka*, 6 October 1974.

26 S. L. Vendrov and K. N. D'iakonov, *Vodokhranilishcha i okru-zhaiushchaia prirodnaia sreda* (Moscow: Nauka, 1976), pp. 122–3; S. L. Vendrov, "Problemy territorial'nogo pereraspredeleniia rechnogo stoka," *Izvestiia Akademii Nauk SSSR, (ser. geograficheskaia)*, No. 1 (1975): 38.

27 G. G. Gangart, "On the Question of Diverting Part of the Unused Runoff of Northern and Siberian Rivers into Regions Suffering from a Shortage of Water Resources," *Gidrotekhnicheskoe Stroitel'stvo*, 8 (1971): 10–13, trans. in *Soviet Geography: Review and Translation*: 13, No. 9 (November 1972), and related articles in the same issue.

28 Voropaev, op. cit.

29 An account of the issues may be found in *Kompleksnoe osvoenie vodnykh resursov obskogo basseina* (Novosibirsk: Nauka, 1970), esp. pp. 7–23 and 237–49.

30  Vendrov and D'iakonov, op. cit., p. 127. See also the discussion in Micklin, "NAWAPA and Two Siberian Water-Diversion Proposals," p. 95, and the collection published by the Arctic and Antarctic Scientific Research Institute, *Otsenka vozmozhnykh ismenenii rezhima nizov'ev i ust'ev rek arkticheskoi zony Zapadnoi Sibiri pod vliianiem vodokhoziaistvennykh meropriiatii* (Leningrad: AANII, 1976).

31  Wimbush and Ponomareff, op. cit.

32  Speech of D. A. Kunaev, *XXVyi. s"ezd, Kommunisticheskoi Partii Sovietskogo Soiuza* (Moscow: Politizdat, 1976), 1: 142.

33  Speech of Sh. R. Rashidov, *XXVyi. s"ezd*, 1: 179–80. Rashidov's strong interest in the Central Asian diversion project continues, as is evident by his presence, together with the presidents of all five of the Central Asian Academies of Sciences and 600 other official participants, at a scientific conference on diversions held in Tashkent in April 1978. See a report in *Vodnye Resursy*, No. 2 (1979): 197–9.

34  Speech of M. G. Gapurov, *XXVyi. s"ezd*, 1: 348.

35  The speeches of the southern party officials suggest that they may have been fighting uphill, trying to reverse an unfavorable verdict. Kunaev said, "The time has come, comrades, to examine the problem of the Aral." Rashidov added, "We ask the CPSU Central Committee and the USSR Council of Ministers to decide the question of completing during the coming five-year plan all the scientific studies, surveys, and hydroengineering design work for the diversion." Gapurov in his speech referred to "Comrade Rashidov's suggestion to accelerate a practical resolution of the question . . . We support this suggestion." Bondarenko talking about the European projects, used similar language: "We support the suggestions made here earlier, that the time has come to determine concrete measures."

36  Speech of A. N. Kosygin, *XXVyi. s"ezd*, 2: 38.

37  That item was apparently judged sufficiently important by the audience (or by the editors of the transcript) to warrant a burst of official applause.

38  "O predvaritel'nykh itogakh vsesoiuznoi perepisi naseleniia 1979 goda," *Pravda*, 22 April 1979, p. 4. For Western discussions of this issue, see, e.g., Grey Hodnett, "Technology and Social Change: the Politics of Cotton Growing," in Henry W. Morton and Rudolf L. Tokes, eds., *Soviet Politics and Society in the 1970's* (New York: Free Press, 1974), pp. 60–117; Murray Feshbach and Stephen Rapawy, "Soviet Population and Manpower Trends and Policies," in U.S., Congress, Joint Economic Committee, *The Soviet Economy in a New Perspective* (Washington, D.C.: U.S. Government Printing Office, 1976), pp. 113–54.

39  One of the first Soviet works devoted explicitly to projections of future population levels is G. A. Bondarskaia, *Fertility in the USSR: Its Ethno-Demographic Aspect* (Moscow, 1977). There have been many since.

40  "Podachi vody iz sibirskikh rek," *Pravda Vostoka*, 24 April 1975.

41  See, e.g., "Napoiat Aral sibirskie reki," *Pravda Vostoka*, 17 August 1978 (interview with K. I. Lapkin, corresponding member of the Uzbek Academy of Sciences). An account of a scientific conference held in Tashkent

in April 1978 refers to "the rapid rate of population growth, together with its low mobility, which engenders a serious social problem of rational use of the region's labor resources." See "Konferentsiia 'Problemy perebroski chasti stoka sibirskikh rek v Sredniuiu Aziiu i Kazakhstan v svete reshenii XXV s"ezda KPSS,' " *Vodnye Resursy*, No. 2 (1979): 197–9.

42  "Perspectivy bol'shoi vody," *Pravda Vostoka*, 30 April 1978.

43  "O provedenii," op. cit.

44  A. N. Kosygin, "Kurs na effektivnost' – vazhneishee zveno ekonomicheskoi politiki partii," *Planovoe Khoziaistvo* 7 (1979): 13.

45  G. Voropaev, "Kuda tech' Obi i Pechore," *Sotsialisticheskaia Industriia*, 7 August 1978.

46  F. Ia. Ukrainskii, "K voprosu o narodnokhoziaistvennom osbosnovanii krupnykh perebrosok stoka," *Trudy Gidroproekta* 29 (1973): 154–8.

47  L. G. Goruleva, "Ekonomicheskaia effektivnost' mnogootraslevogo kompleksa perebroski stoka Pechory i Vychegdy v Volgu," *Trudy Gidroproekta*, 17 (1969): 214–25.

48  L'vovich, op. cit.

49  A biographical sketch of Vendrov appeared in *Vodnye Resursy*, No. 6 (1978): 196.

50  The differences between the two institutes should not be overstated. For example, during the 1970s Vendrov moved from the Institute of Geography to IVP.

51  For summary accounts of this activity, see R. V. Donchenko et al., "Issledovaniia vozmozhnykh posledstvii territorial'nogo pereraspredeleniia vodnykh resursov," *Vodnye Resursy* No. 1 (1977): 30–5. The main findings so far are discussed in Micklin, "Environmental Factors."

52  "Perspektivy bol'shoi vody," op. cit.

53  N. Nekrasov and N. Razin, "Vody severa pomogut iugu," *Pravda*, 11 June 1978. In 1977 V. V. Ivanov, a specialist at the Arctic and Antarctic Scientific Research Institute, wrote that the state of knowledge "was still insufficient for a well-substantiated evaluation of the change resulting from a partial withdrawal of streamflow," *Vodnye Resursy*, No. 5 (1977): 194. It is important to note that the issue is data concerning the possible meso- and macro-scale changes resulting from the changes. Soviet scientists have already fairly conclusively documented the likelihood of many important local environmental effects, particularly those associated with downstream flow reduction and reservoir construction over the long term.

54  Among the articles emphasizing the virtues of the diversion project in improving the drainage of western Siberia, see I. A. Gerardi, "Problema ispol'zovaniia vod obskogo basseina dlia obvodneniia Kazakhstana i Srednei Azii v komplekse s osusheniem zapadno-sibirskoi nizmennosti," in *Kompleksnoe osvoenie vodnykh resursov obskogo basseina* (Novosibirsk: Nauka, 1970), pp. 24–9. The same viewpoint is expressed in L'vovich, op. cit. In a subsequent article, L'vovich seems to argue the other side, pointing out that even under present conditions of water use,

the area covered by swamps in western Siberia is growing by 100 km²
annually ("Razmyshlennia o perebroskakh rechnogo stoka," *Priroda*,
No. 3 [1978]: 100).
On the negative side, see A. Ianshin, V. Saks, and V.
Shirokov, "Potekut reki vspiat'," *Sotsialisticheskaia Industriia*, 7 December
1976, p. 2; Vendrov, op. cit., pp. 35–40. Vendrov is a prominent and
prolific opponent of the Central Asian plan. His concern about the
impact on western Siberia can be found in numerous writings, including Vendrov and D'iakonov, op. cit., p. 123. According to one study,
large canals in the Soviet Union, on past form, lose about 10% of their
water along the way. According to present designs, seepage and evaporation from the Central Asian diversion project could amount to as
much as 500K acre-feet (8 km³) yearly. See M. S. Ivanov, L. S. Ivashenko,
and F. V. Stol'berg, "K voprosu o zashchite ot istoshcheniia i regulirovanii kachestva poverkhnostnykh i podzemnykh vod pri krupnykh
mezhbasseinovykh perebroskakh stoka," *Problemy okhrany vod*, No. 4
(1973): 68–76. Academician A. G. Aganbegian agrees and calls the
official forecast of water losses too low (*Vodnye Resursy* No. 2 [1979]:
198). Still another negative reaction comes from a west Siberian reclamation official (located, perhaps significantly, in the Soviet oil capital,
Tiumen'), I. Rusinov, "Proekt trebuet proverki," *Trud*, 6 December
1977.

55  Rusinov, op. cit. Of the 100-odd institutes involved in assessment of the
    project, some 20 are located in Kazkhstan and Central Asia (*Vodnye
    Resursy*, No. 2 [1979]: 198). Of course, it should be pointed out that such
    a concentration is hardly the result of a sinister plot on the part of the
    design agencies, but simply a reflection of the fact that most research
    and design institutes, and certainly the best ones, happen to be located
    in the two largest cities.

56  Voropaev, op. cit.

57  Nekrasov and Razin, op. cit.

58  V. Kiriasov and V. Mezentsev, "Irtysh v upriazhke," *Pravda*, 26 October
    1978.

59  For example, Academician Abel Aganbegian, director of the Institute of
    the Economics of Industrial Production in Academic City, told a group
    of visiting Americans in October 1976 that he had refused to take on part
    of the impact analysis of the Central Asian project, on the grounds that
    he did not have anyone qualified to undertake the assignment – this
    despite the fact that Aganbegian had the reputation among his col-
    leagues as an opponent of the diversion scheme. (Visit of a National
    Academy of Sciences delegation to Novosibirsk, in which the author
    was a participant.) Nevertheless, two-and-a-half years later Aganbegian
    appeared to be heavily involved in the economic and social evaluation of
    the project.

60  See Jeremy Azrael, *Emergent Nationality Problems in the USSR*, R–
    2171–AF (Santa Monica, Calif.: Rand Corporation, 1977).

6 *Bringing new ideas into Soviet politics*

1 Helen Desfosses, "Demography, Ideology, and Politics in the USSR," *Soviet Studies* 28, No. 2 (April 1976): 244–56.

2 See Mark B. Adams, "Biology in the Soviet Academy of Sciences 1953–1965: A Case Study in Soviet Science Policy," in John R. Thomas and Ursula Kruse-Vaucienne, eds., *Soviet Science and Technology: Domestic and Foreign Perspectives* (Washington, D.C.: George Washington University Press, 1977), pp. 161–88. See also David Joravsky, *The Lysenko Affair* (Cambridge, Mass.: Harvard University Press, 1970).

3 On sociology, see Wesley Fisher and Elizabeth Anne Weinberg, *The Development of Sociology in the Soviet Union* (London: Routledge and Kegan Paul, 1974); Jeffrey Hahn, "The Role of Soviet Sociologists," in Richard B. Remnek, ed., *Social Scientists and Policy Making in the USSR* (New York: Praeger, 1977); Zev Katz, "Sociology in the Soviet Union," *Problems of Communism* 29, No. 3 (1971): 22–40.

4 See Chapter 4, note 2.

5 Erik P. Hoffmann, "The 'Scientific Management' of Soviet Society," *Problems of Communism* 26, No. 3 (May-June 1977): 59–67, and "Technology, Values, and Political Power in the Soviet Union: Do Computers Matter?" in Frederick J. Fleron, Jr., ed., *Technology and Communist Culture: The Socio-Cultural Impact of Technology under Communism* (New York: Praeger, 1971), p. 397–436. Paul Cocks, "The Policy Process and Bureaucratic Politics," in Paul Cocks, Robert V. Daniels, and Nancy Whittier Heer, eds., *The Dynamics of Soviet Politics* (Cambridge, Mass.: Harvard University Press, 1976), pp. 156–78; "Rethinking the Organizational Weapon: The Soviet System in a Systems Age" (*World Politics* 32, No. 2 (January 1980): 228–57; and "Administrative Rationality, Political Change, and the Role of the Party," in Karl Ryavec, ed., *Soviet Society and the Communist Party* (Amherst: University of Massachusetts Press, 1978). Richard Vidmer: "Management Science in the USSR," *International Studies Quarterly*, 24, No. 3 (September 1980): 392–414.

6 Peter H. Solomon, Jr., *Soviet Criminologists and Criminal Policy: Specialists in Policy-Making* (New York: Columbia University Press, 1977). Franklyn Griffiths, "Images, Politics, and Learning in Soviet Behavior toward the United States" (Ph.D. diss., Columbia University, 1972), available from University Microfilms.

7 Solomon, op. cit., p. 125.

8 Ibid., p. 151.

9 Griffiths, op. cit., p. 293.

10 The difficulty in summarizing the views of these two able scholars is that their arguments are carefully measured and qualified. For example, Solomon observes that, "conscious of their situation, some specialists were wont to moderate their advice in anticipation of the reactions of their clients" (op. cit., p. 157), which is the precise equivalent of the tactical interaction that Griffiths is writing about. However, the dif-

ference between the two is in their overall emphasis: Solomon dwells mainly on the role of the specialists in educating the policy makers; Griffiths on their interaction.

11  Griffiths, op. cit., p. 472.

12  Peter Bachrach and Morton S. Baratz, "Two Faces of Power," *American Political Science Review* 56 (September 1962): 947–52, and "Decisions and Non-decisions: an Analytical Framework," *American Political Science Review* 57 (1963): 641–51, and *Power and Poverty: Theory and Practice* (New York: Oxford University Press, 1970).

13  John Newhouse, *Cold Dawn: the Story of SALT* (New York: Holt, Rinehart, and Winston, 1973).

14  Boris Komarov, *Unichtozhenie prirody* (Frankfurt: Possev, 1978), pp. 49–51.

15  Dietrich A. Loeber, "Legal Rules 'For Internal Use Only,' " *International and Comparative Law Quarterly*, (January 1970), p. 77. This practice leads to peculiar courtroom procedures: "The court is bound to apply known unpublished rules. But the court may disregard an unpublished statute if it has not been brought officially to the court's notice . . . In civil cases . . . he who bases his claim on an unpublished statute has to prove its existence by producing the statute in court" (p. 80).

16  "Analysis of 1957 Forecast of 'Low Temperature Physics,' " prepared by Academician A. S. Borovik-Romanov and Dr. L. I. Vinokurova, 1976. Working papers of the US-USSR Working Group on Science Policy, National Academy of Sciences, Washington, D.C.

17  For a good sample, see M. Rakovskii, "Siurprizy elektronnykh mashin," *Pravda*, 2 March 1977.

18  See, e.g., N. V. Makhrov, A. A. Modin, and E. G. Iakovenko, *Parametry razrabotki sovremennykh automatizirovannykh sistem upravleniia predpriiatiiami* (Moscow: Nauka, 1974), p. 81. See also the outspoken memoirs of the founder of Akademgorodok, Academician M. A. Lavient'ev, *Opyty zhizni: 50 let v nauke*, serialized in *Ekonomika i Organizatsiia Promyshlennogo Proisvodstva*, No. 7 (1979) through No. 6 (1980).

19  P. L. Kapitsa, "Energiia i fizika," *Vestnik Akademii Nauk*, No. 1 (1976): 34–43.

20  N. Dollezhal' and Iu. Koriakin, "Iadernaia elektroenergetika: dostizheniia i problemy," *Kommunist*, No. 14 (September 1979): 19–28. See also an interview with Dollezhal', published under the title " . . . Nado nauchit'sia uvazhat' liudei," *Sotsialisticheskaia Industriia*, 27 October 1979. It should be stressed, however, that neither Kapitsa nor Dollezhal' is opposed to nuclear power as such.

21  Grey Hodnett, "Technology and Social Change: the Politics of Cotton Growing," in Henry W. Morton and Rudolf L. Tokes, eds., *Soviet Politics and Society in the 1970s* (New York: Free Press, 1974), pp. 60–117.

22  For a review, see Michael Rywkin, "Central Asia and Soviet Manpower," *Problems of Communism* 28, No. 1 (January-February): 1–13.

23  N. P. Dubinin, *Vechnoe Dvizhenie* (Moscow: Izdatel'stvo politicheskoi literatury, 1973), pp. 368–82.

24 Ibid., p. 357. As early as 1956, Dubinin chaired an advisory committee on hybrid corn in the USSR Academy of Sciences.

25 Ilia Zemtsov, "IKSI: The Moscow Institute of Applied Social Research," mimeographed in Russian (Jerusalem: Soviet and East European Research Center, Hebrew University, April 1976).

26 Loren R. Graham, "Cybernetics," in George Fischer, ed., *Science and Ideology in Soviet Society* (New York: Atherton Press, 1967), pp. 83–106.

27 Cocks, "Policy Process."

28 Desfosses, op. cit.

29 Solomon, op. cit., pp. 58–64.

30 Richard W. Judy, "The Economists," in H. Gordon Skilling and Franklyn Griffiths, eds., *Interest Groups in Soviet Politics* (Princeton, N.J.: Princeton University Press, 1971), p. 230.

31 Emmanuel Belitsky, "TsEMI: The Central Institute of Mathematical Economics," mimeographed in Russian (Jerusalem: Soviet and East European Research Center, Hebrew University, 1974), p. 9.

32 Zemtsov, op. cit., pp. 5, 6, 16.

33 Adams, op. cit.

34 Ibid., p. 164.

35 Ibid., p. 163.

36 Judy, op. cit., p. 224.

37 Dubinin, op. cit., p. 367.

38 Zemtsov, op. cit., p. 6.

39 Ibid., p. 3.

40 Dubinin, op. cit., p. 358.

41 K. M. Sobolevskii, "Nashi usiliia – rodine Oktiabria!" *Avtometriia*, No. 5 (1977): 3–6, and Iu. E. Nesterikhin, "Dva desiatiletiia v Sibirskom Otdelenii AN SSSR," *Avtometriia*, No. 3 (1977): 3–5.

42 See Thane Gustafson, "Why Doesn't Soviet Science Do Better Than It Does?" in Linda Lubrano and Susan Solomon, eds., *The Social Context of Soviet Science* (Boulder, Colo.: Westview Press, 1979), esp. p. 41.

43 Zemtsov, op. cit., p. 2.

44 Hahn, op. cit.

45 See, eg., A. Iakovlev, *Tsel' zhizni: zapiski aviakonstruktora* (Moscow: Politizdat, 1970).

46 See, e.g., Harvey Brooks, *The Government of Science* (Cambridge, Mass.: M.I.T. Press, 1968); Ina Spiegel-Rösing and Derek de Solla Price, eds., *Science, Technology, and Society* (Beverly Hills, Calif.: Sage Publications, 1977); Don K. Price, *The Scientific Estate* (Cambridge, Mass.: Harvard University Press, 1965); and Harvey Sapolsky, "Science Policy," in Fred I. Greenstein and Nelson W. Polsby, eds., *Handbook of Political Science*, Vol. 6 (Reading, Mass.: Addison-Wesley, 1975).

47 See, e.g., a discussion of the role of the *raikom* of the Leningrad district of Moscow in M. F. Tolpygo, *Partiinye komitety i tekhnichkeskii progress* (Moscow: Moskovskii rabochii, 1975), pp. 6–18. Tolpygo mentions the inclusion of engineers in *raikom* inspection of innovation

problems in a furniture factory, and the use of "non-staff instructors" with technical backgrounds to prepare briefings for *raikom* meetings.

48  This theme is discussed in Alexander Yanov, *Détente After Brezhnev: the Domestic Roots of Soviet Foreign Policy* (Berkeley: Institute of International Studies, University of California, 1977).

49  E. E. Schatschneider, *The Semi-Sovereign People* (New York: Holt, Rinehart, and Winston, 1960), p. 68.


7   *Loosening the grip of old priorities: the long struggle against hydropower*

1   This at any rate is the pattern in the Soviet Union. In the United States, in recent years, maximum demand occurs in the summer because of air conditioning.

2   Iu. A. Iukhnov and T. Iu. Kopylova, "Energo-ekonomicheskie predposylki sooruzheniia GAES v ob"edinennoi energosisteme iuga," *Trudy Gidroproekta* 29 (1973): 122–3.

3   T. Dotsenko, G. Kadomskii, and I. Solomentsev, "Narodnokhoziaistvennoe znachenie kaskada dneprovskikh vodokhranilishch," *Biulleten' po vodnomu khoziaistvu* (Soveshchanie rukovoditelei vodnokhoziaistvennykh organov stran-chlenov SEV) 5 (1971): 56–7.

4   M. I. L'vovich, *Reki SSSR* (Moscow: Mysl', 1971), p. 268. Average annual discharge at the mouth of the Dnieper is 41 million acre-feet.

5   Dotsenko, Kadomskii and Solomentsev, op. cit., p. 57. The reduction amounts to a loss of output of about 1.8 billion kilowatt-hours/year and a reduction in firm capacity of 120,000 kw. This reduction means an annual loss to hydropower of 30 million rubles, which is outweighed, according to the source, by an increase of 600 million rubles a year in net income from irrigation. The Dnieper cascade supplied water to 625,000 acres of irrigated land in 1968 – about one-third of the total irrigated area in the Ukraine at that time (pp. 57–8). This curtailment is especially serious in the Southern Power System, to which the Dnieper basin cascade belongs. Hydropower accounted for only 9% of the total capacity of that system – as opposed to a national average of nearly twice that amount – and the resulting shortage of peak-coverage capacity resulted in significant additional burning of fossil fuels through the inefficient use of thermal units. See Iukhnov and Kopylova, op. cit.

6   G. E. Moskalev, "Kanal Volga-Ural i ego rol' v razvitii khoziaistva Severnogo Prikaspiia," in Geografichcheskoe obshchestvo SSSR, zapadno-kazakhstanskii otdel, *Voprosy geografii severnogo Prikaspiia*, No. 1 (Leningrad, 1971): 89.

7   G. L. Sarukhanov, "Perebroska stoka severnykh rek," *Trudy Gidroproekta* 16 (1969): 444.

8   Ibid., and P. S. Neprozhnii, *Gidroenergetika i kompleksnoe ispol'zovanie vodnykh resursov SSSR* (Moscow: Energiia, 1970), p. 126.

9 Soviet sources mention the Sevan-Razdan system in Armenia, the Mingechaur project and others on the Kura River in Azerbaijan, the Bukhtarma Dam on the Irtysh River, and the Tsimliansk on the Don.

10 A. I. Makarov and O. S. Ligun "Nekotorye rezul'taty analiza svodnykh dannykh o vodokhranilishchakh SSSR," *Trudy koordinatsionnykh soveshchaniia po gidrotekhnike*, No. 70 (Leningrad: Energiia, 1972), p. 142.

11 B. V. Vorob'ev, "K voprosu ob uchete trebovanii sel'skogo khoziaistva pri regulirovanii stoka rek gidrouzlami," *Trudy koordinatsionnykh soveshchanii po gidrotekhnike*, No. 70 (Leningrad: Energiia, 1972), pp. 60–2.

12 Ibid.

13 S. L. Vendrov, *Problemy preobrazovaniia rechnykh sistem* (Leningrad, 1970), p. 135, and V. G. Volshanik, "O kompleksnom ispol'zovanii vodnykh resursov i osnovnykh polozheniiakh pravil ikh ispol'zovaniia," in *Kompleksnoe ispol'zovanie vodnykh resursov i rezhimy volzhsko-kamskogo kaskada GES* (Moscow: Energiia, 1967), pp. 19–21.

14 Vorob'ev, op. cit.

15 Ibid.

16 A. M. Rumiantsev, *Regulirovanie ispol'zovaniia vodnykh resursov vodokhranilishch* (Moscow: Energiia, 1966), pp. 60–1.

17 Ibid., p. 64.

18 Ibid., and I. A. Karmazin, "Rezhimy raboty GES kamskogo kaskada," in *Kompleksnoe ispol'zovanie vodnykh resursov i rezhimy volzhsko-kamskogo kaskada GES* (Moscow: Energiia, 1967), pp. 35–9.

19 Rumiantsev, op. cit., p. 62. Of course, only a portion of the land inundated by hydropower stations is agricultural or otherwise valuable.

20 Vendrov, op. cit., p. 135.

21 Rumiantsev, op. cit., p. 64.

22 Ibid., p. 62.

23 Ibid., p. 60, and V. A. Bakhtiarov, "Ekspluatatsionnye parametry vodokhranilishch SSSR," *Trudy koordinatsionnykh soveshchanii*, No. 53 (Leningrad: Energiia, 1969), pp. 29 ff.

24 I. P. Fedorov, "Opyt proektirovaniia vodokhranilishch i problemy ikh kompleksnogo ispol'zovaniia," *Trudy Gidroproekta* 26 (1972): 29.

25 A. B. Avakian and V. A. Sharapov, *Vodokhanilishcha elektrostantsii SSR*, 2nd ed. (Moscow: Energiia, 1968), p. 359.

26 Rumiantsev, op. cit., pp. 62–3.

27 Fedorov, op. cit., p. 29; Bakhtiarov, op. cit., pp. 28 ff. In general, the silt content of Soviet rivers is lower than that of American rivers, and the useful life of Soviet reservoirs is correspondingly longer. However, in recent Soviet projects the rate of loss of useful capacity resulting from silt has been nearly twice what was anticipated in the designs, because of inadequate forecasting of erosion from the banks (Vendrov, op. cit., p. 156). The practice of temporary forcing may be contributing to this problem.

28 Avakian and Sharapov, op. cit., p. 359, and A. B. Avakian, L. N. Shapiro, and V. A. Sharapov, "Razrabotki rekomendatsii po kompleksnomu

ispol'zovaniiu vodokhranilishch," *Trudy koordinatsionnykh soveshchanii*, No. 53 (Leningrad: Energiia, 1969), p. 37.

29  Rumiantsev, op. cit., pp. 60–4.

30  Ibid.

31  G. B. Grin, *Popuski v nizhnie b'efy* (Moscow: Energiia, 1971), p. 34.

32  G. B. Grin, "Analiz rezhimov ekspluatatsii nekotorykh gidrouzlov v navigatsionnyi period," *Problemy ispol'zovaniia vodnykh resursov v narodnom khoziaistve i vodnyi transport* (Trudy tsentral'nogo NII ekonomiki vodnogo transporta) (Moscow, 1969), p. 14. See also N. I. Makaveev, A. B. Gokhshtein, and B. G. Fedorov, "Optimizatsiia ispol'zovaniia resursov vodokhranilishcha dlia tselei vodnogo transporta," in *Raspredelenie vodnykh resursov* (Materialy k vsesoiuznomu seminaru 'Optimal'noe raspredelenie vodnykh resursov i opredelenie raschetnoi obespechennosti vodootdachi uchastnikam vodokhoziaistvennogo kompleksa) (Moscow, 1969), p. 125. See also by the same authors, "Otsenka vliianiia na vodnyi transport razlichnykh variantov ispol'zovaniia resursov vodokhranilishch (na primere nizhnevolzhskogo kaskada GES)," in *Trudy koordinatsionnykh soveshchanii*, No. 53 (Leningrad: Energiia, 1969), p. 163.

33  L. N. Shapiro, "Nekotorye voprosy vliianiia stoka rek vodokhranilishch na ostrasli khoziaistva v nizhnikh b'efakh gidrouzlov," *Trudy koordinatsionnykh soveshchanii*, No. 53 (Leningrad: Energiia, 1969), p. 168.

34  Ibid.

35  Grin, *Popuski*, p. 46.

36  S. N. Kritskii and M. F. Menkel', "Normirovanie obespechennosti i tekhnologiia ispol'zovaniia vodnoi energii," in *Problemy regulirovaniia rechnogo stoka*, No. 7 (Moscow: Izdatel'stvo Akademii Nauk SSSR, 1958), p. 17.

37  See Chapter 8, note 5.

38  Ministerstvo melioratsii i vodnogo khoziaistva SSSR, "Polozhenie o poriadke ispol'zovaniia vodnykh resursov vodokhranilishch SSSR" (Moscow, 1972), p. 3.

39  V. A. Bakhtiarov et al., "Analiz vliianiia ekspluatatsionnogo rezhima vodokhranilishch razlichnogo tipa na ustoichivost' berogov," in *Trudy koordinatsionnykh soveshchanii*, No. 53 (Leningrad: Energiia, 1969), p. 61, and Shapiro, op. cit., p. 168. L. S. Kuskov, "Voprosy metodiki sostavleniia pravil ispol'zovaniia vodnykh resursov kompleksnykh vodokhranilishch," in *Trudy koordinatsionnykh soveshchanii*, No. 70 (Leningrad: Energiia, 1972), p. 26.

40  These have been published as a series of collected papers by the chief agency for this effort, the Vedeneev Hydro-Engineering Institute of Leningrad, as the *Trudy koordinatsionnykh soveshchanii* (Leningrad: Energiia, various years). They are a remarkably frank guide to the lively interagency politics of water use in the 1960s and early 1970s.

41  L. S. Kuskov, "Razrabotka rekomendatsii po proektirovaniiu, stroitel'stvu i kompleksnomu ispol'zovaniiu vodokhranilishch SSSR dlia vodnogo transporta," in *Trudy koordinatsionnykh soveshchanii*, No. 53 (Leningrad: Energiia, 1969), pp. 95–7.

42 L. S. Kuskov, "Voprosy metodiki sostavleniia pravil ispol'zovaniia vodnykh resursov kompleksnykh vodokhranilishch," in *Trudy koordinatsionnykh soveshchanii*, No. 70 (Leningrad: Energiia, 1972), p. 26.
43 Iukhnov and Kopylova, op. cit.
44 I.A. Kuznetsov, "Vodo-zemel'nye resursy volgo-akhtubinskoi poimy i ikh ispol'zovanie," in V. V. Zvonkov, ed., *Issledovanie i kompleksnoe ispol'zovanie vodnykh resursov* (Moscow: Izdatel'stvo Akademii Nauk SSSR, 1960), pp. 173–84.
45 V. V. Delitsyn, "Razmnozhenie ryb na volgoakhtubinskoi poime v usloviiakh zaregulirivannogo rechnogo stoka," in *Volga-1* (Abstracts from a Conference on the Reservoirs of the Volga Basin, sponsored by the Institute of Freshwater Biology of the USSR Academy of Sciences) (Tol'iatti, 1968), p. 167, hereafter cited as *Volga-1*.
46 V. A. Bakhtiarov, "Zadachi regulirovaniia rechnogo stoka i voprosy optimizatsii urovennykh rezhimov kompleksnykh vodokhranilishch i nizhnikh b'efov gidrouzlov," *Trudy koordinatsionnykh soveshchanii*, No. 70 (Leningrad: Energiia, 1972), p. 21; and Ia. D. Gil'denblat, "Proektnyi rezhim raboty vodokhranilishch volzhsko-kamskogo kaskada," in *Raspredelenie*, pp. 135 ff. For characteristics of the Volgograd dam, see *Gidroenergeticheskie Resursy* (Moscow: Energiia, 1967), p. 406.
47 Grin, *Popuski*, pp. 73–84.
48 Ibid.
49 Ibid., p. 62.
50 A. F. Koblitskaia, "Estestvennoe ramnozhenie ryb v del'te Volgi v usloviiakh zaregulirovannogo stoka," in *Volga-1*, op. cit., pp. 174–5.
51 Because of rising Soviet concern over future energy shortages and the congestion of the country's railroad network, inland waterways may take on new importance in the future, thus raising even further competition for water use. See Iurii Kaz'min, "Po rechnym magistral'iam," *Pravda*, 2 July 1978.

8   *The new environmental program: do the Soviets really mean business?*

1 B. N. Laskorin et al., "Kachestvo i okhrana vody v basseine reki-Volgi," *Vodnye Resursy*, No. 4 (1975): 27. A *samizdat* account of environmental problems in the Soviet Union, which is otherwise very critical of Soviet environmental policy, agrees that the condition of the Volga has been stabilized, after an investment of "tens of millions" (Boris Komarov, *Unichtozhenie prirody* [Frankfurt: Possev, 1978], p. 53).
2 A. N. Lavrenov, S. V. Il'inskii, and E. E. Shcherbakov, "Vodoemam byt' chistymi," *Gorodskoe khoziaistvo Moskvy* 4 (1976): pp. 31–2. At the main laboratory facility of the Moscow-Oka inspectorate, the author had the opportunity to study data on changes in biological oxygen demand (BODs) for various points in the city in 1966, 1970, 1973, and 1975. These indicated a steady improvement for the Moscow River below Voskresensk. (The data, unfortunately, do not correct for variations in streamflow by indicating concentration per unit of flow.) The figures do indicate some trouble spots: For example, above Gzhelka

there is a steady worsening of the BOD$_5$ values, owing to the presence of the Zhukovskii industrial complex and heavy agricultural runoff. Throughout the river, BOD$_5$ levels run between 4 and 8 ppm. Despite the general improvement, there has been little progress in dealing with synthetic detergents, which Moscow water-quality officials declare to be their most worrisome problem, for the relevant ministries have done little as yet to develop biodegradable products. See also V. Varavka, "Vniz po Volge," *Ekonomicheskaia Gazeta,* No. 31 (July 1975): 22.

3  During the period 1970 to 1974, according to a deputy minister of Minvodkhoz, industrial wastes increased by 19%, but treatment capacity grew by 37% (I. I. Borodavchenko, "Problemy ispol'zovaniia i okhrany vodnykh resursov SSSR," *Gidrotekhnika i Melioratsiia,* No. 4 (1976).

4  We can perform a crude calculation of our own: The same deputy minister cites the total volume of wastewater produced in 1965 as 150 million m$^3$/day (I. I. Borodavchenko and V. R. Lozanskii, "Aktual'nye voprosy okhrany vodnykh resursov strany," *Problemy okhrany vod,* No. 1 (1972): 8. The estimate they adopt is that of Professor A. I. Zhukov, reported in "Problemy vodnykh resursov," *Trud,* 13 September 1968. This figure is higher than any of the estimates cited in Marshall Goldman, *The Spoils of Progress* (Cambridge, Mass.: M.I.T. Press, 1972), which range from 50 to 100 million m$^3$/day (p. 83). Undoubtedly, the main reason for the wide range of estimates is that most industries have no precise idea how much water they discharge. But assuming that this volume of waste has been growing at 4% annually since then, we arrive at a rough annual increase in effluent in the mid-1970s of 8 million m$^3$/day. This is nearly equal to the planned addition to waste-treatment capacity for 1976, 8.5 million m$^3$/day (P. Poletaev, "Plan i okhrana prirody," *Planovoe khoziaistvo* 4(1976)).

In other words, 1976 was the first year in which planned incremental waste-treatment capacity overtook the annual increase in effluent, at least for the nation as a whole. This assumes, however, that planned construction schedules are actually met; as we shall see, there have been problems on this score. It is probably a safe bet that the construction rate has not yet caught up with the annual growth of waste.

5  The basin inspectorates were created in 1960 (Decree No. 425 of the USSR Council of Ministers, 22 April 1960, "O merakh po uporiadocheniiu ispol'zovaniia i usileniiu okhrany vodnykh resursov SSSR"). Which major agency they should be subordinated to was a controversial issue for a long time. The question was finally settled in 1972 when they were attached to the republic-level Ministries of Reclamation. In the late 1970s there were 105 basin and zone inspectorates, whose activity is "coordinated and directed" by the Chief Inspectorate for the Protection of Water Sources of USSR Minvodkhoz in Moscow (I. M. Kutyrin and Iu. P. Belichenko, *Ohkrana vodnykh resursov – problema sovremennosti,* 2nd ed. [Leningrad: *Gidrometeoizdat,* 1974], p. 49). Needless to say, several years went by before the full network was in place. It was 1967, for example, before a branch office of the Urals basin inspectorate

opened in Magnitogorsk (M. Podgorodnikov and V. Travinsky, "Conflict on the Riverbank," *Literaturnaia Gazeta*, No. 4 [23 January 1974]: 11, trans. in *Current Digest of the Soviet Press* 26, No. 4 (1974): 12. In addition to the basin inspectorates, there is also a network of public-health inspectors with responsibility for water quality.

6 The inspectorates must check each industrial enterprise twice a year, taking samples of effluent for analysis. According to official figures, 34,000 enterprises were inspected and 209,000 water samples were analyzed in 1974 (Alekseevskii interview in *Trud*, 24 January 1976; Iu. P. Belichenko and Iu. G. Egorov, "Ob opyte raboty organov vodnogo nadzora," *Problemy okhrany vod*, No. 5 [1974]: 13).

7 Inspectorates must verify that industrial and municipal waste-treatment plants are operating properly, that industrial wastes entering municipal systems do not contain illegal levels of metals and organic compounds, and that industries and municipalities are submitting accurate water-quality analyses, as current regulations require them to do. The inspectorates are supposed to participate in developing proposals for new waste-treatment facilities and to monitor the progress of construction; they must approve plans for the siting of new enterprises and must certify that new factories have adequate waste-treatment capacity before the plants can be officially "commissioned" and turned over to the relevant ministry for operation. Once new plants are operating, the inspectorates are charged with monitoring their consumption of water, to induce them to economize (Iu. P. Belichenko, "Vode byt' chistoi," *Izvestiia*, 9 October 1974). The general responsibilities of the basin inspectorates were established in the December 1972 joint decree and are described in detail by Belichenko and Egorov, op. cit., pp. 12 ff. It is not clear whether the recent creation of a State Committee for Hydro-meteorology and Oversight of the Environment changes this allocation of duties. A decree of the CPSU Central Committee and the USSR Council of Ministers in December 1978 (the first to describe publicly the functions of the new committee) appears to give it the lead role in dealing with air, whereas it has relatively little to say about water. See Tsentral'nyi Komitet KPSS i Sovet Ministrov SSSR, "O dopolnitel'nykh merakh po usileniiu okhrany prirody i uluchsheniiu ispol'zovaniia prirodnykh resursov," *Pravda*, 6 January 1979, p. 1; hereafter cited as "O dopolnitel'nykh."

8 Such positions would include the director of an enterprise or the general director of an "association" (*ob"edinenie*) and any management positions below them, but not higher.

9 The basin inspectorates have had this authority since 1966 (USSR State Committee on Labor and Wages and All-Union Central Council of Trade Unions, special decree, "O poriadke lishenii premii pri nevy-polnenii v ustanovlennye sroki meropriiatii po predotvrashcheniiu zagriazneniia rybokhoziaistvennykh vodoemov").

10 Increases from 160 to 180 rubles a month were due in 1977, but I have not seen confirmation of this. The staff members of the basin inspec-

torates were the last in the Minvodkhoz system to get raises, which may be an indication of their status in the ministry.

11 For purposes of comparison, a monthly salary of 170 rubles is what would be earned by a junior researcher with a *kandidat* degree in a research institute of the "first category," such as an Academy of Sciences institute.

12 Interviews at the Ukranian Republic Minvodkhoz, Kiev, October 1976.

13 V. Golovin, "Khraniteli chistoi vody," *Kazakhstanskaia Pravda*, 21 January 1975, p. 4.

14 Global figures give a rough idea: If we assume that there are roughly 200 inspectors in the Moscow-Oka inspectorate and that they inspect 6,500 water-using entities twice a year, each inspector must visit 65 per year, not an inordinate number. On the other hand, the laboratories receive effluent-analysis reports from enterprises every ten days, which means a total of some 650 reports a day. This is too much for more than a perfunctory check, to which must be added the 40-odd samples contributed daily by the inspectors, assuming each inspection produces a sample for analysis.

15 Since 1961 it has been forbidden to impose fines by administrative procedure alone. Fines requested by water-quality inspectorates must be approved by the courts. In the past this step slowed down the whole procedure. T. S. Sushkov, "Pravovaia okhrana prirody," *Sovetskoe Gosudarstvo i Pravo* 5 (1969): 3–10, and O. S.Kolbasov, "Conservation Law in the USSR," *Sovetskoe Gosudarstvo i Pravo* 9 (1967), trans. in *Soviet Review* 9, No. 4 (1968): 17–25. Only five fines were approved by the RSFSR courts in 1963, five again in 1965, ten in 1966, and twelve in 1967.

16 Iu. P. Belichenko, "Vode byt' chistoi," *Izvestiia*, 9 October 1974.

17 K. Kornev, "Berech' vodnye bogastva," *Trud*, 8 October 1975, p. 2.

18 Iakovlev interview.

19 Interview with V. N. Cherenichenko, chief of the Main Inspectorate for Water Quality of the Ukrainian Ministry of Reclamation, October 1976.

20 Kutyrin and Belichenko, op. cit.

21 B. Ospanov, "Chistotu – vodoemam," *Kazakhstanskaia Pravda*, 7 May 1976, p. 4. This figure may represent a sizable increase since 1974, because another source reports that in 1974 only 117 fines were requested by the basin inspectorates, out of which 100 were approved and levied (see E. Matskevich, "Slovo o chistoi vode," *Izvestiia*, 9 February 1975). The latter figure, however, refers only to the basin inspectorates, whereas the former may include other agencies with the authority to levy fines, such as the sanitary-epidemiological stations of the Ministry of Health. Therefore, one cannot be sure that there has been any increase at all in the enforcement level.

22 Iu. P. Belichenko, "Za chistotu vodoemov," *Kommunist*, 27 September 1975, p. 2.

23 Interview with K. S. Khilobochenko, deputy minister of the Ukrainian Minvodkhoz, Kiev, October 1976.

24 I. I. Borodavchenko, "Problemy ispol'zovaniia i okhrany vodnykh resursov v SSSR," *Gidrotekhnika i Melioratsiia*, No. 4 (1976): 9.
25 See, e.g., V. Varavka, "Vniz po Volge," *Ekonomicheskaia Gazeta*, No. 31 (July 1975): 22.
26 Iu. Arakelian, "Prikaz podpisan, no...," *Pravda*, 29 November 1978. Earlier articles in *Pravda* on the same plant appeared in August 1977 and February 1978.
27 Boris Riabinin, "Spasennaia reka," *Literaturnaia Gazeta*, 9 February 1977.
28 Interview with USSR Minister of Reclamation E. E. Alekseevskii, "Vodu nado berech'," *Trud*, 24 January 1976.
29 Iakovlev interview.
30 Ibid.
31 See V. R. Lozanskii and I. D. Pichakhchi, "Sotsial'naia znachimost' vodokhrannoi deiatel'nosti," *Problemy okhrany vod*, No. 6 (1975): 7.
32 According to A. K. Kuzin, a staff economist at the All-Union Water Protection Research Institute in Kharkov, water-protection measures accounted for 10 of the 790 pages of the Tenth Five-Year Plan. (Interview in Kharkov.)
33 The *samizdat* author of *Unichtozhenie prirody* agrees: "... The Interagency Council and the Division of Conservation of the State Committee on Science and Technology and the Division of Environmental Protection in Gosplan have practically no power. They are obliged to reckon with the main objectives of the agencies in which they are located, and those objectives are not directed at all toward the preservation of nature" (Komarov, op. cit., pp. 104–5).
34 The two wings are not exactly comparable, because one builds while the other regulates. Minvodkhoz officials, in response to persistent questions, could give no precise answer about the relative size of the two wings. My own estimate is that the reclamation wing is on the order of a hundred times larger.
35 V. Zavarzin and S. Kozhanov, "Ecology and Standards," *Ekonomicheskaia Gazeta*, No. 36 (September 1978): 13, trans. in *Current Digest of the Soviet Press* 30, No. 37 (11 October 1978): 12.
36 V. Shkatov and Z. Zateeva, "Ratsional'no ispol'zovat' bogatstva prirody," *Ekonomicheskaia Gazeta*, No. 27 (July 1976): 13. The worst performance in 1975 came from the Ministries of Light Industry and Food Industry, who met their construction plan by only 80% and 70%, respectively, and their plan for putting waste-treatment facilities into operation by 59% and 78% ("Berech' vodu," editorial, *Izvestiia*, 5 March 1977, p. 1).
37 "O dopolnitel'nykh."
38 There is a bewildering variety of such organizations, often specializing in very different fields from those of their water-quality customers. For example, one of the several hundred assignments contained in the 1972 Volga-Ural decree calls for the Ministry of Agricultural Construction to build a waste-treatment plant for the Aleksandrovskii radio factory in Vladimir province (Iakovlev interview). Also see "Berech' vodu," op. cit.

39  "Berech vodu," op. cit. See also K. Solov'ev, "Vsem mirom," *Izvestiia*, 19 August 1975, p. 5.
40  Podgorodnikov and Travinsky, op. cit.
41  K. Sharonov, "In Complete Sets and on Time: On Accelerating the Construction of Municipal Sewage-Treatment Installations and Deliveries of Equipment to Them," *Ekonomicheskaia Gazeta*, No. 49 (December 1976): 17, trans. in *Current Digest of the Soviet Press* 28, No. 49 (1976): 15. Sharonov repeats much the same criticism in a more recent article in *Ekonomicheskaia Gazeta*, No. 39 (1978): 17.
42  Podgorodnikov and Travinsky, op. cit.
43  "Promyshlennost' i priroda," editorial, *Pravda*, 3 April 1975, p. 1.
44  B. Suleimenov, "Vody Urala," *Kazakhstanskaia Pravda*, 25 June 1976, p. 4.
45  "Vazhnoe zveno okhrany prirody," editorial, *Pravda*, 28 January 1977.
46  For an example described as "characteristic," see T. Mukhamedov, "Khranite vodu v chistote," *Kommunist Tadzhikistana*, 12 May 1976, p. 3.
47  Ibid. In Gorky province, for example, two waste-treatment facilities for the Ministry of Light Industry are being contracted out to the province's agricultural construction trust (*Oblsel'stroi*).
48  Waste-treatment capacity was scheduled to rise at a rate of 12% annually during the Tenth Five-Year Plan. During the period 1972–5, more than 9,000 large new facilities began operation ("Berech'vodu," op. cit.; Poletaev, op. cit.). In addition, the level of treatment is being raised: More and more facilities are based on biological and chemical methods (secondary treatment) rather than mechanical methods (primary treatment). Of the planned capacity scheduled for the Tenth Five-Year Plan, 60% was to be secondary rather than primary treatment (Poletaev, op. cit.). Primary treatment is still the dominant method, but other methods are gaining quickly, with a corresponding increase in the unit costs of waste treatment. (The share of primary treatment dropped from 65% in 1970 to 52.4% in 1975.) The upgrading of treatment levels has been particularly striking in the chemical industry, where the share of primary treatment has dropped from 88% to 54% from 1970 to 1975. Chemical and biological methods rose from 12% to 43% during the same period (O. M. Voronova, op. cit., fn. 11).
49  On the distinction between conservation and environmentalism, see Arthur Maass, "Conservation," in David Sills, ed., *International Encyclopedia of the Social Sciences* (New York: Macmillan, 1968), 3: 271–9.

9   *Slow gains at a high price: the frustrations of reclamation*

 1  See I. A. Gerardi, *Osobennosti prirodnykh i meliorativnykh uslovii zony nedostatochnogo uvlazhneniia i problemy pereraspredeleniia stoki rechnykh basseinov po territorii SSSR*, mimeographed (Moscow, Soiuzvodproekt, 1969); also V. S. Dmitriev, "Melioratsiia zemel' i problema ustoichivosti sel'skokhoziaistvennogo proizvodstva," *Gidrotekhnika i Melioratsiia* No. 7 (1975): 18–21.

2 For discussion of this point, see, e.g., M. N. Loiter, "Rezervy povysheniia effektivnosti ispol'zovaniia vodnykh resursov," in *Intensifikatsiia i rezervy ekonomiki* (Moscow: Nauka, 1970), p. 72; or V. A. Kardash, *Ekonomicheskaia optimizatsiia v oroshenii*, Vol. 2 of L. V. Kantorovich and V. P. Mozhin, eds., *Voprosy analiza planovykh reshenii v sel'skom khoziaistve* (Novosibirsk, 1972), Introduction; or V. N. Polozhii, *Ekonomika orosheniia v novykh raionakh* (Moscow: Kolos, 1974), Introduction.

3 The official conversion rate of rubles to dollars is 1 ruble = $1.48. However, the official rate bears little relation to real buying power. The latter depends closely on the relative efficiency of the USSR and the United States in any given economic sector. For purchasing certain types of consumer goods, the ruble may be worth as little as 25 or 30 cents. But in military procurement, where the Soviet economy is thought to be more efficient, a higher conversion rate applies. Needless to say, the question of conversion rates is highly controversial. I have not attempted to suggest dollar equivalents for the figures given in the text.

4 L. I. Brezhnev, "O dal'neishem razvitii sel'skogo khoziaistva SSSR," *Pravda*, 4 July 1978.

5 See E. E. Alekseevskii, "Tretii god piatiletki i zadachi vodokhoziaistvennykh organizatsii," *Gidrotekhnika i Melioratsiia* No. 1 (1973): 3, and "Melioratsiia v chertvertom gody deviatoi piatiletki," *Gidrotekhnika i Melioratsiia* (1974), p. 8. See also *Sel'skaia Zhizn'*, 12 February 1975, p. 1. For the Tenth Plan see "O plane melioratsii zemel' na 1976–1980 gody i merakh po uluchsheniiu ispol'zovaniia meliorirovannykh zemel'," *Ekonomicheskaia Gazeta*, No. 33 (August 1976): 3–4; hereafter cited as "O plane."

6 Of the net increase in Soviet irrigated area in the last ten years, 75% is located in the European zone. E. E. Alekseevskii, "Melioratsiia zemel' – osnova polucheniia vysokikh i ustoichivykh urozhaev," *Vestnik sel'skokhoziaistvennoi nauki*, No. 5 (1976): 4. During the last five-year plan (1976–80), 600,000 new hectares of irrigated land were scheduled for the Volga basin alone – an increase of 25% over the preceding five-year plan. (A. Vorotnikov, P. Dronov, and G. Ivanov, "Preobrazhenie Povolzh'ia," *Pravda*, 19 and 20 February 1977, p. 2).

7 For discussions of this problem, see E. E. Alekseevskii, "Melioratsiia v pervom godu desiatoi piatiletki," *Gidrotekhnika i Melioratsiia*, No. 3 (1976): 2–12, and V. A. Dmitriev, "Nekotorye voprosy povysheniia ekonomicheskoi effektivnosti orosheniia," *Gidrotekhnika i Melioratsiia*, No. 1 (1975): 83–9.

8 Brezhnev, op. cit.

9 Alekseevskii, "Melioratsiia v pervom," p. 5. One hectare = 0.01 square kilometers = 2.5 acres.

10 Brezhnev, op. cit.

11 E. K. Alatortsev, "Rezervy ispol'zovaniia meliorirovannykh zemel'," *Vestnik sel'skokhoziaistvennoi nauki*, No. 5 (1976): 25.

12  E. E. Alekseevskii, "Melioratsiia v zavershaiushchem godu piatiletki," *Gidrotekhnika i Melioratsiia*, No. 3 (1975): 1–11. On the occasion of the tenth anniversary of the reclamation drive, two journals published special issues that gave a comprehensive review of the state of the program. See *Vestnik sel'skokhoziaistvennoi nauki* 5 (1976) and *Gidrotekhnika i Melioratsiia*, No. 5 (1976). See also *Gidrotekhnika i Melioratsiia*, No. 7 (1975), a special issue in honor of the twenty-fifth anniversary of the International Commission on Irrigation and Drainage.

13  Numerous descriptions of the "industrialization" of the Ministry of Reclamation can be found in the ministry's journal, *Gidrotekhnika i Melioratsiia*. See, e.g., P. P. Ermalinskii and R. Kh. Arabov, "O povyshenii effektivnosti raboty remontykh predpriiatii v vodokhoziaistvennom stroitel'stve," *Gidrotekhnika i Melioratsiia*, No. 2 (1974): 83–8; or "V tsentral'nom komitete KPSS," No. 10 (1973): 1; or S. N. Nikulin and E. D. Tomin, "Napravleniia razvitiia mekhanizatsii meliorativnykh rabot v SSSR," No. 5 (1976): 115–26.

14  M. Pedashenko and M. Gen, "Vodokhoziaistvennoe stroitel'stvo v novykh usloviiakh khoziaistvovaniia," *Gidrotekhnika i Melioratsiia*, No. 7 (1973): 92.

15  Ibid., p. 91.

16  Alekseevskii, "melioratsiia v chertvertom," p. 13.

17  Ibid., p. 10.

18  Loiter, op. cit.

19  K. P. Arent, "Raschetnye zatraty i ikh izmenenie v zavisimosti ot vodopotrebleniia dlia oroshaemogo zemledeliia," in *Raspredelenie vodnykh resursov* (Materialy k vsesiouznomu seminaru 'Optimal'noe raspredelenie vodnykh resursov i opredelenie raschetnoi obespechennosti vodootdachi uchastnikam vodokhoziaistvennogo kompleksa) (Moscow, 1969), p. 75. See also Gosudarstvennyi Komitet pri Sovete Ministrov SSSR and Akademiia Nauk SSSR, *Doklad po probleme Aral'skogo moria* (Materialy k zasedaniiu Biuro i Vremennoi Podkomissii Nauchnogo Soveta "Kompleksnoe ispol'zovanie i okhrana vodnykh resursov') (Moscow, 1970), p. 14. The minister of reclamation has estimated water losses of only 30%, but that seems lower than most estimates (E. E. Alekseevskii, "Vodnye resursy SSSR: Problemy ikh effektivnogo ispolizovaniia i okhrany," *Vodnye Resursy*, No. 2 (1974): 13. At the other extreme, studies in southern Kazakhstan showed losses of from 60% to 75% (G. V. Voropaev, "Rezervy irrigatsii i problemy ikh ispol'zovaniia v usloviiakh irrigatsionnykh sistem iuzhnogo Kazakhstana", *Vodnye Resursy*, No. 1 [1973]: 122).

20  For data on insalination, see Voropaev, op. cit., p. 124; A. M. Mamedov, *Irrigatsiia i irrigatory Uzbekistana* (Tashkent, 1971), p. 100; G. G. Shiler, "Nekotorye voprosy stroitel'stva i sel'skokhoziaistvennogo ispol'zovaniia oroshaemykh zemel' v nizoviakh reki-Volgi," in *Ratsional'noe ispol'zovanie obvodnitel'no-orositel'nykh sistem* (Moscow: Kolos, 1970), p. 23; B. L. Magakian, "Irrigatsiia v SSSR: sovremennoe sostoianie i perspektivy razvitiia," in *Vodnye resursy i ikh kompleksnoe*

*ispol'zovanie, Voprosy Geografii,* No. 73 (Moscow, 1968): 36; and G. V. Kopanev, "Vodnoe khoziaistvo i kompleksnoe ispol'zovanie vodnykh resursov," in Akademiia Nauk SSSR and Soviet po Izucheniiu Proizvoditel'nykh Sil (SOPS) pri Gosplane SSSR, *Razvitie i razmeschenie proizvoditel'nykh sil SSSR* (Moscow, 1972), p. 17.

21 "V Ministerstvakh Melioratsii i Vodnogo Khoziaistva SSSR i Sel'skogo Khoziaistva SSSR," *Gidrotekhnika i Melioratsiia,* No. 10 (1973): 5.

22 "O plane."

23 Brezhnev, op. cit.

24 Loiter, op. cit., p. 73.

25 Kopanev, op. cit., p. 178.

26 Loiter, op. cit., p. 73.

27 I. Rabochev, "Pole v pustyne," *Pravda,* 6 February 1977.

28 A. Kucherenko, "Kak rabotaesh', polivnoi gektar?" *Pravda,* 19 October 1976.

29 E. Nesterov, "Voda v zavolzhskoi stepi," *Gidrotekhnika i Melioratsiia,* No. 11 (1973): 18.

30 V. I. Shlyk and M. I. Krupina, "O preimushchestvakh krupnykh upravlenii orositel'nykh sistem," *Gidrotekhnika i Melioratsiia,* No. 8 (1973): 73. A. Dolgushev, "Nekotorye voprosy ekspluatatsii orositel'nykh sistem," *Gidrotekhnika i Melioratsiia,* No. 6 (1973): 26.

31 Shylyk and Krupina (op. cit., pp. 75–6) give the figure of 1.6 miles of service roads per 10,000 acres of irrigated area. Availability of automobiles ranges from 1 per 35,000 irrigated acres in Turkmeniia to 1 per 108,000 acres in Uzbekistan; 4 to 5 miles of telephone line per 10,000 irrigated acres in Central Asia. These figures appear to apply only to the facilities belonging to the UOS, not to the local farms or other organizations. See also M. F. Natal'chuk, *Vnutrikhoziaistvennaia ekspluatatatsiia orositel'nykh sistem* (Moscow: Kolos, 1969).

32 Shlyk and Krupina give an average of 89% mechanization of cleaning operations in their study of northern Kirgiziia, op. cit., p. 73.

33 K. Umarov and M. Kopylov, "Opyt raboty raionnogo UOS," *Gidrotekhnika i Melioratsiia,* No. 8 (1973).

34 Mamedov, op. cit., p. 111.

35 A. Dolgushev, "Nekotorye voprosy ekspluatatsii orositel'nykh sistem," *Gidrotekhnika i Melioratsiia,* No. 6 (1973): 28.

36 Mamedov, op. cit., pp. 126–7.

37 There is no single, All-Union methodology for drawing up water-allocation plans, and every republic is said to do things somewhat differently. The drawing up of annual water-use plans is described as "very laborious, drawing technicians and engineers away from the management and maintenance of the network at a crucial time of the year" (V. K. Epikhin, V. V. Koshkin, and K. V. Millerov, *Sostavlenie i provedenie planov vodopol'zovaniia [khoziaistvennykh i sistemnykh]* [Dushanbe: Irfon, 1970], pp. 3–4). This suggests that the potential power of the UOSs over the farms, to determine allocations of water as a function of

efficient use, is not exercised in practice because of the lack of full-time specialists in problems of irrigation agronomy.

38  The republic levels and even the USSR ministry play a certain role, either in difficult cases or in the setting of general policy. For example, where scarce water in the lower Amu-Dar'ia basin must be divided among three republics, a special administration has been created for the purpose (Administration of the Irrigation Canals of the Amu Dar'ia Delta – *Upravlenie Amudar' inskikh del'tovykh kanalov*, or "Upradik"), and its annual plans are cleared by the USSR ministry in Moscow (Mamedov, op. cit., pp. 126–7). As an example of central control over general policy, irrigation norms for each region and each major crop, which determine the size of the requests from the local farms, are developed by the ministry's research and design institutes but must be approved by the Scientific-Technical Council of the USSR ministry.

39  Mamedov, op. cit., p. 127.

40  O. S. Kolbasov, *Legislation on Water Use in the USSR*, trans.in Irving Fox, ed., *Water Resources Law and Policy in the Soviet Union* (Madison: University of Wisconsin Press, 1971), p. 135.

41  Such problems caused by lack of full-time ditch-riders are often reported in the press. It should be observed, however, that in some republics, such as Kirgiziia, farms pay a penalty for consumption beyond the approved norm (*Sovetskaia Kirgiziia*, 23 June 1970, p. 2).

42  A. E. Erenov and S. B. Baisalov, "All-Union Water Law Draft Reviewed," *Khabaryshskii Vestnik Kazakhskoi SSR*, No. 12 (1970): 19–26, trans. in *Joint Publications Research Service*, No. 52451, 23 February 1971, p. 26.

43  Iu. Smirnov, "Na trasse Kuibyshevskogo kanala," *Gidrotekhnika i Melioratsiia*, No. 11 (1973): 25.

44  See E. Wimbush and D. Ponomareff, *Alternatives for Mobilizing Central Asian Labor: Outmigration and Regional Development* (Santa Monica, Calif.: Rand Corporation, 1980).

45  "O dal'neishem usilenii rabot po melioratsii zemel' i uluchshenii ispol'zovaniia oroshaemykh i osushennykh zemel'," Joint Decree of the CPSU Central Committee and the USSR Council of Ministers, 2 October 1972, in *Spravochnik partiinogo rabotnika*, 13th ed. (Moscow: Izdatel'stvo politicheskoi literatury, 1973).

46  The "production association" (*proizvodstvennoe ob"edinenie*) in charge of irrigation construction for the middle-Volga Saratov and Kuibyshkev provinces. A production association is the administrative level directly above the firm or enterprise.

47  Nesterov, op. cit., p. 18.

48  Ibid.

49  Loiter, op. cit., p. 73.

50  P. Ia. Polubarinova-Kochina, "Voprosy orosheniia zasushlivykh zemel'," in *Optimal'nye puti orosheniia* (Materialy soveshchaniia v g. Novosibirsk v marte 1967g.) (Moscow, 1968), pp. 28–30.

51  G. V. Voropaev, "Rezervy irrigatsii i problemy ikh ispol'zovaniia," *Vodnye Resursy*, No. 1 (1973): 124–5.

52 S. N. Nikulin and E. D. Tomin, "Napravleniia razvitiia mekhanizatsii meliorativnykh rabot," *Gidrotekhnika i Melioratsiia*, No. 5 (1976): 123.

53 "O plane."

54 See "O plane," and T. P. Senkevich, "Kompleksnoe stroitel'stvo – zalog uspeshnogo osvoeniia zemel'," *Gidrotekhnika i Melioratsiia*, No. 8 (1974): 1–8.

55 A. Vorotnikov, O. Dronov, and G. Ivanov, "Preobrazhenie Povolzh'ia," *Pravda*, 19 and 20 February 1977, p. 2.

56 See, e.g., L. Salazkin and N. Sbitnev, "Deistvuet sluzhba ekspluatatsii," *Sel'skaia Zhizn'*, 3 September 1975, and N. Shevchenko, "Ot etogo zavisit mnogoe," *Sel'skaia Zhizn'*, 30 August 1975.

57 Alekseevskii, "Melioratsiia v pervom."

58 See, e.g., I. Shirshin, "Budet kolos vesomym," *Pravda*, 30 March 1979, p. 1.

59 See Frederic N. Cleaveland, "The Bureau of Reclamation" (Woodrow Wilson School Research Project, Princeton University, mimeographed draft, 1950); and also U.S., Department of Interior, Survey Team, "Organization and Management Survey of the Bureau of Reclamation," mimeographed (Washington, D.C., March 1959).

60 See William E. Warne, *The Bureau of Reclamation* (New York: Praeger, 1973), and Charles McKinley, *Uncle Sam in the Pacific Northwest: Federal Management of Natural Resources in the Columbia River Valley* (Berkeley: University of California Press, 1952).

61 T. H. Rigby, "Soviet Politics Since Khrushchev," *Politics* 12, No. 1 (May 1977): 5–22.

62 Vasil'ev's appointment was announced in *Pravda* on 14 April 1979. For information concerning the upper ranks of Minvodkhoz since Alekseevskii's death, I am grateful to Mr. Werner Hahn.

63 For a defense of this view, which contradicts Karl Wittfogel's well-known, but highly flawed, theory of hydraulic despotism, see Arthur Maass and Raymond L. Anderson, *And the Desert Shall Rejoice: Conflict, Growth, and Justice in Arid Environments* (Cambridge, Mass.: M.I.T. Press, 1978).

10   *Carrying out a third-generation program with second-generation methods*

1 For a review of the current state of the Brezhnev agricultural program, see Part III of U.S., Congress, Joint Economic Committee, *The Soviet Economy in a Time of Change*, 2 vols. (Washington, D.C.: U.S. Government Printing Office, 1979), 2: 1–188.

2 E. E. Alekseevskii, "Melioratsiia v chetvertom godu deviatoi piatiletki," *Gidrotekhnika i Melioratsiia*, No. 1 (1974): 11.

3 I. Ivannikov, "Kapital'nym vlozheniiam v sel'skoe khoziaistvo – effektivnoe upravlenie," *Planovoe khoziaistvo*, No. 10 (1978): 66.

4 E. Nesterov, "Voda v zavolzhskoi stepi," *Gidrotekhnika i Melioratsiia*, No. 11 (1973): 18.

5  See, e.g., K. Solov'ev, "Vsem mirom," *Izvestiia*, 19 August 1975, p. 5, and V. Varavka, "Vniz po Volge," *Ekonomicheskaia Gazeta*, No. 31 (July 1975): 22.

6  V. Pankratov, "Vyshli v pole 'Fregaty'," *Pravda*, 9 June 1979, p. 1.

7  "V Ministerstvakh Melioratsii i Vodnogo Khoziaistva SSSR i Sel'skogo Khoziaistva SSSR," *Gidrotekhnika i Melioratsiia*, No. 10 (1973): 4.

8  See, e.g., a discussion of this problem as it affects the production of advanced new scientific instruments (Iu. E. Nesterikhin, "Novaia forma integratsii nauki i proizvodstva," *Ekonomika i Organizatsiia Promyshlennogo Proizvodstva*, No. 2 (1975).

9  See, e.g., the highly critical description of damage to the Poles'e region of northern Ukraine and southern Belorussia, caused by the mass-production approach to drainage employed by the Ministry of Reclamation. See V. N. Kiselev, "Paradoksy melioratsii Belorusskogo Poles'ia," *Priroda*, No. 12 (1972): 46–51.

10  For example, in the summer of 1979 irrigators in Stavropol' province faced a severe water shortage. The province-level irrigation authority lagged badly in setting new irrigation schedules and allocations. Taking advantage of this, some upstream farms began to cheat on their downstream neighbors (V. Pankratov, "V pole  vyshli 'Fregaty.' " *Pravda*, 9 June 1979, p. 1).

11  Except for a brief period during the First Five-Year Plan. See Marshall I. Goldman, "Will the Soviet Union be an Autarky in 1984?" *International Security* 3, No. 4 (Spring 1979): 18–37.

12  The best discussion of this behavior is still Joseph S. Berliner, *Factory and Manager in the USSR* (Cambridge, Mass.: Harvard University Press, 1957).

13  Geoffrey Levitt of the Harvard Law School has written an excellent study of the spread of such jurisconsults. See "The Legalization Movement in the Soviet Enterprise" (Paper presented at the annual Harvard-Columbia Conference on Soviet Affairs, Harvard University, April 1979).

14  The issues behind these statements are discussed at greater length in the concluding chapter.

15  Mark B. Adams "Biology in the Soviet Academy of Sciences 1953–1965: A Case Study in Soviet Science Policy," in John R. Thomas and Ursula Kruse-Vaucienne, eds., *Soviet Science and Technology: Domestic and Foreign Perspectives* (Washington, D.C.: George Washington University Press, 1977), pp. 161–88.

16  Donald D. Barry and Harold J. Berman, "The Jurists," in H. Gordon Skilling and Franklyn Griffiths, eds., *Interest Groups in Soviet Politics* (Princeton, N.J.: Princeton University Press, 1971), pp. 291–334.

17  P. N. Fedoseev (vice-president of the USSR Academy of Sciences), speech at the General Meeting of the USSR Academy of Sciences, *Vestnik Akademii Nauk* 9 (1976): 22. A. P. Aleksandrov, speech at the General Meeting of the USSR Academy of Sciences, *Vestnik Akademii Nauk* 5 (1976): 17. See also an interview with A. P. Aleksandrov, "Instrumental'nyi tsekh nauki," *Komsomol'skaia Pravda*, 23 June 1979.

18 A particularly interesting case is provided by the problems the Soviets have encountered in the construction of Atommash, a large complex designed to mass-produce light-water-reactor nuclear-power plants. Atommash has been extensively covered in the Soviet press. See, e.g., V. Shilov, "Svet atoma: komu byt' dirizherom?" *Pravda*, 5 August 1977. In addition, see Gloria Duffy, *Soviet Nuclear Energy: Domestic and International Policies*, R-2362-DOE (Santa Monica, Calif.: Rand Corporation, December 1979).

19 See the discussion of this point in Andrew S. McFarland, *Power and Leadership in Pluralist Systems* (Stanford, Calif.: Stanford University Press, 1969). There has been enormous controversy in the Western literature over what constitutes "key" issues and whether research on political power should be confined to those alone. One of the earliest definitions, to which other scholars have been reacting ever since, was that of Peter Bachrach and Morton S. Baratz, "Two Faces of Power," and subsequent articles (see note 12, Chapter 16). Further discussion can be found in Raymond E. Wolfinger, "Nondecisions and the Study of Local Politics," (pp. 1063–80), Frederick W. Frey, "Comment: On Issues and Non-issues in the Study of Power" (pp. 1081–1101), and Raymond E. Wolfinger, "Rejoinder to Frey's Comment" (pp. 1102–4), *American Political Science Review* 65 (December 1971). For useful reviews of the whole subject of power, see Robert A. Dahl "Power," in the *International Encyclopedia of the Social Sciences* (New York: Macmillan and Free Press, 1968), 12: 405–15, and also Stephen Lukes, *Power: A Radical View* (London: Macmillan, 1974).

20 These differences are usually unstated and therefore unanalyzed. One of the very few attempts to grapple explicitly with problems of definition is Hough's *The Soviet Union and Social Science Theory*, especially the last chapter.

21 Zbigniew Brzezinski and Samuel P. Huntington, *Political Power USA/ USSR* (New York: Viking Press, 1964).

22 Juan Linz, "Totalitarianism," in Fred I. Greenstein and Nelson W. Polsby, eds., *Handbook of Political Science* (Reading, Mass.: Addison-Wesley, 1975), 3: 175–251.

23 Zhores Medvedev, *The Rise and Fall of T. D. Lysenko* (New York: Columbia University Press, 1969).

11 *Conclusion: lessons of the Brezhnev policies and the future of reform*

1 See Seweryn Bialer, *Stalin's Successors* (Cambridge: Cambridge University Press, 1980).

2 On upcoming energy problems, see Central Intelligence Agency, National Foreign Assessment Center, *The World Oil Market in the Years Ahead*, ER 79-10327 (Washington, D.C.: U.S. Government Printing Office, 1979); and J. Richard Lee and James R. Lecky, "Soviet Oil Developments," in U.S., Congress, Joint Economic Committee, *The Soviet Economy in a Time of Change*, 2 vols. (Washington, D. C.: U.S. Government Printing Office, 1979) 1:587–99; hereafter cited as *Time of Change*.

On manpower, see Murray Feshbach and Stephen Rapawy, "Soviet Population and Manpower Trends and Policies," in U.S., Congress, Joint Economic Committee, *The Soviet Economy in a New Perspective* (Washington, D.C.: U.S. Government Printing Office, 1976), pp. 113–54.

3  Seweryn Bialer, "The Politics of Stringency in the USSR," *Problems of Communism* 29 (May-June 1980):19–33.

4  Roy D. Laird and Betty A. Laird, "The Widening Soviet Grain Gap and Prospects for 1980 and 1990," in Roy D. Laird, Joseph Hajda, and Betty A. Laird, eds., *The Future of Agriculture in the Soviet Union and Eastern Europe: The 1976–1980 Five-Year Plan* (Boulder, Colo.: Westview Press, 1977), pp. 27–48. For recent comments on continuing controversy over clean fallow in the Virgin Lands, see A. Baraev, "Vazhnyi rezerv," *Pravda*, 19 August 1980.

5  See Padma Desai, "Estimating Soviet Grain Imports in 1980–85: Alternative Approaches" (Occasional Paper of the Russian Research Center, Harvard University, Cambridge, Mass., revised 1980). The Soviet Union drew 16 million tons of grain out of its reserve in 1977, restored 19 million tons in 1978, and drew down 17 million tons in 1979 (Robert L. Paarlberg, "Lessons of the Grain Embargo," *Foreign Affairs* 59, No. 1 [Fall 1980]:156–7). The U.S. Department of Agriculture's figures are 14, 19, and 16 million tons, respectively. See U.S. Department of Agriculture, Foreign Agriculture Service, *World Grain Situation: Outlook for 1980/81* (Washington, D.C., 1980), p. 18.

6  David W. Carey and Joseph F. Havelka, "Soviet Agriculture: Progress and Problems," in *Time of Change*, 2:55–86. A valuable Soviet source is A. M. Emel'ianov, ed., *Kompleksnaia programma razvitiia sel' skogo khoziaistva v deistvii*, 2nd ed. (Moscow: Ekonomika, 1980), p. 42.

7  See Michael D. Zahn, "Soviet Livestock Feed in Perspective," in *Time of Change*, 2:165–87.

8  Carey and Havelka, op. cit., p. 66.

9  David M. Schoonover, "Soviet Agricultural Policies," in *Time of Change*, 2:105. See also Judith G. Goldich, "USSR Grain and Oilseed Trade in the Seventies," in the same collection, pp. 133–64.

10  Daniel L. Bond and Herbert S. Levine, "Energy and Grain in Soviet Hard Currency Trade," in *Time of Change*, 2:244–90.

11  Paarlberg, op. cit. The U.S. Department of Agriculture takes a slightly different view, based on a belief that the Soviets intended to import 37.5 million tons and that the real shortfall has consequently been 6 million tons, which was concentrated primarily in the spring months of 1980. The USDA reports declines in Soviet animal weights and in milk and meat production, and it points to the possibility that some distress slaughtering may take place. Paarlberg believes the USDA has exaggerated the extent of the Soviet import shortfall. See U.S. Department of Agriculture, "Impact of Agricultural Trade Restrictions on the Soviet Union," Foreign Agricultural Economic Report No. 158 (Washington, D.C., April 1980), and same, "Update: Impact of Agricultural Trade

Restrictions on the Soviet Union," *Foreign Agricultural Economic Report* No. 160 (Washington, D.C., July 1980).

12  This conclusion is shared by Paarlberg, op. cit., p. 159.

13  For recent statistics, see Emel'ianov, op. cit., pp. 78–81, 89.

14  I. Ivannikov, "Kapital'nym vlozheniiam v sel'skoe khoziaistvo – effektivnoe napravlenie," *Planovoe Khoziaistvo* 10 (1978): 65–6.

15  Address by Professor Gale Johnson of the University of Chicago at the Faculty Club, Harvard University, 5 February 1979. A summary is available under the title "Economic Results in 1978: Is There a Slow-Down in the Soviet and East European Economies?" (Occasional Paper of the Russian Research Center, Harvard University, Cambridge, Mass., February 1979).

16  Emel'ianov, op. cit., p. 209.

17  S. Enders Wimbush and Dmitry Ponomareff, *Alternatives for Mobilizing Soviet Central Asian Labor: Outmigration and Regional Development*, R–2476–AF (Santa Monica, Calif.: Rand Corporation, 1979).

18  Emel'ianov, op. cit., pp. 68, 208.

19  See, e.g., the comments by Brezhnev in the chapter of his autobiography devoted to the Virgin Lands ("Tselina," *Novyi Mir*, No. 10 [1978]:3–55).

20  Wimbush and Ponomareff, op. cit.

21  Emel'ianov, op. cit., p. 251. The share of private activity in the total income of collective-farm families has declined from 36.5% in 1965 to 25.2% in 1978.

22  See note 2.

23  See George Breslauer, *Dilemmas of Leadership in the Soviet Union Since Stalin: 1953–1976* (Berkeley: University of California Press, forthcoming).

24  M. Fedin, "Ot delianki do polia," *Pravda*, 20 June 1979.

25  Central Intelligence Agency, National Foreign Assessment Center, "Biological and Environmental Factors Affecting Soviet Grain Quality" (Washington, D.C.: December 1978).

26  Philip Hanson, "Soviet Strategies and Policy Implementation in the Import of Chemical Technology from the West, 1958–1978" (California Seminar on Arms Control, Pasadena, Calif., 1980).

27  The Western scholar who has made the most of this concept is Seymour Goodman in his brilliant work on Soviet computers. See N. C. Davis and S. E. Goodman, "The Soviet Bloc's Unified System of Computers," *ACM Computing Surveys* 10, No. 2 (June 1978): 93–122.

28  Fedin, op. cit.

29  Emel'ianov, op. cit., p. 75.

30  P. I. Simush, "Social Changes in the Countryside," *Kommunist* 16 (1976):61–73. Abstracted in *Current Digest of the Soviet Press* 28, No. 49 (5 January 1977):1.

31  Emel'ianov, op. cit., p. 172, gives a total of 466 billion rubles invested between 1966 and 1977 in the entire "agro-industrial complex."

32 Ibid., p. 75.

33 This idea is developed further in a forthcoming analysis by Nancy Nimitz of the Rand Corporation on the implications of the July 1979 decree and the future of Soviet economic reform.

34 Industry in the USSR consumes a larger amount of energy than in the United States, even though Soviet industrial output is some 20% smaller than that of the United States. See Robert W. Campbell, *Soviet Fuel and Energy Balances*, R-2257 (Santa Monica, Calif.: Rand Corporation, 1978). The best overall account of Soviet energy problems is that of Leslie Dienes and Theodore Shabad, *The Soviet Energy System* (Washington, D.C.: Winston, 1979).

35 Gertrude E. Schroeder, "The Soviet Economy on a Treadmill of 'Reforms,'" in *Time of Change* 1:312–430.

36 George Breslauer, *Five Images of the Soviet Future: A Critical Review and Synthesis* (Berkeley: Institute of International Studies, University of California, 1978), writes about the possibility of "changes in regime-type that come largely from above or through political forces within the Establishment that are strengthened by crisis situations" (p. 4). Included as a factor in Breslauer's analysis are the domestic conditions that may facilitate the realization of one or another scenario.

37 F. Douglas Whitehouse, "Soviet Resource Allocation in the 1980's: Some Speculation" (Paper prepared for the Council on Foreign Relations' Study Group on Domestic Sources of Soviet Foreign Policy, November 1979).

# INDEX

Abalakovskoe Dam, 48
Academy of Medical Sciences, 89
Academy of Pedagogical Sciences, 89
Academy of Sciences, 23, 31, 43, 44, 154
  and hydropower, 46
  Central Econometric Institute, 91
  Institute for Concrete Sociological
    Research, 89, 90, 91
  Institute of Economics, 57, 59
  Institute of Electrometry and
    Automatic Systems, 91
  Institute of Genetics, 88
  Institute of Geography, 46, 79–81
  Institute of Philosophy, 89, 90
  Institute of Water Problems (IVP), 46,
    79, 80
  Institute of the World Economy and
    International Relations (IMEMO),
    91
  and leadership constraints and
    objectives, 144
  Presidium, 42
  Scientific Council on Water
    Resources Management (Nauchnyi
    Soviet po Vodnomu Khoziaistvu), 48
  Scientific Council on Water Transfer
    Problems, 81
  Siberian Department (SOAN), 41–2,
    81, 88, 90, 91
  USA Institute, 90
Aganbegian, A. G., 92
agreement (soglasovanie), basin
  inspectorates, 112
agricultural science
  inadequacies, 154–5
  revival, 29
agriculture
  Brezhnev's policy, 8–9, 26–8, 133,
    141; evaluating, 150–6; political
    lessons of, 156–61
  demotion of hydropower, 103–4
  investment in, 19–20, 25, 49, 151, 155
  Khrushchev's policy, 16–24

specialists, and policy-making, 17, 25,
    28–32, 84–5, 92–3
  and third-generation reform, 7–10,
    153–61
  traditional policy and its
    consequences, 7–8, 15–16, 18, 28,
    31, 156
agro-industrial complex, 9–10
agronomy, 89
Alekseevskii, E. E., 133
All-Union Conference on Questions of
  Capital Effectiveness, 57
Americanology, in Soviet Union, 84
Amu-Dar'ia River diversion project, 76
And Quiet Flows the Don (Sholokhov),
  41
animal husbandry, 25, 150
Aral Sea, and Central Asian diversion
  project, 76
Arbatov, G. A., 90, 92
associations (ob'edineniia), 5
Atomizdat, 89

Baikal, Lake, 40–6, 85, 92
Baikal-Amur Mainline construction
  project, 45
Baraev, A. I., 30, 31, 89, 91
basin inspectorates, and water quality,
  112–15
Berliner, Joseph, 160
Beschinskii, A. A., 57, 62
Boguchansk reservoir, 48
Bondarenko, I. A., 77
Breslauer, George, 19, 21, 22
Brezhnev, Leonid, 131
  agricultural specialists under, 28–32
  agriculture policy, 8–9, 26–8, 133,
    141; evaluating, 150–6; political
    lessons of, 156–61
  bill of particulars against Khrushchev,
    23
  and Central Asian diversion project,
    77